DANGER
on the
RIGHT

*

DANGER ON THE RIGHT

by *Arnold Forster*
and *Benjamin R. Epstein*

Random House   *New York*

SECOND PRINTING

© *Copyright, 1964, by Anti-Defamation League of B'nai B'rith*

All rights reserved under International and Pan-American Copyright Conventions. Published in New York by Random House, Inc., and simultaneously in Toronto, Canada, by Random House of Canada Limited.

Library of Congress Catalog Card Number: 64-7549

MANUFACTURED IN THE UNITED STATES OF AMERICA

Authors' Acknowledgment

Those who are unfamiliar with the structure of the Anti-Defamation League of B'nai B'rith and the responsibilities of the undersigned might erroneously conclude that *Danger on the Right* is the product of their exclusive effort. As with the four previous books in this series, which began in 1948, this volume is the end result of a combined staff effort. Situated strategically in twenty-seven cities across the country, and in the national offices of the Anti-Defamation League in New York City, are men and women whose daily assignment is the accumulation of data about extremist movements on the American scene. The resulting documentation on the activities of the so-called Radical Right in the United States led our agency's program director, Oscar Cohen, to suggest that the importance of the current Extreme Right phenomenon warranted the organization of our data into a readable book. We hope we have accomplished this.

Written as part of ADL's total public service program, and in no sense whatever a commercial venture, *Danger on the Right* was written under the supervision of an ADL lay committee that gave unstintingly of its effort and intelligence to perfect the document. Thus, our profoundest appreciation to: Marvin Berger, Bernard Nath, Lawrence Peirez and Henry Edward Schultz.

Our deepest gratitude goes to Jerome Bakst, ADL's director of research and evaluation. Ably assisted by Mortimer Kass, he devoted long days and nights to this endeavor and made relatively simple the otherwise overwhelming task of organizing the mass of details into a manuscript. To Jerry, and to the many others whose arduous work built the foundations for this study, we extend our deepest gratitude and affection.

A. F.
B. R. E.

To the Memory of John F. Kennedy

Ignorance and misinformation can handicap the progress of a city or a company—but they can, if allowed to prevail in foreign policy, handicap this country's security. In a world of complex and continuing problems, in a world full of frustrations and irritations, America's leadership must be guided by the lights of learning and reason—or else those who confuse rhetoric with reality and the plausible with the possible will gain the popular ascendancy with their seemingly swift and simple solutions to every world problem.

There will always be dissident voices heard in the land, expressing opposition without alternatives, finding fault but never favor, perceiving gloom on every side and seeking influence without responsibility. Those voices are inevitable.

But today other voices are heard in the land—voices preaching doctrines wholly unrelated to reality, wholly unsuited to the sixties, doctrines which apparently assume that words will suffice without weapons, that vituperation is as good as victory and that peace is a sign of weakness. . . .

We cannot expect that everyone, to use the phrase of a decade ago, will "talk sense to the American people." But we can hope that fewer people will listen to nonsense. And the notion that . . . strength is but a matter of slogans is nothing but just plain nonsense.

—Excerpt from text of undelivered speech scheduled for presentation in Dallas, Texas, on November 22, 1963, by the late President John F. Kennedy.

Foreword

The authors of *Danger on the Right* have attempted to write a definitive book on the attitudes, personnel, and influence of the Radical Right and the Extreme Conservatives on the American scene. I believe they have succeeded.

The depth of the Far Right has not been fully explored, as has the depth of the Far Left. At a time when the strongest threat to our democracy is the force of communism in the world, we are engaging all our defenses to contain and contest it.

In the years of Fascist and Nazi aggression, all our energies went into that struggle. In that time we found strange allies, and the thrust of the Communist conspiracy became strong in American political life. It took a good deal of realignment after World War II to straighten out the line of resistance. The aftermath of that readjustment brought on the McCarthy era and its hysteria and terror.

Left over from those days is the simple truth that the Communist world presents a danger and poses a serious challenge. Once again we have strange allies in the United States who befog the real issue by unrealistic and reckless accusations.

It is difficult to accept Westbrook Pegler, Robert Welch, and General Walker as comrades-in-arms in the cold war against communism. It becomes impossible when they charge Presidents and secretaries of state and senators as Communist dupes.

It becomes impossible when they use divisive tactics that, albeit unwittingly, abet rather than abate the threat of communism. It was Paul Hoffman who wrote persuasively during the McCarthy days that the senator from Wisconsin was—by weakening our faith in government, the military, the clergy, our educational resources and our political parties—actually doing what the Communists would like to do. Senator McCarthy, walking a shadowy road, loaded with a shotgun that he fired from the hip at any target that came into sight, was following a strict Marxist line in making us doubt the integrity and validity of our democratic process.

Today, the Radical Rightists are following the same path. They resist the civil rights movement by saying it is Communist-inspired, yet, by their violent opposition, degrade and humiliate us in the newly free nations which must be convinced by us if they are not to be convinced by the Communists.

They, the Radical Rightists, attack our Supreme Court and our clergy and our educational system. They belabor the United Nations and belittle the danger of nuclear war.

They are, in short, irresponsible and, therefore, necessarily dangerous.

It has been estimated that some 20 percent of the American electorate can be grouped as Extremists on the Right Wing. Therein dwell the Radical Rightists and the Extreme Conservatives. Therein also can be found those who would vote for a candidate who ran on an anti-Semitic or anti-Negro platform. Such a candidate would attract the racists, the bigots, the kooks and the yahoos to be found among the Extremists who are tempted into accepting the phony nostrums and panaceas of any or all fake medicine men who range the political scene in America.

Opposing them all with real conviction are some 25 to 30 percent of Americans. The remaining 50 or 55 percent of American citizens are the prize to be won. The moderate and liberal constituency struggles to win this majority over from the Radical Right, or to insulate the majority against it.

A book such as *Danger on the Right* has that purpose as its arrow. I hope it will hit its target by touching the mind and conscience of the uncommitted American citizen. I believe it will.

DORE SCHARY

New York
June 29, 1964

Contents

Preface

The Anti-Defamation League of B'nai B'rith is deeply concerned with the American political process, but does not engage in partisan politics. Our interest is democracy, which includes our system of public elections insofar as the political process can be misused to destroy our democracy.

Many Americans have the inaccurate impression that the Anti-Defamation League's sole concern is anti-Semitism. Even in its beginnings, at the turn of the century, this agency was not concerned solely with anti-Semitic activities. We believed at the time, as we believe now, that to defend and strengthen the rights of any group of Americans reinforces the rights of all—and therefore the very structure of our democracy.

Citizens who have observed our activities must have noticed our continuing concern with domestic extremist political movements. In the thirties the ADL fought communism and Nazism in this country, not only because these movements victimized minority groups, but because ADL recognized that they tore at the democratic structure of our society. Over the years the League joined in the struggle against an amorphous isolationist movement crystallized at different times in an America First Committee, a Christian Front, and in McCarthyism. ADL fought the resurgence of the Klan after the Supreme Court desegregation decisions, as well as the anti-Catholic propaganda which made its appearance in the 1960 election.

Today the United States faces new attacks on our democracy by an extremist movement which has mushroomed in the past few years and which is broadly referred to as the Radical Right. This movement, together with its allies among Right-Wingers, now spends a minimum of $14,000,000 a year in an assault on our democratic progress; consequently, the Radical Right, its conservative allies and those who support them, become a vital concern.

Considerable research by ADL's staff into the operations of this movement turned up no evidence that the Radical Right—as distinguished from its conservative allies—should be regarded as part of this nation's responsible political fabric. On the contrary, the evidence is that in reality it is a fringe political activity, and no more sound as a political position than the troublesome Communist conspiracy. The Radical Right sometimes has surrounded itself and often functions with certain characteristics of secrecy, furtiveness, and hidden motivation—marks of an organized conspiracy, which it is not. Ironically, the Radical Right's analysis of all national and international problems is rooted in a conspiratorial concept. Everything is blamed on a "Communist conspiracy."

In the eyes of the Radical Right, the American Republic is imperiled on almost every front by this Communist conspiracy which, says the Radical Right, has been entrenched in Washington for the last thirty years, and which has been softening up the country for an imminent "Communist take-over." The softening-up process, in the mythology of the Radical Right, has resulted from the advocacy by the "conspiracy" of socialism in domestic policy, and sellout and softness in foreign affairs.

This Radical Right mythology differs in degree and intensity, but not in kind, from the viewpoint of the Extreme Conservatives. The latter also view American domestic policy of the last thirty years as socialistic and dangerous, and our foreign policy of the same period as prone to softness and appeasement in dealing with the Communist threat.

The basic difference is that, unlike the Radical Right, the Extreme Conservatives generally do not tend to ascribe the alleged socialism and softness to any sinister plot in high places, but rather to blindness, stupidity, and bungling on the part of four Presidents and their liberal advisers.

Nevertheless, if there are some differences in interpretation of recent history between the Radicals of the Right and the Extreme Conservatives, there are also similarities which are noteworthy. If these two wings of the American Right differ on the *reasons* for the fancied perils and problems the country faces, they agree basically on the nature of the "evils" they fight—Federal taxes, Federal spending, Federal social welfare programs, and Federal regulation of private business, as well as foreign aid, UN activities, and negotiations with the Soviets.

This basic similarity of viewpiont has led to an ideological blur between these two segments of the American Right. The less extreme often "fellow-travel" with the Radicals of the Right, much as some Liberals fellow-traveled with the Communist Left twenty or thirty years ago. As a result, individual Conservatives today often lend their names, their sponsorship, and their financial support to organizations and causes of the Extremists.

Since 1960, the Radical Right and the Extreme Conservatives have been pouring millions of dollars into a propaganda campaign aimed at influencing American public opinion, often by disseminating pure fright along with distrust of respected American leaders and established institutions. These Radical Rightists, all too often aided by their conservative allies, pose a threat to our democratic institutions. They undermine confidence in the integrity and patriotism of our elected leaders, our judicial system, our military leaders, our educators, our clergy, our labor leaders—from Washington all the way out to the smallest community in the country. They attack the integrity and patriotism of local officials, clergymen, teachers, and librarians.

This multimillion-dollar-a-year propaganda campaign is financed by an impressive but comparatively small number of tax-exempt foundations, business corporations, and wealthy individuals—plus the one- to five-dollar contributions of hundreds of thousands of average citizens who have been frightened by this propaganda barrage and who, to an alarming extent, have succumbed to it.

The rabble-rousing gutter bigot, who combines political extremism with promoting racial and religious hatred, is often classified as part of the Radical Right. That is an easy error, for the peddlers of racial and religious bigotry who have sullied the national scene in the last thirty years have been, almost without exception, far to the Right in their political thinking. These racists and anti-Semites, like the Radicals, believe the Republic has been and is being sold out from within by a sinister conspiracy, deeply entrenched in the national capital. But their view of recent American history differs again from the picture of the alleged conspiracy which is painted by the Radicals of the Right, who do not normally peddle race and religious hate. In the eyes of the rabble-rousers, the fancied sellout of the American Republic over the last three decades results not from the mere presence in powerful positions of leaders who are pro-Communist, but from a sinister, secret, powerful pro-Soviet Jewish conspiracy. The bigots equate liberalism, socialism, and communism with Judaism. Often they chide the Radical Rightists for "pussyfooting" and for failing to brand Jews as the real culprits in American political life who have, since the days of the New Deal, instigated the policies at home and abroad that have brought the Republic to the brink of an internal Red take-over.

The conspiratorial theory of the bigots is the same as that of the Radical Right, but with that extra noxious ingredient of racial and religious hatred.

In the gradations of American Right Wing activity, the opinions of the Radical Right, expressed by men such as Robert Welch, Founder of the John Birch Society, may blur with those of the Extreme Conservative. This "blurring" merits study and is examined in this book. But, to repeat, neither the Birchers and their like-minded Radical Right allies, nor the Conservatives who often fellow-travel with them, should be confused with gutter-type extremists like George Rockwell, head of the miniscule American Nazi Party. Rockwell is a publicity-seeking nuisance, a concern only at the police precinct level, and forms no part of the really capable, efficient, well-financed, and truly dangerous movement of the Radical Right, which, quite unlike Rockwell, poses a very real threat to American democracy.

The Anti-Defamation League has continuously fought against all racial and religious bigotry. Anti-Semitism is one aspect of such bigotry. Anti-Jewish discrimination still persists in American life. But despite Rockwell and a handful of similar gutter-level bigots, there is no such thing in the United States today as an effective, nationally organized anti-Semitic movement. Such scattered overt activities as do exist are carried out by a corporal's guard of rabble-rousers, street-corner hoodlums, and old-time platform spellbinders and pamphleteers.

The dozen or so professional hate racketeers such as Rockwell, Gerald Smith, and the late Conde McGinley will therefore not be the measure of this book's concern. The Radical Right (and its conservative allies) will be—because it is a force that receives and spends millions of dollars every year to influence untold numbers of Americans with extremist propaganda.

There can be no doubt Radical Rightists are motivated by a hatred and fear of many twentieth-century developments in the economic and political life of our nation and the world, in which we Americans now play a major role. They make a profession of warning America about hazards they think they see. They urge people to watch out lest coddling of labor unions brings the welfare state one step closer. They sound the warning that fluoridation is but a chemical softening-up process preliminary to Communist brainwashing. They shout to beware of social security as a large step forward in socializing the Republic. They signal an alarm that the income tax is simply a means of pauperizing the rich in favor of the poor in order to communize the United States. They admonish in urgent voice for all to believe that the United Nations is a weapon the enemy is using to destroy American sovereignty and deliver us to the Bear.

Their fears and warnings are, to all purposes, baseless. The real danger is that in continuing endlessly to cry wolf, they confuse and divide America, diminishing her ability to recognize a real peril when it appears on the horizon. They constitute a serious threat to our democratic processes. The Radical Right (and their conservative supporters) are the real and proper concern of this book, as they should be the concern of all Americans.

*

The Radical Right

1

Radicals of the Right

It happened in Amarillo, Texas—population 140,000.

A shadow of fear and suspicion moved in across the city, in 1961, pitting people against people, and setting off a wave of antics so bizarre it appeared that some outlandish circus had encamped in town.

Brigadier General William L. (Jerry) Lee, a retired Air Force officer who was the area co-ordinator of the John Birch Society, the growing phenomenon of America's Right Wing, charged that a local clergyman was a Communist sympathizer. Shortly thereafter, he proclaimed that the National Council of Churches, representing an overwhelming proportion of the nation's Protestants, was infiltrated by Communists—for almost a decade a favorite and never-documented allegation of certain fundamentalist preachers and Extreme Rightists.

The community was immediately up in arms, disbelief fighting credence, townsman debating townsman. Leading Amarillo clergymen demanded that General Lee present to the Federal Bureau of Investigation his professed evidence that Communists had infiltrated the National Council of Churches, or keep quiet. But Lee only repeated the scandalous charges and ignored the cries for proof.

Amarillo's mayor, Jack Seale, was an avowed member of the John Birch Society. With his help, and that of a strong Birch membership in the city, General Lee's charges were spread everywhere and reached everyone. Before long, members of congregations delivered angry ultimatums to their pastors demanding that they break with the National Council of Churches or suffer the stoppage of contributions in the collection baskets. The ministers, fortunately, stood firm, insisting that first they be shown evidence of the charges. Proof, uncharitably, was never forthcoming.

While the split grew worse, Birchers instigated a second drive, this one to get rid of "Communist" reading matter in local schools and libraries. As a result, nine books were removed from the city's four high schools and from the library at Amarillo College—among them four Pulitzer Prize novels: John Steinbeck's *The Grapes of Wrath,* Oliver LaFarge's *Laughing Boy,* MacKinlay Kantor's *Andersonville,* and A. B. Guthrie's *The Way West.* Ironically, another of the purged novels was George Orwell's *1984,* a book generally regarded as a devastating critique of life under communism. Amarillo College eventually cleared all the books for general circulation except *Andersonville* which, peculiarly, was placed on the reserve shelf.

The book-purging campaign and the search for Reds fell with an upsetting impact on many Amarillo high school students. Suddenly they "discovered" they had teachers who were Communists, and they leveled accusations of disloyalty and dark hints of treason. In a town torn by hatred, recriminations, and wild, unsupported Birch charges, many old friendships were soon broken.

As an almost palpable hostility crept across the small city, even the local Girl Scouts were drawn into the fight when Birchers questioned the patriotism of scout leaders. At that juncture, Amarillo's Birchite mayor, Jack Seale, decided to run for Congress against the incumbent Democrat and, in the ensuing campaign, received the enthusiastic help of the Birchers and their fellow travelers. Before election day finally arrived, the Birch Society and charges of "communism" had become the major issues in the bitter campaign, and politics in Amarillo might never be quite the same again.

This was not an isolated instance. Similar frenzy has not been wholly unknown to other communities in the United States. The circus encamps for a while here, for a while there, arousing the citizenry and then leaving bitterness and unresolved suspicions in its wake. It has been part of the pattern of the current resurgence of the Radical Right in this country.

And this is where it has been happening—not on Capitol Hill but in Amarillo, in Midlothian, in Levittown and Los Angeles. Not so often in the far-off halls of political theory, it's usually found just down the block, particularly if there is a school, a church, or a charitable institution there. And when the circus comes to town, everybody gets caught up in it.

The climate is right.

In the long history of the United States, extremist groups—born of the problems of their times—have played a recurrent role. Most of these have been transients on the national scene. Some have lasted for a short time, others have stayed on longer. Eventually, as the real or the fancied need for such organizations has dwindled, most of them have disintegrated and have disappeared—to become short chapters or footnotes in the history books.

Today's Radical Right is the direct lineal descendant of ultra-Rightist organizations that flashed across the national scene in the 1930's and the 1940's—from the Liberty League to the isolationist America First Committee and the Constitutional Educational League, and thence to the whole amorphous carload of patrioteers and Communist-hunters that came to be called the McCarthy movement, or McCarthyites, after the late senator from Wisconsin.

Many of those whose names stud the rolls of today's Radical Right are veterans and leaders of those earlier political wars, and of those propaganda campaigns to save the nation from the "evils" of the New Deal, or the Fair Deal, or from "Communist infiltration" in Washington—particularly in the State Department. These old-time leaders have been joined by countless thousands who marched in their ranks in bygone years. They march today along with younger recruits who share the view of a United States heavily infiltrated by Communists and pro-Communists, and ripe for an imminent Red "take-over."

Still the question remains: Why did the Radical Right, which in various forms had been kicking and screaming about for many years, emerge around 1960 as a force to be reckoned with in American life?

In 1963, a group of social scientists from Stanford University, Washington University in St. Louis, and the California Department of Public Health published a depth study of the kind of American who is drawn to a Radical Right organization, and provided some clues on the question of why the Extreme Right Wing soars higher and higher at certain times. The study was made at one of the "schools of anti-Communism" conducted by Dr. Frederick C. Schwarz, head

of the Christian Anti-Communism Crusade, an organization which
will be considered in a later chapter.

One conclusion drawn by the study was that those who paid
to attend a Schwarz school in Oakland were in the majority Republican. It was possible, then, that the presence in the White House
of a Republican President from 1952 to 1960 had acted as a restraining factor on the Radical Right.

"The allegations of Communist influence that play so large a part
in right-wing propaganda," the study said, "are less convincing to
the public when a Republican is President. Hope, party loyalty and
organizational alliances all restrain right-wing leaders at this time."
And it added: "All these conditions are reversed when the White
House changes hands. There is no incumbent President to restrain
right-wing dissidents. . . . During a Democratic administration,
alarmism about Communism is more plausible to many people,
particularly those with very conservative ideas.

"Recent fluctuations in radical right activity conform to this
pattern. The current resurgence occurred after the 1960 Presidential election. While the John Birch Society was founded in 1958, it
was not until 1961 that it grew enough to attract public attention.
The Christian Anti-Communism Crusade was an obscure organization for the first seven years of its existence, but in the first year
of the Kennedy Administration its income increased 350%."

There are, of course, reasons other than Democratic Party
dominance for the upsurge of the Radical Right in the last four or
five years. A complex of factors seems to have converged with
unusual impact since 1960:

The cold war frustrations of the American people and the recurrent international crises and confrontations with the Communists
in Korea, Berlin, Laos, Vietnam, and Cuba, together with the lack
of clear-cut American "victory" in a number of these crises—a new
kind of experience for Americans, accustomed to climactic
triumphs on the battlefield and unprepared for "a long, twilight
struggle" lasting years. Then there have been crises and tensions at
home: the need for high taxes to support the nation's defense,
rising costs of living, the conflicts of the racial struggle over integration—not to mention the return to Washington of a Democratic
administration generally regarded as "liberal." For political or propaganda activity which flourishes in a climate of frustration and confusion, the climate was indeed right.

Some five hundred Right Wing organizations, national and local,
have been identified on the American political scene in recent years.
By 1964 many were inactive or moribund, but some were louder and

lustier than ever. These groups have ranged from somewhat right of center to the Extremists of the Radical Right, and beyond—into the lunatic fringe, where racism and religious bigotry of the gutter variety supplement the Radical Rightist gospel.

Of these hundreds of organizations only twenty-six or twenty-seven can be considered major groups, and of these, perhaps fourteen can be viewed as Radical Right. The others, often less extreme, are the conservative allies of the Radical Right who, through a lavish lack of discrimination or through an excess of zeal, are sadly "soft" on Radicals of the Right and prone to make common cause with them.

These two dozen or so organizations manifestly make an impact on the nation, and on the Republican Party in particular. Their activities reflect dissatisfaction with the course of national policy in the past three decades, and their propaganda thunders that GOP leaders are only "me-too" with respect to Democratic Party policies at home and abroad. The greater number of Republicans are undoubtedly embarrassed by their self-appointed supporters from the extreme edge of the political spectrum, having grown up in a complex, twentieth-century world that has ceased looking for final answers in the waving of a flag or in hair-raising escapes from responsibility.

Many of these outfits of the Radical Right and its conservative fellow travelers enjoy tax-exempt status. A number of them have been incorporated as "educational," "charitable," or "religious" organizations, which qualifies them for tax exemption by the United States Treasury, although in fact much of their activity, and most of their publications and materials, appear to be at all times essentially political and partisan.

Virtually the only thing the Internal Revenue Service requires of a tax-exempt body is an annual report on its income and expenditures. Such reports show increased receipts and expenditures by Right Wing organizations in 1958 and 1959. As the 1960 Presidential campaign went into its final lap, the contributions reached a peak, and after the votes were in, contributions dwindled. In 1961 they began to rise again, and reached another high point in 1962, a congressional election year. Reports for 1963 indicated another sharp rise and, as this is written, point to a high level in the 1964 Presidential election year. It is not unfair to conclude that one immediate aim of those who contribute the money, and of those who spend it, is to influence the outcome of political elections.

As to political philosophy, the Right Wing ranges extremely wide as well as extremely far out. On one hand, the minions of the Radical Right, armed with those peculiar powers of intelligence denied most of us, see the country as ripe for a take-over by an internal conspiracy of secret Communist agents and socialist planners who have craftily burrowed into every facet of American life, saddling us with a domestic tyranny and a foreign policy made in Moscow. The Extreme Conservatives, on the other hand, are quite convinced that since the Roosevelt New Deal, America has been going socialist and that its foreign policy has been at least soft on communism. But, whereas the Radical Right blames an internal conspiracy for the alleged sorry situation, its conservative allies attribute it to blindness, stupidity, and bungling on the part of Liberals who they say have controlled the nation's affairs these three decades.

From either viewpoint, however, the look of things is obviously frightening, and in the ideological war the Extremists are now waging, fear itself is a basic weapon. To convert Americans to their alarmist views, the crusaders of the Extreme American Right—the Radicals and their conservative allies—are currently spending at least $14,000,000 a year. In addition, about $1,300,000 goes to an ignoble potpourri of anti-Semitic, racist, and other fanatical bodies which also would like to make a hard Rightist impact on American political life.

A substantial portion of the $14,000,000 that goes to the Radical Rightists and their conservative allies comes from the wellsprings of 70 foundations (almost all of them tax exempt), 113 business firms and corporations (most of which can deduct contributions to "religious" or "educational" organizations), 25 public utility companies, and some 250 individuals who have been identified as contributing at least $500 each to Rightist causes in the last few years. The names of some of the foundations, companies, and individuals will be found throughout this book and in the Appendix.

Another sizeable portion of the total is scared up from ordinary citizens—through dues, appeals at rallies, mailing-list pleas, etc.— literally scared up, so potent is the pull of fear, and so fearful is the Rightist view of things.

In addition to these offically reported millions, other money is poured into the American Right Wing for specific projects such as TV and radio programs, special broadcasts, publications, and reprints—all of which are charged off as business expenses. Such costs, met by business firms, are not always reported by Right Wing organizations because the money does not pass through their hands. It is difficult to estimate such "side" expenditures precisely, but the total is known to be substantial.

Some of the nationally known organizations—for example, Dr.

Schwarz's Christian Anti-Communism Crusade and Billy James Hargis' Christian Crusade—encountered difficulties in maintaining membership and financial support after a nation-wide avalanche of critical publicity directed at the Radical Right during 1961 and 1962.

Hargis' crusade grossed almost $1,000,000 in 1961. The evangelist reasonably anticipated a million and a quarter in the following year, but instead he had to cut his operations for a time.

Schwarz suffered even more serious difficulties. But even with the widespread criticism of the Radical Right, Schwarz and Hargis might not have encountered such reversals were there not a basic difference between their operations and those of the Birch Society. Neither Schwarz nor Hargis sought to build a permanent membership organization from the grass roots up, but instead merchandised anti-communism by hitting the sawdust trail. Their unending appeals were for money for the cause, not permanent members. They sought to mobilize dollars to support their crusades. The John Birch Society, on the other hand, sought to mobilize the people whom it wanted to participate in an action program—a program in which money is only one necessary ingredient. As a result, the Birch Society grew, despite hostile publicity, while the Schwarz and Hargis crusades dwindled. (The Birch strategy for mobilization and the cash sale techniques of the two "Christian Crusaders" are subjects to be dealt with later on in these pages.)

Politically, it was the 1962 congressional election which provided the first real test of Radical Right strength. Although most of its candidates were defeated, the Radical Right made its presence obvious in the political picture in a number of states, and in some of them exerted a political impact far out of proportion to its numerical strength.

In California, where the Radical Right in general and the John Birch Society in particular were strongest, the two known Birch members in the Eighty-seventh Congress—Representatives John Rousselot and Edgar Hiestand—were defeated in their bids for re-election. Superficial observers concluded that the Birchers and their allies had suffered a resounding defeat. The conclusion was not justified; the Rousselot and Hiestand districts had been redrawn by the California state legislature and neither of the men was given much chance of winning. Despite this handicap, the two ran surprisingly strong races, Rousselot polling 46 percent and Hiestand 45.5 percent of the vote cast. A third Bircher—H. L. Richardson, later to become one of the Society's paid co-ordinators—polled 44.2 percent in still another district.

In other primary and general election campaigns that year—

including those in such politically important states as New York, Texas, Michigan, Wisconsin, and Washington—the John Birch Society and its Rightist allies wrought an impact on the course and the character of the campaigns far greater than the numerical strength and voting power of their adherents. The Birchers themselves became fired up with hopes for future victories.

In the June, 1964, California primaries at least five members of the Society were successful in bids for Republican nominations as candidates to the House of Representatives and to the state legislature; three others publicly reported to have ties to the Birch Society were also victorious. Assessing the results of the 1964 primaries in California, Rousselot, as western states governor for the Birch Society, rejoiced—declaring that "it was a good day" for the cause.

Despite their political impact on the 1962 elections, and even in the face of the successes of Birchite candidates in the June, 1964, West Coast primaries, Radical Right groups do not essentially seek to create new political parties. Rather, they seek by concerted propaganda drives to change the political climate in the United States, to turn the winds slowly their way. They do so by penetrating and influencing both major political parties. And in this effort, the John Birch Society has emerged as the strongest of such organizations, geared as it is for the long pull, and growing as it is, slowly but steadily, in membership and in the influence of its propaganda activities.

Thousands of words have been published in the last few years exposing and criticizing the John Birch Society and its Founder, Robert Welch. The late President John F. Kennedy, former Vice-President Richard M. Nixon, and United States senators in both political parties have assailed the society and its leader, as have the National Council of Churches, the United Presbyterian Church, the General Assembly of the Southern Presbyterian Church, leading Episcopalian clerics and prominent Catholic churchmen and laymen, and leaders in business, labor, and education. Even such Right Wing publicists as William F. Buckley, Jr., and Russell Kirk have added their own sharp criticism. Yet, despite this national wave of rebukes, the Birch Society is still in business. It is still expanding its operations year by year, and growing ever more arrogant against the dupes, cowards, atheists and traitors that it sees directing the main stream of American life.

2

The John Birch Society
— Robert Welch

"I want to convince you, as I am convinced," says Robert Welch, the John Birch Society's Founder and leader, "that only dynamic *personal* leadership offers any chance for us to save either our material or our spiritual inheritance. . . . I intend to offer that leadership to all who are willing to help me."

The John Birch Society is a monolith from top (Welch's "dynamic personal leadership") to bottom. The latter end of the Birch setup is comprised of its great grass-roots strength, a legion of dedicated, active, mostly overwrought, superpatriotic Rightists 20,000 to 50,000 strong.*

The semi-secret organization (it carefully conceals its member-

*Estimates of the membership by the press and other observers have varied from 50,000 to 100,000. Edgar W. Hiestand, himself a Birch Society member and a congressman at the time, told the House Rules Committee that he, personally, placed the figure at 40,000 men and 20,000 women. This 1961 figure conflicted with the number of members reflected by the dues reported in the Society's financial statements to the Attorney General of Massachusetts. From studies of these official reports, the highest possible estimate of membership at the close of 1962 would have been 24,000.

ship lists and the names of its heavy financial contributors) seeks
to recruit a million persons into its ranks, eventually doing so by
convincing the American people, who are quite properly concerned
about the dangers of communism, that time is running out and
that it is almost zero hour in the fight to save America from an
internal Communist take-over. (Just what remains to be taken over
is not too clear. Welch's latest estimate figures the United States to
be "50%–70% Communist-controlled." The cold war apparently is
a sort of civil war in the Birch logic, and patriotism thus becomes
something of a paradox.)

In the oppressing atmosphere of fright that can be summoned by
the vision of enemies so snugly within, wild emotion and suspicion
will thrive—as they did in Amarillo. And since it organizes on the
local level, the Birch Society is able to marshal and direct these un-
savory forces into strong, pinpointed action at any time and in
almost any place.

It was so in that Texas city in 1961 and in 1962 as has been
described earlier.

Amarillo had been torn apart by the winds of suspicion. The
permanent damage that could be seen even after the storm had sub-
sided is a graphic illustration of the bitter and disruptive effects of
Rightist extremism. The climax here had come only after a long,
febrile season in which clergymen and teachers had been accused of
spreading communism, the libraries and schools had been purged
of certain outstanding books, and many a long friendship had been
severed by hate. It was then that the city's Mayor Seale, a member
of the John Birch Society, had decided to run for Congress on the
platform of the Radical Right.

Amarillo's responsible civic leaders were aghast at what local
elements in the Birch Society had done. The city's power structure,
composed mostly of conservative businessmen, at long last recognized what damage the extremist organization had wrought. They
understood that the community itself could be destroyed, and threw
their combined support to the incumbent, Congressman Walter
Rogers, hoping that Seale's defeat would end Birch influence in the
frightened community. At the end, Birchite Mayor Seale was defeated, although he ran a strong race, polling 42 percent of the
total vote.

The Birchers remain an influential factor in Amarillo to this day,
and all the hatreds they engendered are still there, waiting for something to touch them off again. This is the unlovely impact that the
Society and its allies had on a good-sized American city not very
long ago.

In smaller communities, where almost everyone knows his neighbors, the bitterness becomes even more personal. In Midlothian, for example, a Texas town of some 1,500 normally peaceful residents, a heavy dose of Birchist tactics was all that was needed to bring the community to the point where the local anti-Birch newspaper office was bombed.

The hatreds had caught fire during a campaign for a school board election. On March 19, 1962, Edgar Seay, a leading Bircher in the town, had delivered an extremist speech in the Midlothian high school. He had charged the late President Franklin D. Roosevelt with the responsibility for the existence of communism, and had labeled former President Harry S. Truman a cold-blooded murderer. He had also urged that the United States Constitution be drastically revised in line with Rightist dogma.

A prominent local citizen then demanded that a well-informed United States District judge be given equal time to answer the wild statements. Sides were quickly chosen. Faced with a divided opinion, the school superintendent passed the request to the high school principal. The principal declined to let the Federal judge speak on the grounds that to do so would improperly introduce "an outsider."

The school board election was won by the Extremists. When Penn Jones, the local newspaper editor, wrote an editorial critical of the Birchers, Edgar Seay called on the editor to complain about it. In the course of the discussion, Mr. Jones's patriotism was called into question. Apparently cast in the mold of the Old West's independent newspaper editor, Penn Jones resented the slur on his loyalty. The Bircher, in turn, resented what he said had been an intolerable insult by the editor. Tempers flared and the discussion ended in a brawling fist fight.

Not long afterward, a brick was thrown through the window of the newspaper office. Then a crude fire-bomb was tossed through the shattered glass, causing considerable damage. Lie detector tests absolved both Mr. Seay and the editor, but Midlothian was by then a divided and bitter town—and another showcase of Birch Americanism.

Such examples of communities split down the middle by bitterness and dissension point to a sequence of local events which, however spectacular, certainly are not uncommon in America since the resurgence of the Radical Right. And quite often the spark which ignites such fiery events is a sharp word received through the mails in the bulletins of the John Birch Society, from a far distant community—the town of Belmont, Massachusetts.

It may be one of the "suggestions" in the official monthly Agenda. Birchers normally take these "suggestions" as orders.

"Join your local PTA at the beginning of the school year," wrote the leader, Robert Welch, in an apparent burst of good citizenship, but then he added this clincher: ". . . and go to work and take it over."

Such "suggestions" have set the stage for turmoil in many a town. And the man who issues them has become, through his "dynamic personal leadership," probably the most powerful single force that has ever functioned on America's Far Right Wing.

Robert Welch is a short, slightly built, white-haired man in his sixties, reportedly gentle and thoughtful in personal relationships but publicly brusque, finicky, and short-tempered. He is nervously energetic, speaks rapidly in a throaty monotone that carries traces of a Southern accent. Welch likes to talk, and will often wander through the rooms of his Belmont headquarters to chitchat with his employees, all of whom appear to regard him with some fondness. At mealtime, he likes to be surrounded by close friends, not so much to discuss the bothersome inroads of communism as for a little small talk and conviviality. Yet with all this, he is a tireless toiler who often will work sixteen or twenty hours at the day's tasks.

Welch makes efforts at a pixieish sense of humor and apparently loves the practical joke. Once on a trip in India, he is said to have airmailed instructions to his staff in a memo he had persuaded someone to write for him in Sanskrit. For days after his return he could not decide whether to be disappointed because he had not stumped the staff, or to be pleased at their efficiency in getting the memo translated and in carrying out his instructions. In some ways Welch appears to be a frustrated scholar. He loves books, especially the works of minor poets who sing of simple emotions. His personal office at the Society's headquarters is a book-lined study resembling that of a small Midwestern college dean. Only when a visitor stands at Welch's desk with its neat piles of paper, and looks at the gigantic map of the world the Founder has before him, does one sense the single-minded driving force which seems to animate the man. Behind his desk are pictures of his heroes, nicely framed and so hung that they seem to look benignly down upon him. One is a photograph of the late General Douglas MacArthur and the other of Senator Joseph R. McCarthy. On another wall is an oil painting of John Birch, for whom Welch named the Society.

Welch thinks that the "intellectuals" look down upon poets like Longfellow, and he calls attention to the simplicity of a poem's message seemingly to avoid derision for his poetic tastes. Every John

Birch Society Bulletin, the official monthly organ of the Society which Welch writes personally, begins with a couplet or a quatrain that speaks a message. For example:

> Let us, then, be up and doing,
> With a heart for any fate;
> Still achieving, still pursuing,
> Learn to labor and to wait.

When he uses such quotations, he often makes an apologetic comment, such as: "Naturally the above quatrain will seem 'corny' to a generation which accepts Archibald MacLeish as a poet."

When he goes on speaking tours, Robert Welch is a man completely preoccupied with the Communist conspiracy he sees everywhere. He is fearful and suspicious of newsmen and strangers. At times, this attitude has infected his aides. At the end of one public meeting a reporter started swiftly for the platform to try for an interview as Welch's admirers swarmed around him. A co-ordinator seeing the swiftly advancing reporter obviously thought it was an attack on the Founder, and held out a hand in horror, crying, "No!"

The New York Times described Welch in the various settings of a typical tour:

> The visitor . . . had slipped quietly into town, linked hands piously with his hosts around the dinner table to offer family grace. The sound of crickets relayed across Louisiana bayous and neat, clipped lawns, broke the night's stillness outside. . . . One of those at the dinner table addressed Mr. Welch by the wrong name. But he was in good spirits, laughed over the mistake, and launched into a detailed discourse on the etymology of his name. He concluded by explaining, quietly, that the root word for Welch means "stranger." . . .
>
> The "Stranger" has just completed a number of quick visits to towns around the country. He travels alone, and is so close-mouthed about his schedule that even his chapter chiefs are not sure of his precise arrival time until shortly before he comes to town. When he alights from his plane (usually a commercial liner but occasionally a private plane put at his disposal by one of his wealthy sponsors), Mr. Welch, carrying his briefcase and suggesting in his appearance a worn Southern preacher, gets into a waiting car and takes off for a private home that is seldom identified. And somewhere in town— again an unidentified place—he meets with his chapter leaders and members, talking softly through puffs of cigar smoke. . . .

When Welch travels on speaking tours, he draws large audiences, most of them middle-aged and from the upper middle class. They are not unemployed malcontents or crackpots; they are patient and enthusiastic men and women, willing to wait on a line, four abreast, for an hour, to buy tickets to hear him. Reporters who have talked to them say many speak like educated people. From their dress and social poise most of them seem economically well off.

Seth Kantor, a reporter from the *Dallas Times Herald* covering a Welch speech at the Baker Hotel in Dallas, asked the Founder to substantiate some of his wilder charges.

"I have nothing more to say," said Welch.

The reporter tried again. Would Mr. Welch "clear up some points about his statements?"

"No!" Welch exploded.

When the ballroom was emptied of all but a handful of Birchers who stayed close to their leader, the reporter asked him again for a press conference. "I don't give press conferences," Welch answered, "in cities where the newspapers have not printed what I think they should. Dallas is one of those cities. Good night."

A *Houston Chronicle* reporter who did get an interview was quoted by Kantor: "It looked like cloak and dagger stuff. I was told to stand in front of the Baker Hotel in Dallas at an exact time in the morning. A car pulled up with two men. One got out. He walked past me, then came back. He asked me my name, the town I was from, then if I could name the newspaper that had sent me."

The newspaperman was driven to a private home where he was given a tape-recorded interview. In it Welch refused to disclose the strength of his following in Texas, although he told the *Boston Sunday Herald* months earlier that Texas was a major stronghold of the John Birch Society.

Welch's suspicions show on the lecture platform. *Time* magazine reports that when someone in the audience coughs or moves about during a speech, Welch will look up from his text and say that walking or coughing is a "dirty Communist trick." His suspicions of the press are not limited to requests by reporters for statements and interviews; but to he hates being photographed. This suspicion of reporters and photographers stems from a belief that the nation's press is in the grip of Communists and pro-Communists and that newsmen will therefore twist his answers to questions to make him look ridiculous.

A reporter once cornered the Founder, as he was leaving the platform, to ask: "Do you still stand by your opinion that Eisenhower is a Communist agent?" The *Pasadena Independent Star-News* reported: "Welch did not answer. . . . He hurried from the room head down, his nearly-bald head ringed with grey hair. His round, lined face was set and grim."

The Founder of the John Birch Society is descended from settlers who came to America from Wales in 1720. He himself was born in North Carolina in 1899, was educated at the University of North Carolina and at Harvard, and spent two years at the United States Naval Academy. He lives in Belmont, not far from his national headquarters, and has lived in the Boston area for about forty years. In a biographical sketch he once wrote in the third person, he boasted of "one wife, two sons, a Golden Retriever dog and 14 golf clubs—none of which he understands, but all of which he loves."

As vice-president of a firm of candy manufacturers, Welch did well financially. (He left the company for the ideological wars in 1956, and has no known connection with it today.) As a business-man, he was active in the National Association of Manufacturers, of which he was both a director and a vice-president.

In 1946, and again in 1948, Welch went to England to study the effect of socialist government on the country. In 1949 he made a one-month flying trip around the world, devoting most of the time to Asia. When he returned, his political views were slipping further to the Right, and his fears for the nation's future led him to enter politics. He sought the Republican nomination for Lieutenant-Governor of Massachusetts, unsuccessfully. In 1952, he ardently supported the late Senator Robert A. Taft for the Republican Presidential nomination. He now insists that the nomination was stolen from Taft by the "Communists" and the "One Worlders" who had picked and secretly primed General Eisenhower as their man. Until then, Welch claims, "it was still possible to have saved our country, from the immediate Communist danger anyway, primarily by political action."

In 1955, he went to Asia again to visit President Syngman Rhee of Korea and Generalissimo Chiang Kai-shek on the Nationalist island of Taiwan. In 1956, he called on Chancellor Konrad Adenauer in West Germany. From his travels and reading, Welch became convinced that it would be necessary that he devote the rest of his life to fighting communism. For two years after leaving the candy business, he pondered the "Communist conspiracy" in the United States, and concluded that only "dynamic *personal* leadership" offered any chance to "save either our material or our spiritual inheritance"—and that he was the man to supply that leadership.

In his years as a vice-president of the National Association of Manufacturers, and through personal business contacts, Robert Welch had made friends with men of industry who shared his political views. Late in 1958, he asked eleven such men to meet with him in an Indianapolis hotel. The men who gathered there on Monday morning, December 8, had come from nine widely scattered states.

For two days Welch delivered a breathless monologue—it was recorded and has been published as the John Birch Society's *Blue Book*. He traced the advance of communism, offered his peculiar analysis of the existing situation, and outlined the aims and the structure of an ambitious national Right Wing organization he proposed to form. Welch decided that the organization should be called the John Birch Society because a twenty-six-year-old soldier named John Birch had been "the first American casualty in World War III." The *Blue Book* quotes Welch:

"You will find that John Birch, a young fundamentalist Baptist preacher from Macon, Georgia, who did as much as any other man, high or low, to win our war and the Chinese war against the Japanese in China, was murdered by the Chinese Communists at the first opportunity after the war because of the powerful resistance he would have been able to inspire against them. You will find, and I believe, agree with me, that John Birch possesses in his own character *all* of those noble traits and ideals which we should like to see symbolized by the John Birch Society."

In his book, *The Life of John Birch*, Welch wrote:

"We have built this sermon around John Birch, for in one blade of grass lies the key to all creation, could we only understand it; and in the forces that swirled around John Birch lay all the conflicts, of philosophy and of implementation, with which our whole world is now so imperatively concerned. Therein lay the signficance of his life and death. Actually we must choose between the civilization, the form of society, and the expression of human life, as represented by John Birch, and their parallels as envisioned by Karl Marx and his spiritual successors. There is no middle ground. . . ."

At the Indianapolis meeting Welch told his eleven friends just how he saw himself in this struggle, and of the grand organization he thought possible. He said: "If I were the 'man on the white horse' on our side in this war, *which is still political and educational rather than military*; if I had sufficient resources available and sufficiently accepted authority over one million dedicated supporters out of at least five times that many militant anti-Communists who are already enrolled in, or contributing to, hundreds of ineffectual 'freedom' groups—so that I could coordinate the activities of those million men and women with some degree of positiveness and efficiency approaching the coordination by the Communists of their members and fellow-travelers; if, though recognized as the leader for the sake of positiveness and direction and coordination of effort and resources, I still had the dedicated advice, counsel, help, organizing ability and executive know-how offered by the ablest men in America among the staunch anti-Communists whom I would gather around me; if I had this kind of realistic force with which to fight the Communists, here are some of the things I would do."

And he offered a ten-point program, most of which is now being carried out by Birch chapters throughout America, and which is essentially a tough campaign of membership recruitment and ultra-reactionary propaganda. Its operation ranges from issuing Far-Rightist publications to establishing reading rooms and libraries. It includes the booking of Far-Rightist speakers before civic groups across the country, firm support for the radio programs of broadcasters such as Fulton Lewis, Jr., and Clarence Manion, the use of "the powerful letter-writing weapon," the organization of front groups (a favorite tactic also of the Communists), and the exposing of alleged Communists wherever they may turn up next. The stated Birch objective is to change the pattern of American thinking, to "awaken an apathetic American people," and to build "the cumulative total of anti-Communist resistance."

This is to be achieved by organizing chapters of "from 10 to 20 dedicated patriots" to exert an impact at the local community level —on the schools, libraries, church groups, PTAs, and thus on the whole nation—and to shock the people into enlightenment by exposing the supposed extent of the Communist conspiracy.

Eventually, in the opinion of its Founder, the Birch Society would put its weight "into the political scales in this country just as fast and far as we could" to "reverse by political action the gradual surrender of the United States to Communism. . . ." Welch believes that the kind of painstaking organizational work at the precinct levels that wins elections could not be carried out by the existing Republican Party, nor "by anything that can come out of the present shattered Republican Party in the foreseeable future." If the Republican Party stood for "any Americanist principles whatsoever," he said, it still could not win *"unless* it has strong help and backing from forces outside of the straight political organization— such as the Democratic Party has on the other side in Walter Reuther's Committee on Political Education." He said that the Democrats were winning elections despite their own internal splits because of COPE's organizational activities.

"We are at a stage," he concluded, "where the only sure political victories are achieved by non-political organization; by organization which has a surer, more positive, and more permanent purpose than the immediate political goals that are only means to an end; by organization which has a backbone, and cohesiveness, and strength and definiteness of direction, which are impossible for the old-style political party organization. . . . with a million men and the resources consistent with the dedication of those men which we are presupposing, we could move in on the elections thereafter with both more man power and more resources than Reuther will be able to marshal. . . ."

There have been indications, however, that since that protracted two-day presentation at Indianapolis, the members Welch recruited have become far more eager to engage in political action than the Founder himself. On more than one occasion, Welch has found it necessary to warn his members not to dilute the scope and impact of their Birch barking by excessive and premature political action.

This was especially true in the summer of 1963, when the Goldwater-for-President boom was shifting into high gear. Welch prepared a four-page memorandum (he explained that he was getting "so many requests for comments concerning Senator Goldwater that it has seemed advisable to prepare this brief memorandum") in which he wrote that Senator Goldwater "obviously and honestly feels that 'direct political action' is the most important part of any total program for saving our country from either the menace of Communist terror and tyranny, or the more gradual disaster of Socialist stagnation. We disagree."

Efforts by Conservatives in political campaigns, he wrote, were wasted because they were wishful thinking. "For what is our problem? It is to stop the Communists from continuing and completing their take-over of our own country, which is going on right now. And what is the answer?"

Welch provided it. It was "to wake up enough patriotic American citizens to what is really happening . . . to put most of our money and effort into a massive educational campaign on many fronts. . . ." Welch said that some political activities would be justified by the extent to which "even these political campaigns can be made basic parts of a huge educational program. . . ."

As to Senator Goldwater, he wrote: "I personally think Barry Goldwater is a very patriotic American and a very able politician, who is determined to use his political skill to do all he can towards saving our country from the dangers now closing in from every side. As made clear in the *Blue Book,* four years ago, I don't think political action alone can do it, or is even the most important of the efforts which must be combined to save us."

Goldwater "would even be a far smarter politician if he were less of a politician," Welch wrote, but added: "Let's not lose the benefit of whatever Barry Goldwater can do, in the way he thinks best, to make political action and solidity on behalf of the Conservative cause a very helpful part of that total combination."

In his long-winded soliloquy at Indianapolis, Welch had claimed that he knew Senator Goldwater fairly well, and that he was "a great American," one he'd "love to see" as President of the United States. But then he commented, in a significant and revealing statement on his attitude toward political leaders: "Goldwater, by the very circumstances of his political success, present prestige, and the expectations of his supporters, will inevitably think and move in terms of *political* warfare."

He went on to say: "As you look more and more carefully into the hopes that have been bred, and the disappointments that have followed, throughout the political performances of . . . twenty years, you come increasingly to realize the wisdom of the old advice: 'Put not your faith in politicians.' We shall have to use politicians, support politicians, create politicians, and help the best ones we can find to get elected. I am thoroughly convinced, however, that we cannot count on politicians, political leadership, or even political action except as part of something much deeper and broader, to save us."

Welch's fear that his members may become excessively involved in purely political activity probably stems from a realization that this could divert them from building a million-member Birch Society, a giant movement which, by the impact of its propaganda activity, could convert American thinking to the Robert Welch line.

Toward the end of his marathon speech, Welch pictured the kind of organization he wanted to establish:

> The John Birch Society is to be a monolithic body . . . democracy is merely a deceptive phrase, a weapon of demagoguery, and a perennial fraud.
>
> . . . The John Birch Society will operate under completely authoritative control at all levels . . . no collection of debating societies is ever going to stop the Communist conspiracy. . . .
>
> . . . The men who join the John Birch Society during the next few months or few years are going to be doing so primarily because they believe in me and what I am doing and are willing to accept my leadership anyway. . . . Whenever and wherever,

either through infiltration by the enemy or honest differences of
opinion, that loyalty ceases to be sufficient to keep some frag-
ment in line, we are not going to be in the position of having
the Society's work weakened by raging debates. We are not
going to have factions developing on the two-sides-to-every-
question theme.

Those members who cease to feel the necessary degree of
loyalty can either resign or will be put out. . . .

When the two-day meeting at Indianapolis ended, the John
Birch Society had been established as a secretive body, resolved
to operate quietly, without publicity, to carry out the aims laid
down by its Founder. Besides Robert Welch himself, and the
original incorporators, the leadership included a national council
of twenty-six, from which Welch later selected five members to
serve as his executive committee. This leadership group is composed
in substantial measure of businessmen who share Welch's extremist
views on government, politics, and his estimate of the internal
Communist menace confronting the country. Three former presidents of the National Association of Manufacturers have served on
the organization's national council. Other council members were
leaders in the NAM, or in state associations of manufacturers. Of
the three former NAM presidents only W. J. Grede of Milwaukee
remains active in the Birch Society.

Just outside this inner circle of the Society are Committees of
Endorsers in the various states, many of whom can be considered
among the Society's leaders, although some so listed have even
denied actual membership.

Paid area organizers, or "major co-ordinators," as they are
called, are appointed by Welch personally, and either Welch or
these co-ordinators select all local chapter leaders. There are no
elections anywhere in the Society's structure. Everything operates
from the top down—or from the center outward, actually, for
Founder Welch stands at the hub of a group of concentric circles,
controlling their movements because the leadership and the members willingly allow him to do so.

Area or local co-ordinators are given an intensive course of special
instructions. Prospective or new members are indoctrinated either
by reading the entire *Blue Book,* or listening to and watching Welch
recite on film a condensation of his Indianapolis monologue. No
new member can, thereafter, possibly be uncertain about where
power lies in the Society. In his long talk Welch said:

"It is imperative that all the strength we can muster be subject to smoothly functioning direction from the top. . . ."

The chief stance of the John Birch Society is, of course, open hostility to United States foreign and domestic policies of the last thirty years, policies which have been, in the suspicious Birch view, elements of Bolshevik strategy. Manifestly, Birchers would like to set the clock back at least three decades, repealing American political and economic history from the 1930's to the present. The domestic reforms of the last three decades, many of them instituted clearly to preserve the free enterprise system in a workable form, are seen as service to the enemy. So, too, are the programs of military preparedness for the United States and its allies. So, too, are the far-reaching provisions for foreign military and economic aid to allies and underdeveloped countries. So, too, is the bipartisan United States policy of support for the United Nations, from which Robert Welch would have the United States withdraw. As he puts it: "Get the U. S. out of the U. N. and the U. N. out of the U. S."

A suspicious man, a man as suspicious as Founder Welch himself, let us say, would have reasonable grounds to wonder whether the Birch Society program of undoing thirty years of America's effort to improve herself at home and help others abroad, would not really achieve precisely what the Communists wish:

—The Communists want the United States to recall its troops from Europe, which would render NATO, the free world's protective shield in Western Europe, impotent. The Birch Society wants to see the end of NATO.

—The Soviet Union has sought to dominate the United Nations by its use of the veto, and by seeking to create a "troika" in place of the position of secretary general. The Birchers would abandon the UN to the Soviets by pulling the United States out of UN membership.

—The Soviet Union tries to persuade underdeveloped countries to reject American aid and accept Communist aid, thus enabling the Soviets to establish firm footholds in those lands. The Birchers would end American aid to underdeveloped nations and thereby throw them into Moscow's clutches.

—The Soviet Union has repeatedly denied that it constitutes any kind of external threat to the United States. Birchers in effect agree with this Russian pose when they assert that the threat from communism is not wholly from the Soviet Union, but almost entirely from traitors within, along with dupes and sympathizers. In diverting attention from the Communist military threat posed by Moscow and Peking, one might argue, the Birchers play the Red game.

—The Soviet Union is spending huge sums and has assigned countless secret agents and open propagandists to its unending effort to turn dark-skinned Asians and Africans against the United States. The Red theme is that the United States is a hotbed of racial discrimination. Birchers would impeach the Chief Justice of the United States for the Supreme Court's desegregation decisions and some of its other enlightened judgments. The campaign against the Supreme Court's order for racial integration provides valuable grist for the Red propaganda mills.

Actually, of course, the Birchers are seriously dedicated to what they believe to be the great fight against the Reds. Their anti-Communism is, in fact, extreme almost to the point of paranoia. For example, the Society regards as treacherously un-American the business of selling products made in the Iron Curtain countries, even though such imports actually benefit American business. In 1962, a Miami chiropractor named Jerome Harold organized The Committee To Warn of the Arrival of Communist Merchandise on the Local Business Scene. Enthused with what he immediately saw as a fine project, Welch praised the idea highly, and in the Society's Bulletin he advised members to get in touch with Harold.

The response was instantaneous. The Founder's suggestion to Birch members, said Harold later, insisting he wasn't a member of the Society, "swamped us with mail." Welch urged Birchers to spread the boycott drive across the nation, and in city after city Society members vigorously spearheaded local "card parties," drawing Birch fans and fellow travelers into an ever-widening circle of activity.

A card party seemed almost always to be organized by a Birch chapter representative with all the trappings of a conspiratorial act. A leader would summon members to a closed meeting without revealing its purpose. Attendees would be given batches of printed flyers, about the size of postcards, which had been made in great secrecy. On each flyer was a hammer and sickle, and the legend "Always Buy Your Communist Products At——." Then followed the names of large local retail stores which allegedly sold goods imported from eastern Europe.

The Birchers and their aides were to pour unobtrusively into the offending stores, accidentally drop cards on counters, and furtively tuck others under merchandise, all the while taking great care not to be caught in the act. The game was for unknowing shoppers to find the cards when looking at wares on display. If intercepted, a "cardplayer" was to apologize and say it was all quite accidental and he'd be glad to go quietly. To play it safe, everyone undertaking the work was given the name and phone number of a lawyer to call in case of arrest.

Plagued with the petty annoyance, or perhaps seriously concerned that sales would fall off, department store owners appealed to the United States Government. To stem the boycott, a Federal agency issued a public statement that it was to the country's advantage to maintain a certain amount of peaceful trade with Soviet-dominated nations, and that importers were conforming to American foreign policy. They pointed out that the quantity of merchandise brought in from Communist countries was less than 1 percent of what this country exported to them.

The government appeal had no effect on the Birchers. The campaign spread to fifty cities in Florida, Ohio, Minnesota, New York, Massachusetts, California, Illinois, Michigan, Maryland, Texas, and Virginia, and to the District of Columbia. The Miami chiropractor's group said it had 264 affiliated committees, which meant that this was the number of cities where merchants were being bedeviled.

From card parties, the next step was for the Society's members and their friends to exert pressure upon local and state agencies. Legislators were urged to pass laws which would impose prohibitive taxes on stores carrying goods from Soviet-bloc countries. Birmingham, Alabama, adopted a local ordinance requiring any merchant who wished to sell merchandise from a Soviet-controlled country to get a license, the fee for which was $5,000. Similar legislation was passed, generally with $1,000 license fees, in such widely scattered places as Columbus, Georgia, Montgomery and Phenix City, Alabama, and Butte, Montana. An added provision of the Columbus ordinance was the requirement that after a store paid the exorbitant fee, it was required to display a sign reading, "Licensed To Sell Communist Products."

Some of the biggest names in America's retail industry felt the impact of this organized Birch campaign and yielded under the intimidation. Sears, Roebuck, F. W. Woolworth, S. S. Kresge, the Walgreen Company, and others were constrained to stop stocking Red goods. Smaller chain stores, supermarkets, and department stores, as well as numerous individual merchants, were forced to withdraw all Eastern European products.

In the end, card party operators did not have things all their own way. Protests by angered merchants finally resulted in arrests for disorderly conduct of those caught distributing the boycott cards. Many store owners, big and small, would not surrender to the organized pressure, and their firm refusals reached a climax when Bullock's Department Store in Los Angeles obtained a court injunction against further card distribution. The West Coast retailer sued the local card party committee and two of its leaders for the unlikely sum of four million dollars, an amount apparently imposing enough to give the boycotters pause.

Faced with angry businessmen now fighting them, the Birchers reluctantly abandoned the campaign. Word about the court suit had spread throughout the country and Birchers everywhere retreated hurriedly. It certainly had been fun, and it was surely patriotic to terrorize retail merchants who did not retaliate; it was somewhat different when those they clandestinely attacked hit back hard.

But this has been the history of most pressure groups that use the economic blackjack to frighten the enemy (their own neighbors) into surrender without opposition. This and other techniques used by Birchers surely created dissension among ordinary people— between storekeeper and customer, between teacher and student, between elected official and voter, between librarian and parent, between government and citizen. The method was to cast doubt on the patriotism and loyalty of the man next door. This has been the effect of the Radical Rightists on the country they profess to love and serve.

The steamy brew of dissension is never more poisonous than when injected with unadulterated hate.

Always a refuge for suspicious minds, the John Birch Society has been plagued by the problem of religious bigotry—by anti-Semitism, in particular—since it was founded. Welch himself is not an anti-Semite, and anti-Semitism is not a part of his Society's program and never has been.

It is not startling, however, that these historic hatreds have been a chronic problem for the Birch Society. Organizations of the Far Right, past and present, have always been magnets for anti-Semites and have frequently been tainted by anti-Semitism. More often than not, anti-Semites in the United States are Far Right in their political thinking and so are naturally attracted to Radical-Rightist movements. Anti-Semites also accept the conspiracy theory of history. Like Welch and other leaders of the Radical Right, they see the country as the victim of an internal Communist conspiracy, but unlike Welch and other Radical-Rightist leaders who do not preach anti-Semitism as a stock-in-trade, the anti-Semites equate Communism with Judaism (or Zionism). In the eyes of the anti-Semite, therefore, the betrayal of the United States in the last thirty years is not the result of a mere Communist conspiracy, but of a "Communist *Jewish* conspiracy."

Welch and other leaders of the Radical Right have a blind spot that makes it possible for some anti-Semites and a degree of anti-Jewishness to creep into the membership and activities of their organizations. In 1961, and again in 1963, Welch wrote long advisory memoranda for his membership on the problem of anti-Semitism. Welch denied that he, himself, was an anti-Semite and declared that he would never allow the Birch Society to become an anti-Semitic organization as long as he was at the helm. In the 1963 article, he warned that Communist plants and *agents provocateurs* would try to divert good Birchers into a misguided campaign against Jews in order to neutralize the work of the Society and its fight against the Communist conspiracy.

Though Welch voiced his concern, awareness of the problem was insufficient to keep his organization clean. Some Birch leaders have records of involvement in anti-Semitic activity—for example, the late Merwin K. Hart, head of the anti-Semitic National Economic Council.* Before his death in November, 1962, Hart was leader of Chapter 26 of the Birch Society in New York. Two Birch council members, one a resident of New York, the other of Los Angeles, were also listed as directors of Hart's Economic Council. Birch Council member A. G. Heinsohn, Jr., of Tennessee ran an ad in the *Wall Street Journal* soliciting funds for Hart's organization, assuring readers that its activity "merits your support." Another Birch Council member, Paul Talbert, of Beverly Hills, was a contributor to Gerald Smith's anti-Semitic Christian Nationalist Crusade.†

Birch "Endorsers," such as Miss Olive Simes of Boston and Petersham, New Hampshire, contributed to the Smith Crusade for years. Endorser Theodore W. Miller, a Chicago attorney, has long been identified as a lawyer for anti-Semites and anti-Semitic causes. Miller has represented or associated with such notorious bigots as Joe McWilliams of the Christian Mobilizers, Elizabeth Dilling, and Gerald Smith.

Manifestations of anti-Semitism or the presence of anti-Semites in the Birch Society at the membership level are frequent:

—In 1962, Fred Huntley of Berkeley, California, a self-described Birch Society member, promoted the sale of the long-discredited anti-Jewish forgery, *The Protocols of the Learned Elders of Zion.* Huntley placed advertisements in a local newspaper, asking readers to call two telephone numbers. Those who did heard a three-

---

* See *A Measure of Freedom* by Arnold Forster (Doubleday and Company, Inc., 1950), and *The Troublemakers* by Arnold Forster and Benjamin R. Epstein (Garden City, N.Y.: Doubleday and Company, Inc., 1952).
† *Ibid.*

hundred-word recorded message advertising the *Protocols*. When a news story was published that Huntley was promoting the *Protocols*, he made another recording to explain why he was doing it. A reporter from the *Alameda Times-Star* quoted the new recording:

"According to unconfirmed reports, something of a furor has been occasioned by our mention of *The Protocols of the Learned Elders of Zion*. Why all the fuss anyway? All this book does is pinpoint the conspiracy against the liberties and independence of these United States. . . . It is . . . un-American to suppress books, especially a book as important as *The Protocols of the Learned Elders of Zion*."

—Frank Ranuzzi, a member of the John Birch Society, runs the Poor Richard's Book Shop in Los Angeles, a major center for Radical Right literature in Southern California. He carries a full line of Birch Society material. Ranuzzi sold an anti-Semitic book called *Pawns in the Game*, a rehash of *The Protocols of the Learned Elders of Zion*, but apparently he did not have the courage to peddle it openly. He kept it under the counter, evidently for sale only when specifically requested by a customer.

—In Welch's own bailiwick in Boston, two Birch chapter leaders joined with five other Birchers to organize the so-called Boston Forum to hear speakers on subjects of interest to Birchers and their friends. The first speaker invited was Kenneth Goff, a notorious professional anti-Semite.*

—In December, 1962, Birch member Speros Lagoulis, possessor of a police record dating back to 1934, and publicly identified in Boston newspapers as an associate of American Nazi Party leader George Rockwell, opened a so-called Joe McCarthy Book Store in South Boston. Despite Lagoulis' notorious reputation, Philip K. Langan, a New England co-ordinator for the Birch Society, urged Birch members to volunteer to work in Lagoulis' store and asked the wholesale book department of the Society to sell stock to Lagoulis.

When the *Boston Herald* published a news item about this, Welch admitted that one shipment of books had been made to Lagoulis, but claimed that neither he himself nor any member of the Society's national council had ever heard of the man. The Founder conceded, however, that co-ordinator Langan should have investigated more thoroughly before urging Society members to help Lagoulis. The organization revoked the membership of Rockwell's friend and said that he would be sold no more books from Belmont.

* *Ibid.* See also *Cross-Currents* by Arnold Foster and Benjamin R. Epstein. (Garden City, N.Y.: Doubleday and Company, Inc., 1956).

—In Tacoma, Washington, a lady dedicated to the Radical Right joined the Birch Society not long after it was formed, only to find anti-Semitic propaganda being disseminated in her chapter. She complained to Welch personally about it. Shortly thereafter she was expelled from the organization. Though the complaint to Welch went by registered mail, there is no certainty that he ever saw her letter, although the Founder reportedly tries to keep close tabs on what his chapters are doing. With the publicity that followed her expulsion, it is difficult to believe the matter did not come to his attention.

The lady was Mrs. Virginia Shackelford of Tacoma, long a leading spokesman for the Far Right in the Northwest. She had watched with dismay the infiltration of her chapter by anti-Semites who, instead of spreading the alarm about the Communist conspiracy, devoted their energies to spreading anti-Semitic propaganda. She protested to Welch. At the same time Mrs. Shackelford's chapter and several others requested "home chapter" status—a special category for Birchers not affiliated with a local chapter. The other members who requested "home chapter" status received it. What Mrs. Shackelford received was formal notice of her expulsion from the John Birch Society.

—In a speech on the Senate floor, Senator Thomas Kuchel (R-Calif.) quoted a letter from a self-described (he may not have been) Birch Society member in Westminster, California. The letter spoke of "the grip that Jew Communism . . . has on our country and government" and went on to refer to "the Jew press, radio, TV and papers." It also declared that integration ought to start "with the Jew schools. And synagogues. . . ."

The blind spot on anti-Semitism that plagues Founder Welch and the Birch Society led to other embarrassing little episodes. One of them, which took place late in 1963, centered around the "Israel Cohen" hoax, involving the dissemination of a canard which originated in the nether regions of the anti-Jewish hate movement in America. The hoax had been thoroughly exposed in 1958 by the *Washington Evening Star,* an eminently respectable, conservative newspaper, and this was fully five years before Robert Welch's *American Opinion* put it back into circulation via a quotation from the fraudulent document by critic Jack Moffitt, who reviews movies for Welch's magazine.

The canard itself pretended that an English Communist named Israel Cohen, back in 1912, had written a blueprint for Communist incitement of racial strife and violence in the United States. The nonexistent document was allegedly entitled, "A Racial Program for the 20th Century"—and when the report of it was originally foisted upon the nation in the mid-1950's, some bigots and Jew-baiters tried to pass it off as the Red master plan for the racial unrest just then beginning to mark the American scene.

The Washington *Star*, however, found that eight hundred main libraries in the United States had never heard of "A Racial Program for the 20th Century," and that no record of a Communist named Israel Cohen could be found in England. The newspaper, after its exhaustive investigation, concluded that the Israel Cohen document was a fraud; it was satisfied that the hoax had been the work of professional bigots. The *Evening Star's* exposé, however, had apparently not reached critic Moffitt, let alone the editors of *American Opinion*, who had presumably read Moffitt's scrivenings before publishing them. In January, 1964, following receipt of a letter from a reader questioning the authenticity of the Israel Cohen hoax, *American Opinion* stated simply that that reader was correct. The caption over the reader's letter and the editorial note was "Gulp!"

Tom Anderson, a member of the John Birch Society's National Council and a frequent public speaker on its behalf, apparently had not read the Washington *Star*—or *American Opinion*. Two months after Welch's magazine had gulped over Moffitt's boo-boo, Anderson quoted from the fraudulent Cohen document in "Straight Talk," a column he writes for newspaper publication. The Anderson article was on civil rights, and the columnist prefaced his quotation from the Cohen fabrication by declaring that "A leading English Communist, Israel Cohen, wrote more than 50 years ago. . . ."

The blind spot of the Birchers on anti-Semitism, and their inability to recognize it, was strikingly illustrated in the relationship of the Society and its Founder with former columnist Westbrook Pegler. Pegler joined the Birch forces late in 1962 after his connection with the Hearst newspapers was severed. Amidst appropriate fanfare and breathless announcements, it was disclosed from Belmont that he would write a regular monthly article for *American Opinion* and would also be available as a lecturer through the offices of the "American Opinion Speakers Bureau."

The relationship lasted only a year and some uneasy months. Pegler's articles were, with few exceptions, marked by a noticeable recklessness and a frequent lack of good taste—directed at such long-time targets of his wrath as the late Eleanor Roosevelt, the late Herbert H. Lehman, Adlai Stevenson, David Dubinsky, Robert F. Kennedy, and the late President John F. Kennedy.

A cowardly attack by Pegler upon Mrs. Roosevelt shortly after she died brought protests to Belmont even from faithful readers of *American Opinion.* In a subsequent issue of the Birch Society Bulletin, Robert Welch tried as best he could to excuse the article, in which Pegler had charged that the former First Lady had prostituted the Presidency of the United States "with advancing impudence, rising to imperial arrogance." Pegler had added that the prostitution of Polly Adler, a former madam, was of a more honest kind.

In another article during 1963, Pegler lamented that Giuseppe Zangara, who tried to assassinate President-elect Franklin Roosevelt in February, 1933, had not been a better marksman. Zangara, he wrote, "would have been a great benefactor of mankind if he had shot better. . . ."

In other articles, Pegler developed the line that Americans with Jewish-sounding names who came to these shores from countries such as Russia and Poland were often instinctively sympathetic to communism. He contrasted this with the pure Americanism of immigrant and second-generation Americans of Anglo-Saxon and Irish stock—like himself.

Eugene Lyons, a well-known anti-communist and a senior editor of the generally conservative *Reader's Digest,* is reported to have exploded in an outrage of disbelief when he found himself among some of the foreign-born denounced by Pegler. He wrote to some acquaintances at *American Opinion,* asking that they choose between Pegler and himself. Two staff members, J. B. Matthews and Rodney Gilbert, resigned as a result.

The increasing recklessness of Pegler's fulminations reached the first of a series of terminal climaxes in November, 1963, when he wrote an article for *American Opinion* on bigotry—which he defended, declaring that it was "clearly the bounden duty of all intelligent Americans to proclaim and practice bigotry."

The article was marked by some ill-concealed prejudice in regard to the late Senator Herbert H. Lehman (he was then still living). Pegler referred to the "enormous" power of Lehman's money. "His specialty," Pegler explained, "is judges." Lehman was, he wrote, "the prophet of a sect of pushcart sophists who wouldn't be judges if they did not share his bigotries and morals. Honor and conscience are no more thinkable in such pettifoggers than in the dregs which are found in the tank of a county jail on a Monday morning."

Pegler also declared himself a racist, explaining that the term was "a common but false synonym for Nazi, used by the bigots of New York. . . ." He said a racist is "one who is content to be what he is, whether a white man, or a Negro or Chinese."

Pegler's thinly veiled anti-Semitism was apparent in the same article when he referred to the appearance in 1962 of American Nazi Party leader George Rockwell at San Diego State College, where a Jewish student took a punch at the would-be American *Führer*. Pegler wrote: "If there had been a bad riot, instead of a little shoving match, the publicity would have emphasized a horrible threat to a persecuted minority of innocent Americans, who never had more liberty, money, and power anywhere in the world than they enjoy today in the United States."

Pegler argued that what the Jews call bigotry and persecution is really "retaliation, or punishment" because, he wrote, "persecution connotes injustice."

Founder Welch apparently was uneasy about printing this Pegler article and prefaced it with an italicized statement which he himself signed. In it Welch wrote that "the basic purpose of this magazine is to offer information and create understanding. . . . Our guiding motto is: Lay it out straight." On the other hand, Welch wrote, Pegler "is a brilliant and cutting satirist who advances to attack through circuitous paths of *ad hominem* reminiscences. . . . This is anything but 'laying it out straight.' And obviously, by strict logic, Mr. Pegler has no place in the pages of *American Opinion*."

Welch added that Pegler, moreover, "has the temerity to hold a few prejudices that do not coincide with my own. There are certainly some made visible, for instance, in the very article which follows, that are quite contrary to opinions of this editor, often and strongly expressed. But this is a magazine for the general public, not a society bulletin for its members. . . .

"In the essay below he plays a number of variations on the theme that any American, of any race, color, or creed, should have the unqualified right to like anybody he pleases, to dislike anybody he pleases, and to get himself disliked in turn by anybody he pleases. The steps to that end fall properly within man's natural right, known as the 'freedom of choice.' Our esteemed fellow-editor, Tom Anderson, once put it that 'only morons and prostitutes fail to discriminate.' Mr. Pegler takes the positive side, for the nonce, and praises the 'bigotry' of those who pick and choose."

For a man who claims that the aims of his John Birch Society are to promote "less government, more responsibility and a better world," Welch's tortured editor's note to the Pegler article was a rather revealing case study of the evasion of individual responsibility. As editor of *American Opinion* Welch is presumably responsible for what appears in the pages of his magazine, and it is a responsibility which he has exercised when it suited him, for in succeeding months Welch did kill several Pegler articles.

Pegler can boast the admiration of Gerald Smith, the long-time anti-Jewish rabble-rouser. In February, 1964, Pegler made a speaking appearance at the Hollywood Women's Club before an organization calling itself "Friends of Westbrook Pegler," a hastily whipped-up name for an obvious Gerald Smith front organization. Charles Winegarner and Mrs. Opal Tanner White, both Smith intimates and associates of many years, sat on the platform with Pegler, and the meeting itself was entirely staffed by personnel from Smith's Los Angeles headquarters.

Pegler was equal to the audience and to the occasion. He delivered a blatant, gutter-level, anti-Jewish speech, replete with references to "kikes" and "sheenies" and to "geese"—a term Pegler applied to Jews because, as he explained, the Jew talks with a hiss like a goose, devours everything in front of him, and fouls up everything in back of him. (Pegler even went so far as to define "kike" and "sheenie" for the receptive audience. He said the term "kike" was not derogatory, and only referred to those persons in or from central and eastern Europe, and that the term "sheenie" referred to cloth popular in the 1920's which had a sheen to it—and since Jews were associated with the garment industry, the term "sheenie" developed. Pegler characterized such terms as "purely innocent.")

He made reference to the Leo Frank lynching in Georgia some fifty-years before. Frank, a Jew accused of the rape-killing of a young girl, was taken from his cell by a mob which then, in Pegler's words, hung him to a tree and he couldn't be unhung.

The audience greeted this statement with laughter and cries of approval. Winegarner, Smith's associate, was so convulsed that he had to remove his glasses to wipe the tears of mirth from his eyes.

Pegler also referred to the Nazi effort in Germany to exterminate Jews. He said Hitler and Goebbels were so worked up that they began stuffing the poor Jews into gas ovens. Pegler added sarcastically that the victims were of course Communists, but that didn't count, did it?

The erstwhile columnist, in his rambling remarks, also told his audience that showman Billy Rose had once asked him why he didn't print something good about the Jews. Pegler said he had replied that he'd never heard anything good about them, and that if he had, he wouldn't have believed it.

Finally, Pegler said, the Jews had "suckered" Americans into fighting "their war," and that the *real* Americans one day woke up and found themselves on the beaches of Normandy. When the

Americans came home, he added, they found the best homes and the best jobs already taken by Jews and the only thing the suckers could do was to re-enlist to keep from starving.

And there was more of the same.

There had been evidence, even a few months earlier, that in addition to his written bigotry, Pegler was descending to the depths on the lecture platform. In December, 1963, the columnist addressed a crowd of seven hundred at an Americanism Forum in Houston, Texas. This was shortly after President Kennedy had been assassinated, and Pegler told his listeners that the violence in Dallas stemmed from the fact that "we got used to violence under Roosevelt." He referred to FDR as a "fathead" and a "louse," and attacked the Anti-Defamation League, declaring that if American Jews had any wisdom, they would wipe out the ADL or "they're going to be in trouble in our country." The Jews, he added, both in Israel and the United States, were the subjects of Senator Lehman and "his associates in international finance in New York." Because Lehman had died only a week earlier, Pegler sarcastically proposed "three minutes of silence."

A reporter for the *Houston Chronicle* noted that at this point "the audience laughed."

When Robert Welch added the caustic Pegler to the team at Belmont as a writer and speaker, there already had been rumblings indicating that Pegler's attitude toward Jews was a little less than objective. As far back as 1944, Pegler had complained in his column that anti-Semites were deluging him with letters of praise after he had criticized Jews on what may, perhaps, have been minor grounds: supporting Zionism and adopting Anglo-Saxon names. But Pegler insisted he was not an anti-Semite, and most Americans and the national Jewish agencies seemed ready to take him at his word.

Yet about the same time Pegler's name was first linked to the John Birch operations, an unpublicized incident took place in New York on Thanksgiving Day, 1962, which revealed the depths of Pegler's anti-Semitism. At the Stork Club, Pegler became so boisterous in discussing David Ben-Gurion, the former Israeli Prime Minister, that the Stork Club's owner, Sherman Billingsley, had him escorted to the street by three table captains. Pegler sat on the sidewalk and when newspaper columnist Leonard Lyons emerged from the posh night club with a group of friends, Pegler called him a "kike son-of-a-bitch" and "that Jew-Communist Lyons." The once-respected writer then shouted "nigger bastard" at a Negro chauffeur who tried to help him to his feet, and was finally poured into a cab by a group of bystanders.

Pegler's prejudices also were showing throughout 1963 in arenas other than the Birch Society's magazine or the sidewalks of New York. He had for some time asserted that the New York court which in 1956 had found him guilty of libelling Quentin Reynolds in that now-famous case, had been controlled by Jews conspiring against him. Late in 1963 when a dramatic restaging of the Reynolds trial opened on Broadway—a play called *A Case of Libel*—Pegler, in an interview, called the New York Federal Courts "the Southern district of Tel-Aviv."

James Oviatt is not well known throughout the nation, as Westbrook Pegler is, but in Los Angeles, Oviatt's haberdashery store is a fancy emporium known for its fine British woolens and other expensive merchandise. It was once a status symbol to be a charge customer at Oviatt's—until 1962, that is, when the high-class customers began receiving low-class hate propaganda in Oviatt's envelopes.

Oviatt, a man in his seventies, had been in the business of selling clothing for fifty years—but that apparently was not his only business. He found time, not only to peddle hate, but to be a member of the John Birch Society, a defender of General Edwin A. Walker, and a patron to Wesley Swift, the latter a West Coast bigot who once served as Gerald Smith's bodyguard and who founded the scandalous Christian Defense League.*

When Oviatt started pinning anti-Semitism to his business, he went all-out and peddled some of the choicer merchandise of hate. His clients received the late Conde McGinley's notorious anti-Jewish hate sheet, *Common Sense;* the Benjamin Franklin Forgery, a series of anti-Jewish statements falsely attributed to Franklin; a canard purporting to "prove" that Jews plotted world domination, based primarily on *The Protocols of the Learned Elders of Zion*; and of course, the "Israel Cohen Hoax."

Customers receiving this gutter-level propaganda began to complain. And just before Christmas, 1963, a Beverly Hills columnist accused Oviatt of sponsoring a flyer urging people to "Wake Up! Buy Your Christmas Gifts from Christians." The Southern California office of the Anti-Defamation League had held a meeting with Oviatt in 1962, when complaints had first been received about the distribution of the anti-Jewish hate materials in his envelopes. At that time, Oviatt denied that he had mailed out *Common Sense*.

In January, 1964, when Oviatt was still peddling similar propaganda, the ADL's West Coast director, who had met with Oviatt in 1962, wrote to accuse the storeowner of having lied during their

* See *Cross-Currents*.

earlier meeting. Oviatt replied, in effect, that what he mailed out was his own business.

ADL's charges were then made public. Oviatt's attorney immediately demanded a "correction of libel" from the newspapers carrying the charges, but so far as is known, none of them complied. Oviatt's attorney was Jack B. Tenney, a former California state senator who once had been chairman of the California Un-American Activities Committee, and who, in 1952, was a candidate for Vice-President of the United States on the ticket of Gerald Smith's Christian Nationalist Party. (In 1953, a pamphlet bearing Tenney's by-line and entitled "Zion's Fifth Column" was mailed to members of the Congress bearing a notation that additional copies could be obtained from Smith's organization. A second Tenney pamphlet, "Zionist Network," appeared in July, 1953, and the Arab League bought 10,000 copies. These were distributed throughout the Middle East and in the United States.)

In May, 1964, Oviatt sent out a neatly printed little booklet of anti-Semitica reproduced from a March, 1942, issue of Father Charles E. Coughlin's long defunct *Social Justice*. Attached to the booklet was a neat card which read: "Compliments of James Oviatt."

Because Oviatt had publicly declared that he was a member of the John Birch Society, ADL in September, 1963, wrote to former Representative John Rousselot, then western states governor of the Society (with a copy to Robert Welch), citing Welch's declaration that he could never allow the Birch Society to become a haven for anti-Semitic feeling as long as he was at its helm. The ADL letter inquired whether Oviatt's distribution of hate materials disqualified him for membership in the Society.

Rousselot made a noncommittal reply some two months later. Welch responded a full eight months later—only after ADL had published an article on the whole sorry Oviatt story, making reference to Oviatt's membership in the John Birch Society. Welch's letter dealt not only with the Oviatt question; he wrote of the Pegler problem as well, because Pegler's descent into anti-Semitism had also been the subject of an ADL article earlier in the year.

With respect to Pegler's article on bigotry, Welch wrote that "we were already becoming quite unhappy ourselves over some of the attitudes expressed in Mr. Pegler's writings, and were starting to hold up publication even of material for which we were paying him." Welch said he probably should have written ADL earlier about the ADL article on Pegler, but that his thought was, "Why bother to explain an unfortunate incident that is now already in the past?"

Welch went on to say that "in view of our long past record of complete freedom from religious or racial bias, it was rather surprising that you would pick up and make so much out of this incident." But because the ADL's publication appeared with the Oviatt article, he added, "Perhaps I had better put the facts on the record."

Welch wrote that early in February, 1964, Rousselot's office had advised Birch headquarters that Oviatt had declared that "for several months he had neither paid any dues to The John Birch Society nor considered himself a member." Welch added: "While we had received no formal resignation, therefore, on February 16 we simply dropped this man's name from our membership rolls. We had certainly never approved of his activities which your correspondence protested; we were unwilling to allow the Society to be a haven for a man engaged in such activities; and this action seemed to us to close the matter as far as we were concerned."

Enclosed in Welch's letter was a copy of his pamphlet, "The Neutralizers," which, he said, indicated that "one of our most damaging detractors is the Rev. Wesley Swift," and he protested the fact that ADL had run Welch's picture in its publication alongside pictures of Swift, Oviatt, and Tenney.

Welch's letter concluded: "We are not anti-Jewish, and by the very nature of things we cannot be made anti-Jewish. We are not anti-Catholic, nor anti-Protestant, nor anti-Negro, nor anti-Mongolian, nor anti any member of any race or creed. We *are* anti-Communist, to the extent of being anti *all* Communists. . . ."

Welch's letter, dated May 4, 1964, reached the ADL national office in New York a few weeks after Pegler had publicly indicated that his relationship with the Birch Society and its magazine had come to the end of the line. Newspapers carried the story. Welch's letter did not quite go that far, but it was clear that he had been unhappy over Pegler.

What Welch did not answer, perhaps because he could not do so, was the question of why the Birch Society attracts the likes of Oviatt and Pegler.

The New England center from which the Birch Society exerts a certain impact on American life is a beehive of activity. The national headquarters at Belmont, Massachusetts, located in a red-brick, two-story building which the Society shares with an insurance company, is the biggest client of the local post office, situated close by. Welch uses the street floor and the basement, and the offices of *American Opinion*, the Society's official magazine, are in the basement of an adjoining building. Of approximately 125 full-time paid employees throughout the country, the headquarters employs about sixty-five.

The country is divided into four sections for Society administrative purposes and for efficiency of operation in the face of a massive amount of paper work. The steady growth of the Society has created a tremendous backlog, and so the lights in the Birch Society office often burn late. The office itself is cluttered with filing cabinets stuffed to overflowing. Bundles of printed mailings and old Birch chapter reports are stacked on the metal cabinets and on the floor. About a dozen desks are jammed together on one side of the cabinets, where staff members sit sifting through piles of communications and relaying them to the proper executive. On the other side are three rows of desks for the large secretarial pool.

The atmosphere is also hectic next door, where the *American Opinion* staff of ten is housed. The mailing and shipping departments are piled almost to the ceiling with an accumulation of books, old records, and office material. The mail room often operates full speed on Saturdays. In 1962, the Society spent $33,000 for postage, and the figure rose sharply in 1963.

The Belmont headquarters does not house all activities of the Birch Society's total national operation. The American Opinion Speakers Bureau, for instance, is run in Brookfield, Massachusetts, in the office of Gavitt-Morse Associates. The printing operations of the Society are handled by a company in nearby Lowell, Massachusetts, and have provided a substantial booster shot for that city's economy. In 1962, the Society reported a $55,000 printing expense, and this has probably climbed much higher since, with all the other organizational activities having so greatly expanded.

Unlike many other organizations of the Radical Right, the Society does not file reports as a tax-exempt organization with the Internal Revenue Service. It has never applied for such status. Welch once explained why he does not want contributions to the Society to be tax-deductible, and why he had not applied for tax-exemption for the Society: he is opposed to tax-exemption as a form of government subsidy, a form of statism. (The Founder, incidentally, draws no salary from the Society and just how much of his own money has been contributed to the cause is not known. The $1,000 fees he receives for speeches before Rightist and civic groups around the country are turned over to the Society.)

The Society's expanding activities are mirrored in its financial reports to the state of Massachusetts. In 1959, the organization's first full year of operations, it reported no paid officers but 14 paid employees. The total income was $129,000. In 1960, it was $198,000. In 1961, the Society nearly tripled its gross income—to more than $534,000—and sharply increased its staff. In 1962, gross income rose to $737,000, and in 1963 passed the million-dollar mark.

The financial reports filed in Massachusetts supply an insight to the membership status of the Society, the most closely guarded secret in the whole Birch picture. The Society publicly boasts chapters in forty-eight states and members in the other two. Welch says there are "a few thousand chapters." But revealing the actual number of members is another matter. At a meeting Welch addressed in Houston, a Birch chapter leader, in the presence of a reporter from a Dallas newspaper, said to Welch: "We have fifty members in Beaumont."

"Don't talk!" Welch said quickly. "Don't disclose the number of members. We never do that. You are among enemy ears!"

Birch strength is scattered unevenly throughout the country. The biggest stamping ground is California, which probably has nearly 10,000 Birch members. Texas is next. Florida, Michigan, and Tennessee are strong in Birchers, as are Wisconsin, Ohio, Indiana, Kansas, and perhaps a dozen other states. In 1963 the Society made some progress in the Deep South, especially in Alabama and Georgia. The Society is weakest on the northeastern seaboard and in the Middle Atlantic states. Several new co-ordinators were hired in 1963 for recruiting work in these areas.

The two metropolitan centers which probably have the biggest concentrations of Birch strength are Greater Los Angeles and Greater Houston. Dallas has substantial membership. Wichita, Milwaukee, and Columbus have considerable strength, as do some areas of Greater New York, particularly Nassau and Suffolk counties on Long Island. Stamford, Connecticut, and Amarillo, Texas, are small strongholds. In Florida, the main pockets of Birch membership are in Greater Miami, Palm Beach, Fort Lauderdale, and St. Petersburg.

While Welch makes no secret that his membership aim is 1,000,000, he is obviously far from his ambition. The expansion of the Birch Society is marked more in its publishing and propaganda than in its membership. The increase in the Birch organization's publishing, library, and recruitment operations has been meteoric.

In a report delivered on June 8, 1963, in Chicago to the national council of the Society, Welch said that in its four years of operation the Society had emerged as a " 'pilot operation,' that not only works, but which contains all of the parts and processes required for stopping the Communists, if we now construct a working model of sufficient size from exactly this same design."

At the close of 1963, Welch revealed in a report to his members that the Society was spending two million dollars a year to bring its message to the American people. The picture of Birch operations is of a substantial organization unique among Radical Right movements—and this accounts in large measure for the Society's ability to survive the critical publicity in recent years. It is the first extremist group in years to be well organized, and to have any degree of success in recruiting members at the grass-roots level. It is financed by dues and contributions received on a continuing basis, in contrast to many other Radical Right groups which have languished for lack of quick-cash support. The Society has a continuing program of activity for its members, using its official monthly Bulletin to issue assignments to members who meet regularly at chapter meetings. It not only has "chiefs"—it has "Indians" too.

At the grass roots, Birch leaders are generally people of some social and financial status. Regardless of their extremist viewpoints, Birchers are often sufficiently respectable and influential to win a hearing for Welch's propaganda, and to put the screws on with considerable pressure when they wish to.

If Robert H. W. Welch had never written a weird manuscript called *The Politician*, he and the John Birch Society might never have come under such sharp focus of national attention and controversy. In the summer of 1960, the *Chicago Daily News* disclosed the substance of the book's fantastic allegations. The waves of profound shock that gradually covered the country drew serious attention to Welch, to his Society, and to the new Radical Right itself.

It was in *The Politician*, which had been written during the years 1954-1958, that Welch had charged President Dwight D. Eisenhower (the "Politician" of the title) with being a "dedicated, conscious agent of the Communist conspiracy."

Here is an important passage from the book, illustrating the charge:

"At this stage of the manuscript, however, perhaps it is permissible for me to take just a couple of paragraphs to support my own belief. And it seems to me that the explanation of sheer political opportunism, to account for Eisenhower's Communist-aiding career, stems merely from a deep-rooted aversion of any American to recognizing the horrible truth. Most of the doubters, who go all the way with me except the final logical conclusion, appear to have no trouble whatever in suspecting that Milton Eisenhower is an outright Communist. Yet they draw back from attaching the same suspicion to his brother, for no other real reason than that one is a professor and the other a president. While I too think that Milton Eisenhower is a Communist, and has been for 30 years, this opinion is based largely on general circumstances of his conduct. But my firm belief that Dwight Eisenhower is a dedicated, conscious agent of the Communist conspiracy is based on an accumulation of detailed evidence so extensive and so palpable that it seems to me to put this conviction beyond any reasonable doubt."

To the accusations against the President and his distinguished brother, Welch added the charge that Eisenhower's Secretary of State, John Foster Dulles, and his brother, Allen Dulles, then head of the Central Intelligence Agency, were also important cogs of the Communist apparatus in America. The late General George C. Marshall was similarly accused.

An angry outcry rose across the nation as news of the treason charges against Eisenhower and other Americans spread.

Some prominent Birch Society members went to painful lengths to disassociate themselves from Robert Welch's appalling accusations. Welch himself protested that the book had been intended as a confidential letter meant only for the eyes of understanding friends. Welch's associates in the leadership of the John Birch Society insisted that the charges expressed were Welch's personal view, and were no part of official Society policy.

Yet Welch *is* the Birch Society and the Society *is* Welch. He is the same man who said at Indianapolis: "The men who join the John Birch Society . . . are going to be doing so primarily because they believe in me and what I am doing and are willing to accept my leadership anyway. . . ." The very men who now tried so hard to disassociate the Society and its viewpoint from that of Founder Welch and his personal viewpoint, had presumably joined the Society because they believed in him, and in the things he was doing, and had been willing to accept his leadership. Not only was the man whose statements they tried to disavow the moving spirit of their organization, but the view he expressed in *The Politician*— that the country is in the grip of an internal Communist conspiracy reaching into the White House—was actually the essence of their belief. And this belief is the essence of the whole Radical Right doctrine in the United States today.

Excuses and disavowals were laid aside, more or less, late in 1962, when *The Politician* was officially published under the imprint of a corporation called Robert Welch, Inc., but actually controlled by the John Birch Society.

"Read it and judge for yourself," read the full-page ads, which were placed in *The New York Times* and other leading American newspapers. The book's price tag was $8—this designed to create the impression that a collector's item was at long last available to an eager public. But neither the waiting populace nor the Birch Society's own members were told that this new edition was a sterilized, expurgated, emasculated, edited, dressed-up, toned-down version of the original. Just how much "sterilizing" *The Politician* went through can be gleaned from this excerpt in the public version:

> In the second stage, Truman was passively *used* by the Communists, with his knowledge and acquiescence, as the price he consciously paid for their making him President. In the third stage, the Communists have installed in the Presidency a man who, for whatever reasons, appears *intentionally* to be carrying forward Communist aims. And who, in situations where his personal effort and participation *are* needed, brings to the support of those aims all of the political skill, deceptive cunning, and tremendous ability as an actor, which are his outstanding characteristics.
>
> With regard to this third man, Eisenhower, it is difficult to avoid raising the question of deliberate treason. For his known actions and apparent purposes certainly suggest that possibility of treason *to the United States*, no matter how he may rationalize it to himself as loyalty to an international dream.

Now here is the way the very same point was printed in the original:

> In the second stage, Truman was *used by* the Communists, with his knowledge and acquiescence, as the price he conciously paid for their making him president. In the third stage, in my own firm opinion, the Communists have one of their own actually in the presidency. For this third man, Eisenhower, there is only one possible word to describe his purposes and his actions. That word is treason.

Also in the original version, Welch wrote: "In my opinion the chances are very strong that Milton Eisenhower is actually Dwight Eisenhower's superior and boss within the Communist Party."

In a new edition, this latter phrase is changed to: ". . . boss within the whole Left Wing establishment."

So great was the criticism of *The Politician* and of Welch's "conspiracy theory of history," that many embarrassed Conservatives urged publicly that the Birch Society get rid of its Founder and leading spirit.

One of these was William F. Buckley, Jr., publisher of the *National Review*, who noted that a number of other conservative spokesmen were also criticizing Welch. He named Russell Kirk, Representative Walter Judd of Minnesota, Senator Barry Goldwater, and broadcaster Fulton Lewis, Jr.—all of whom, he said, had raised questions as to Welch's judgment and leadership. Buckley emphasized that Senator Goldwater had stated flatly that Welch should resign. It was the Senator's view, said Buckley, that if he refused to do so, the Birch Society should disband and reorganize under different leadership. It was the editor's own view that Welch had been "damaging the cause of anti-Communism" because he persisted in distorting reality, refusing to make a moral and political distinction between a pro-Communist and what Buckley called "an ineffectually anti-Communist Liberal." Buckley criticized Welch for branding anyone who disagreed with his interpretation of history as blind and idiotic at best, or at worst a Communist or a "Comsymp"—the latter is Welch's own word for a Communist sympathizer. To agree with Welch, wrote Buckley, is to accept his thesis that the United States Government is "under the operational control of the Communist Party."

Those who disagree with Welch, Buckley declared, "are not excused if, by our silence, we egg him on."

Buckley added that it was widely known that "some members of the National Council of the John Birch Society are at their wits' end, and one or two have quietly resigned." He wrote that their lamentable dilemma was very simple: "How can the John Birch Society be an effective political instrument when it is led by a man whose views on current affairs are, at so many critical points, so critically different from their own, and, for that matter, so far removed from common sense?"

The Buckley piece, like most of the other conservative attacks, was aimed at Welch, not at the Society. This was true of the Judd, Goldwater, and Fulton Lewis, Jr., criticisms. Russell Kirk went beyond the others, criticizing the "fantastics" of the Right, but even his statement was not an all-out condemnation of the Society or its membership—just Robert Welch. Nevertheless, the chorus of criticism was widely interpreted as a conservative assault on the Birch Society and its members, which it was not.

The anti-Welch statements from conservative leaders appeared to be a co-ordinated effort to persuade the rank and file of the Birch Society to abandon extremist leaders and to follow true Conservatives such as Senator Goldwater—and the effort failed. There were, however, some indications that the monolithic structure of the Society, under Welch's leadership, had been slightly modified as a result of all the criticism. The Society's national council met more often than before. A five-man executive committee was created and Welch now appeared to be in frequent consultation with this group. Welch indicated that the contents of the monthly Bulletin, in which he personally interpreted the Birch party line, were now being cleared by the newly created executive committee.

But the melancholy fact is: the Founder was, and is, still the leader.

And to the Founder, this tide of hostility was easily explained: The attack was all a dirty, Communist-inspired smear campaign to destroy the Society, as ordered by Moscow in December, 1960. He asserted that the signal for the 1961 onslaught had been given by the West Coast Communist newspaper *People's World*, in a malicious article about his organization on February 25, 1961.

Welch charged that an attack in *Time* magazine, which followed in March, had been inspired by that of the Communist newspaper. He completely ignored the fact that unfavorable reports about the Birch Society had appeared in newspapers long before the story in the *People's World*. Besides the *Chicago Daily News*, the *Boston Herald* had run a series at the end of August, 1960. In January, 1961, the *Santa Barbara* (California) *News-Press* had published a series of articles on the Society—several weeks before that of the Communist paper. But to Welch, the wave of condemnation was triggered by *People's World* as part of a centrally directed Red campaign. The Communists, Welch believed, had trapped the Conservatives into attacking him. He added:

"This is no place for us to try to identify the reasons, some sordid and selfish, but mostly idealistic and sincere, which prompted Conservatives of such stature and standing to participate in this concerted attack on myself. And on the Society. For let there be no mistake on that score. Despite the theme of 'Welch must go!' the ultimate purpose of some of these attackers, though not of all, was to destroy the Society itself."

Welch did, however, try to identify some of the reasons later in 1962—with typical snide innuendo:

"Now we all know what strange companionships politics can arrange, especially in a campaign year. But when Gus Hall, Mike Newberry, Gene Grove, Marquis Childs, Drew Pearson, Ralph McGill, Eleanor Roosevelt, Pat Brown, Robert Kennedy, Richard Nixon, Bill Buckley, John Tower and Barry Goldwater all find themselves energetically shooting at the same victim, somebody is wrong. And it's not likely to be the Communists at the left end of the firing squad."

Robert Welch has developed a theory of analysis he calls the Principle of Reversal, which he claims the Communists employ to deceive and confuse their opponents. According to Welch, it works this way: The late secretary general of the UN, Dag Hammarskjöld, was one of the most contemptible agents of the Kremlin ever supported by the American taxpayers. Moscow levels violent denunciations against Hammarskjöld—ostensibly to precipitate his removal. But the real Kremlin objective is to force the United States and other Western nations to come to Hammarskjöld's defense and fight to retain him in his UN post. This, Welch claims, is exactly what the Communists really want, Hammarskjöld being one of the Kremlin's very own agents.

The Principle of Reversal is a handy tool for Welch and his followers. If the Communists adopt a certain position which does not square with Welch's expectation, that Red line is explained by the Principle of Reversal.

There are compelling resemblances between Welch's Principle of Reversal and the "doublethink" of totalitarianism so vividly depicted in George Orwell's *1984*. Nothing can be trusted any more, not even one's reason. Reality is in reverse. Or, to quote Cole Porter: "The world has gone mad today, and good's bad today, and black's white today, and day's night today. . . ." *

This is the world of Robert Welch. The political phantasmagoria which he constructs, in his freneticism about the alleged workings of the Red conspiracy, were explained by the Founder himself, when the Birch Society was first established. As he traced the world situation and the forward march of the "conspiracy" within the United States, he told his listeners: "Everything I am talking is fantastic. We are living in fantastic times and a fantastic situation. . . . we are in circumstances where it is *realistic* to be *fantastic*."

Actually, the members of the Birch Society have terrorized themselves. They have saturated themselves with false propaganda about an overwhelming, domestic Communist conspiracy, about treason in high places, and about an imminent Red take-over of the United States. The measure of success they may have with others is the extent to which they may paralyze with fear the ability of Americans to confront real problems of international communism. Dominated by the Founder in his book-lined office in Belmont, Massachusetts, the John Birch Society's destructive political propaganda is responsible for a good part of the existing fright.

* Copyright 1934 by Harms, Inc. Used by permission.

Some other organizations have used education and religion to fill the gaps in the broad-scaled effort of the Radical Right to undermine America's confidence in itself.

Because of the considerable criticism of the Birch Society, and even before the avalanche of national denunciation swept over it, most other Radical Rightists have been hesitant about co-operating with, or even approving of, the Birch Society. At least one such Rightist, who had corresponded with the Founder of the Society, sought to keep such communication secret. He even went so far as to instruct an aide to remove from the files literature and other materials which would show any kind of connection with the Birchers or other organizations of the Radical Right.

He was Dr. Frederick Charles Schwarz, a once-practicing M.D. in Australia who now directs a tax-exempt corporation known as the Christian Anti-Communism Crusade, with international headquarters in Long Beach, California.

It is to Dr. Schwarz that we shall now turn.

3

The Christian
Anti-Communism Crusade
— Dr. Frederick C. Schwarz

"I am a specialist on the popularization of Marxist-Leninism," says Dr. Frederick C. Schwarz. "You can't fight Communism unless you understand it."

And apparently you can't understand it unless you attend the rallies, conventions, seminars, forums, and "schools" promoted by the leaders of the Radical Right—Dr. Schwarz's own "schools of anti-Communism," for example. "Knowledge is power," Dr. Schwarz reminds us—and for the student, it is also frightening and quite expensive.

There are times when the good doctor is even more lurid than Birchers in persuading listeners to give him generous "offerings." Like all Radical Rightists, Schwarz disseminates fear—but he has been perhaps the most influential practitioner of that specialty, and he has had an undeniable impact on a large number of Americans. An alien in this country, he has nevertheless been "saving America" for the past twelve years, and in that time he has been given millions of dollars by our citizens to save our nation from Communists, Socialists, and the intellectuals.

America's fear spreaders—the Birchers, the "Christian" Crusaders, and others of their ilk—have worked with such divisive effects that on May 2, 1963, Senator Thomas H. Kuchel (R.-Calif.) took the Senate floor and addressed his colleagues on the disturbing elements of the situation.

". . . In every day's deluge of mail at my office, which sometimes means as many as 5,000 letters, telegrams and postcards," he said, "there are generally 100 and even 200 letters which I describe simply as 'fright mail'. . . .

". . . I have, in the past, attempted to reply calmly and factually to 'fright mail,' mustering all the reason and reserve I could summon . . . For most fright mail writers will come right back a week later, terrified about something else, urgently stating that they do not believe me—and that I am either misinformed or worse. Sometimes, they darkly insinuate that treason has prompted the reply they have received. . . .

"In recent months, I have been casually accused of ignorance or of a desire to sell my country down the river because I have written, for example, that: 'It not only seemed untrue on its face, but was demonstrably untrue, that thousands and thousands of Chinese Communist troops were poised on the Mexican border for an attack on California.' "

In another instance, the Radical Rightists had reported that Operation Water Moccasin—a routine Army military training operation in Georgia—was actually a devious maneuver by the United Nations to get foreign troops onto our soil and take over the United States. In one letter he received, the senator read:

"I am writing you this letter of protest, to the presence of foreign troops on American soil. That there are African Negro troops, who are cannables [*sic*], stationed in Georgia."

Another letter read: "It is unconstitutional to quarter American troops in American homes, so how come these pagan, ruthless, brutal, Godless savages? Yes, we know of the U.N. plans to place Mongolian and Congolese troops over our dear United States (the kind of troops which ravished Katanga) if the U.N. can swing their damnable world police force plan, so undoubtedly these moccasin troops are to be the same."

And others: "Sixteen thousand African troops already in Georgia, with rings in their noses and ears." "A war to invade America." "The United Nations take-over." "Integration part of the disarmament program." "Let's get out of the U.N." "Investigate NATO." "Abolish the income tax."

Said Senator Kuchel: "Clutching at half-truths and downright falsehoods, the fright peddlers fabricate hoaxes, as we have seen, which frighten Americans and divert their attention from the real menace. They sow suspicion and hatred. They attempt to undermine faith in Government, its institutions, and its leaders. They preach resistance to the laws of our land. They degrade America and Americans, and do it as well as—or better than—the Communists do."

Dr. Schwarz's technique is more subtle. In the course of his activities he delivers several hundred talks a year, mostly to middle-class, middle-aged audiences. The tenor of such "educational" talks is illustrated by two of recent vintage. At one, he stated as an undisputed fact that the Communist take-over of the United States is set for 1973, a date which almost all America-savers have agreed on, and proceeded to terrifying details of what his listeners faced when the Reds seized power. He grew dramatic, stepped close to the edge of the platform as if to bring the Reds nearer, and told them that a basic aim of the enemy is "to liquidate the bourgeoisie."

"If you own shares of common stock, it means you! Now, fifteen million Americans own common stock! If the Reds win, it means the gallows!"

At another meeting, Schwarz's Reds were evidently short of rope and had to rely on revolvers. After working his listeners to the edges of their seats with horrendous tales, with the pauses and the studied emphasis of the trained performer, the Doctor said: "When they come for you . . . on a dark night, in a dank cellar, and they take a wide bore revolver with a soft nose bullet, and they place it at the nape of your neck. . . ."

Everyone contributed generously to save himself and his country from the fate pictured for the listener by the evangelist from Down Under.

It seems wholly incredible that Americans in this day can be frightened by this kind of arrant nonsense, yet thousands and thousands of Americans have been influenced by the Extremists of the Radical Right and are pouring millions of dollars a year into the laps of these self-appointed America-savers. Their followers have actually been convinced that every facet of American life is permeated by Communists and pro-Communists. And to save the country from the fancied threat, these beguiled Americans have become willing followers of a Radical-Rightist thrust which itself may provide something of a threat to the Republic its adherents think they are saving.

The Australian who has influenced many Americans was born

in Brisbane on January 15, 1913, the son of a Viennese Jew who emigrated to England, where he was converted to Christianity. Schwarz's father had married an English girl, active in the Methodist Church, and eventually had become a Pentecostal preacher. He emigrated to Australia and, after World War I, prospered as a dealer in surplus goods.

Frederick Charles Schwarz had a normal education and, as he tells friends, he made "a personal commitment to the Christian doctrine and the Christian manner of life" when he was seventeen. He went to college and acquired degrees in both science and liberal arts, taught school, and lectured on mathematics and science at the Queensland Teachers College. While teaching, he studied medicine and graduated from the University of Queensland Medical School in 1944, served his internship at two reputable hospitals, and bought a medical practice in Sydney, which is still his legal residence.

While practicing medicine and psychiatry in Sydney, Schwarz preached in various churches. His wife Lillian May, a former pupil, and his three children live in Sydney, and about once or twice a year the Doctor visits them briefly before flying back to "save America."

This prophet of doom is considerably less honored in his own country than in the United States. An American reporter in Australia wrote that when Dr. Schwarz visits his native land he receives scarcely any public attention. "I called on an Australian editor and asked how he was received. . . . [In Sydney] he conducted a long dull meeting before 200. His Sydney collection was $70 . . . not enough to pay the meeting expenses."

From his Christian evangelism Schwarz went on to the problem of communism, publicly debating on the subject and attacking the atheism of the Marxist ideology. It was during one such debate in 1950 that two fundamentalist preachers who were touring Australia attended a meeting and found the Doctor an energetic man with a folksy way of speaking and an infectious, waggish grin on a ruddy face. His platform manner was that of a scholar in the field under discussion, yet the man was capable of the old-fashioned fire-and-brimstone exhortations. The two visitors were impressed and invited Schwarz to visit the United States for a two-month speaking tour under the auspices of the American Council of Christian Churches, a small and ultraconservative wing of American Protestantism.

The two men were the late Dr. T.T. Shields of Toronto, Canada, an old crusader who opposed "modernism" in religious teachings, and the Reverend Carl McIntire of Collingswood, New Jersey. The latter is a dedicated foe of the National Council of Churches, which he claims is Communist-infiltrated. After being expelled from the Presbyterian Church in 1936, McIntire had organized the American Council of Christian Churches. (McIntire and Dr. Schwarz seem to have drifted apart. Though both are engaged in the same effort of "saving America," they no longer appear to have personal contact.)

Schwarz accepted the invitation and began a two-month tour of the United States, which included visits with a number of evangelists, including the late Dr. William Pietsch, a fundamentalist radio preacher of Waterloo, Iowa. In 1952, Schwarz returned to this country and was offered time on Dr. Pietsch's radio broadcast. Subsequently, the American evangelist gave his listeners some joyous tidings: "A group of Christian men have felt the need of alerting the nation as to the perils of Communism. God has raised up Dr. Fred Schwarz from Sydney, Australia, as a special messenger on this vital subject. We are organizing the Christian Anti-Communism Crusade, a nonprofit Christian organization."

The articles of incorporation for the nonprofit body were filed in 1953 with Iowa's Secretary of State. The objectives that were stated: "To combat communism by means of lectures in schools, colleges, civic clubs, servicemen's organizations, and other similar organizations and through radio and television broadcasts and by providing courses for missionaries and others to be used in Bible schools and seminaries and the holding of religious and evangelistic services in churches, and through the publication of books, pamphlets and other literature and by all other appropriate means."

Three years later (1956) the Crusade moved to San Pedro, California, and in another two years to Long Beach, California, where it now has its international headquarters. Currently it has regional offices also in Houston, Texas, and in Sydney, Australia.

By 1958, when the Christian Anti-Communism Crusade was garnering large sums of money, one of the three original directors was replaced by Dr. Schwarz, and the articles of incorporation were then amended to allow the corporation "to acquire, own and hold personal property and to transact all business relative thereto which may be proper and necessary for the best interests of the corporation. . . ." They further stated that "the property of this corporation is irrevocably dedicated to religious, charitable or scientific purposes. . . ."

Nothing in the original or amended articles says that money collected by the Crusade may be spent for political objectives.

Such objectives, however, appear to be present in the thinking of Dr. Fred C. Schwarz, and he more often becomes involved in the political dialogue than in the spiritual.

On September 19, 1960, Schwarz wrote as follows to Robert Welch:

> I find this letter very difficult to write. It would probably be better for me to make a special effort to come to see you, and I hope to do that before too long. I am glad that you have written to me and expressed yourself so fully, and I regret that we have not met before this. It does seem strange that we have not come face to face as we have so many mutual friends, such a common interest and concern and, as you say, our works complement each other very much. . . .
>
> I would like to say as simply as I can the following things:
>
> (1) I believe the John Birch Society has in it some of the finest, most patriotic and most dedicated people in America.
>
> (2) The program of action of the John Birch Society has been highly commendable.
>
> (3) I have never questioned for one moment your complete sincerity and devotion. Your leadership and literary eloquence speak for themselves.
>
> (4) To my knowledge, the Christian Anti-Communism Crusade has received the honest and wholehearted support of members of the John Birch Society right across the country. I believe also that we have been instrumental in stimulating the concern of people who have been recruited into the John Birch Society.

Times changed, and some anti-Red faces got red. On December 4, 1961, Schwarz wrote to Dr. Joost Sluis, a close associate:

> As a Christian Anti-Communism Crusade, we are under thorough investigation by hostile forces desiring to discover something they can use to attack us. The things they are seeking are:
>
> (1) Links that can tie us to other organizations whom they classify as right wing.
>
> (2) Attacks on individuals or other organizations.
>
> (3) Interference in political issues.
>
> (4) Over-simplified national programs.
>
> We must be careful to avoid giving them ammunition. If interviewed by a representative of the national press, it is wise to keep a tape recording of the interview. Avoid criticism of

all individuals, organizations and government agencies such as the State Department.

Please remove from our official recorded list literature of any other organization. Please do not officially show or advocate the films "Communism on the Map" or "Communist Encirclement."

Emphasize the fact that we are Christian and Anti-Communist. We are not related to the political or economic spectrum apart from this. . . .

The wise and wary doctor has put on a little weight since he was discovered in Australia back in 1950. Today he seems somewhat dumpy because of a noticeable middle-aged spread. His face is nondescript except for animated eyes behind prominent horn-rimmed spectacles—eyes that dart from side to side when he is engaged in personal or public talk, giving him the look of being constantly alert, as though expecting someone to pounce on him. He rarely smiles, but when he makes a point and it is well received, the eyes twinkle with mirth.

Schwarz is self-possessed on the platform, a positive speaker who has mastered the technique of capturing the attention of an audience and of sensing the effects his words produce. Like a good performer, he rarely goes into his major speech without first warming up his listeners with a folksy joke about his Australian accent or a deprecatory comment about himself, so they can feel he's human. Not long ago, he adopted the TV-star technique of sitting on a stool before the microphone while lecturing at one of his anti-Communism "schools." He speaks with the ease of a professional who has rehearsed what he wants to say in words, gesture, inflection, and with just the proper timing with which to play on his audience's emotions. He is a confirmed name-dropper; he does it casually as if he had just in passing remembered what some high-ranking statesman or general had said in a personal conversation. The impression left is that he moves in top circles and that important men come to him for advice.

He seems to be two Fred Schwarzes, the first an impassioned orator who frightens his listeners and thunders on the urgent need to save "our" country by making "offerings" to the Crusade so that he may continue and expand his work. At such times, seeming to forget that he is an alien, Schwarz keeps talking about "our" country. Off the platform his self-assurance vanishes and the fire-and-brimstone evangelist becomes a second man—retiring, mild-mannered, but with an irascible temper that he shows mainly to those who depend on him for their jobs. At Crusade headquarters he keeps to himself; he rarely drops in to see or talk with those who work with him. Co-workers have commented on his frequent lack of common courtesy and on his rudeness, especially when he is upset by some annoying incident in the office, or even by a letter he has received.

In the opinion of his employees, Dr. Schwarz sees himself as incapable of error and is thus intolerant of the mistakes of others. He is, as one employee phrased it, "a fussy autocrat" who can throw a childlike temper tantrum over a typist's error. Once, when his staff failed to have enough collection envelopes for the whole audience at a rally, he raged for hours about the stupidity of his help. Others who know him report that despite his air of self-confidence Schwarz is a nervous man who seems insecure, and that when unsure of himself he either bites his fingernails or cracks his knuckles.

Schwarz is not always meticulously precise with facts in his efforts to sell his product and collect the offerings. He has not even hesitated to imply that the United States Government, or at least one of its agencies, actively co-operates with him on projects involving foreign language translations of his book, *You Can Trust the Communists*, and he has used this claim in solicitation of money for further translations into Portuguese for distribution in Latin America. In the course of this plea he announced that the United States Information Agency "is assisting in the translation and publication of the book *You Can Trust the Communists*, around the world."

Normally, it is not the province of the U.S. Information Agency to comment on America-savers hard at work in this country, but when Schwarz boasted that this arm of the Government was co-operating with him in expanding his Crusade to Latin America and "around the world," Stanley Plesent, general counsel for the USIA, wrote Schwarz as follows (June 7, 1963):

"This Agency has recently received copies of a brochure announcing your fund raising banquet, to be held this Monday, June 10. The brochure is headed 'Anti-Communist Literature for Latin America Banquet.'

"While it is true this Agency did facilitate your publication efforts in a few countries, it is not at all true as stated in your brochure that your project has the active cooperation and support of this Agency.

"We, therefore, strongly object to the use of the name of this Agency in furthering your fund raising efforts. . . ."

It is probably natural to wonder why a citizen of Australia decided to "save America" instead of his own country, and a newsman asked Schwarz this question. The doctor had been denounced by a prominent American as operating a "patriotism for profit" organization. A reporter from the *Alameda* (California) *Times-Star* asked why, since Americans are so overwhelmingly against communism, Schwarz felt it necessary to come here to "educate" them with lectures, mass rallies, and anti-communism "schools"— especially since this country had its own home-grown America-savers. So far as he could see, the reporter continued blandly, Schwarz's purpose was not to save America but to take "lots of money from lots of communities" in the United States.

The evangelist seemed slightly irritated by the reporter's combined statement and question, and answered with some words about freedom of speech. Then, pressed on the specific question, he replied:

"The United States saved Australia from Japan at the beginning of World War II . . . it was then that I decided to fight Communism with the base set up in the United States."

The Christian Anti-Communism Crusade, says Schwarz, is built on the foundation of education, dedication, and evangelism. His lectures, writings, and "schools" expound, among others, three basic premises: that communism exists, that it is evil, and that the dimensions of its threat are alarming. Defensive programs, including those of the United States Government, have proved inadequate and alone are not sufficient; hence, both governmental and non-governmental action is necessary. And all such action depends on knowledge of what communism is—its philosophy, morality, organization, deceitful techniques, and objectives.

Dr. Schwarz advises that study groups be established and students get sets of basic materials available at Crusade headquarters. These materials consist of writings and tape recordings by himself and others; there is, for instance, a beginners' special for $50, made up of twelve publications and one set of taped speeches by Dr. Schwarz; by William Strube, Jr., Schwarz's disciple in Texas; by Richard Arens, former counsel to the House Committee on Un-American Activities; and by Herbert Philbrick, who was an FBI counterspy in the ranks of Boston Communists twenty years ago.

In his talks to his students Dr. Schwarz sometimes advises that they forget certain Constitutional guarantees (Americans should be willing to renounce "a certain measure of personal freedom" in the battle against Communism), and tosses out glib overstatements and startling assertions, which can neither be proved nor disproved, but which leave his gullible audiences ripe for the "message." The Australian physician, according to the *Chicago Daily News,* asserted that Communist children were forced to witness mass executions as part of their education. Schwarz was quoted as saying: "Communists believe they must put about half the world's population to death and the children are being conditioned for their role as adults."

At Phoenix, Arizona, Schwarz said: "The hour of their [the Communists'] final conquest draws near. I think my prediction of world conquest for the Communists for 1973 was too conservative. They are running ahead of schedule. There are one billion people in Communist laboratories today being organized and exploited for world conquest. This is six times the population of the United States. . . . Their Godless doctrine of Communism is being taught children at a ratio of 5 to 1 over doctrines taught in any school anywhere. . . . If Communism takes the world, it will be unrestrained. People will be animals, to be disposed of. Imagine them coming for you."

At San Francisco he told an audience: "I believe he [Khrushchev] has chosen San Francisco as headquarters of the world Communist Dictatorship. The Mark Hopkins Hotel will make splendid offices for him . . . the people of San Francisco—those they don't dump in the Bay—can be put in the Nevada desert, which is quite handy."

Schwarz has not hesitated to repeat the long-discredited slander that 7,000 Protestant ministers in the United States have been involved in the "Communist apparatus." He has said that he himself has found the churches to be significantly infiltrated by practicing Communists. As usual, he offers little proof, but does succeed in planting suspicion of their ministers in the minds of his listeners, a favorite technique of Radical Right Extremists. From the clergy, he proceeds to a harum-scarum assault on other Radical Right targets, such as socialists, pacifists, "pseudo-liberals," and "intellectuals"— all of whom he says are used as part of the Communist plot.

The "intellectual" is his special hate—those men and women "found in the ivy cloisters of colleges and universities, frequently occupying professorial chairs, and usually characterized by a pseudo-intellectual outlook." Schwarz speaks of these intellectuals as the people who become Communists.

Dr. Schwarz usually opens and closes the day's studies with one of his talks, filled with his pious platitudes, such as "Knowledge is power," "We must know the enemy," "We must pay the price for knowledge." One of his favorite opening lectures is entitled "Communist Appeal to the Intellectual," which is sometimes called "Why

Millionaires, College Professors and Ministers of Religion become Communists."

A "seminar" is a one-day session, usually held on a Saturday, and conducted by a single speaker using films and tapes. Students are urged to continue their studies at home, which they can do by buying a tape with two speeches on it for only $5, or a set of recordings of all the sessions for $75.

In addition to income from tuition and sales, the usual banquet at the end of each "school" brings in additional cash. Here, the graduating class is urged to make generous contributions. In Omaha, for instance, the cash receipts from the banquet were $17,565, and from donations and the sale of literature, $19,644.

The faculty of the Schwarz "schools" is a miscellaneous catch-all of former employees of the Government, field informants once used by the Federal police agencies, former congressional investigators, retired military officers who are genuinely worried about our country's future after hearing Radical Right propaganda, Schwarz staff people, and others specially selected by the Doctor.

The Reverend James D. Colbert, formerly in the trucking business, a pastor who is vice-president of the Crusade, says that it has founded 5,000 study groups. Many of these local anti-Communist study groups have become recruiting grounds for the John Birch Society and other Radical Right groups who sell a "cure" for the disease that Schwarz only diagnoses. The Reverend Colbert, who once served a church in Pedley, California, is often a faculty member at the Schwarz "schools."

Very few teachers in these "schools" are teachers by accepted academic standards or state licensing requirements. The faculty is hand-picked by Dr. Schwarz and is given leeway—in the name of "academic freedom"—to attack United States domestic and foreign policy, which Schwarz, as an alien, tends to avoid. In his own talks, the Doctor exercises some restraint, and when he is not concentrating on fund-raising, he usually discourses on the philosophy and tactics of Communists. But from time to time, Schwarz also makes direct and indirect attacks on United States policy.

Some faculty regulars go about the country to lecture to the students. One of them is William P. Strube, Jr., a Texas insurance executive who attended a Schwarz rally and there saw the light, which, he says, left him shivering. Strube describes himself modestly as "one of America's leading authorities" on the subject of "the Communist tactics in the cold war." Another faculty member is John Drakeford, an Australian citizen and former Schwarz patient, now a professor at Southwestern Baptist Theological Seminary in Texas.

Lecturing on the *Communist Manifesto* and *Das Kapital,* the professor declares: "Karl Marx was a Jew"—he adds that he was short
and ugly, lazy and slovenly, and had no desire to go get a job.

Guest experts include men such as Richard Arens, who once
was on the staff of the House Committee on Un-American Activities.
In his lectures, Arens says there are three to five million illegal
aliens in the United States, all with Communist leanings or criminal
Communist backgrounds. He adds: "There are nine million Communist agents in Africa, and the House committee knows for a fact
that some African witch doctors have been taken to Moscow,
trained, and returned to Africa, loaded with a new and terrible Soviet
drug from which there is no point of return." Besides teaching at
Crusade "schools," Arens has been a paid consultant for a bio-
logical research study which seeks to prove that Negroes are
genetically inferior to whites. He has also acted as advisor to
H. L. Hunt, a superpatriotic Texas multimillionaire, on grants for
"patriotic projects." John Birch Society chapters have often heard
tape recordings of Arens' speeches. And because Arens has spoken
so often at Dr. Schwarz's "educational" endeavors, many Birchers
have heard him before.

In what was certainly a more scientific educational endeavor,
Stanford and other social scientists made a study of the Christian
Anti-Communism Crusade and the persons it attracted. They found
that, "despite continued protestations of political neutrality from
Crusade officials, the organization has several characteristics that
place it on the radical right."

These conclusions, made public at a meeting of the American
Political Science Association in New York in September, 1963, were
based on the following findings: (a) Most of the faculty members
at Schwarz's "schools" of anti-Communism clearly express Right
Wing points of view; (b) Schwarz himself has taken conservative
positions on several major issues; (c) by inference, the central message of Schwarz's Crusade is an insinuation of important Communist
penetration of American institutions; and (d) a tendency to brand
criticism of the Crusade as stemming from Communist influence.

The Stanford study found that Schwarz supporters tend to come
from an upper status group. More than half are business or professional people, 41 percent with incomes of more than $10,000
a year. More than half are college graduates. Almost half of those
attending an anti-communism "school" in Oakland were opposed
to Federal aid to education; a substantial majority opposed Medicare, and believed that trade unions do more harm than good.

Most significantly, most of the Schwarz followers believed that a great many people in the United States were Communists who were concealing this allegiance. They said they feared internal Communist subversion more than the external threat from Russia or Red China. Ninety percent thought "Communist professors" had a great deal of influence in the United States, and 50 percent thought Communists had exercised continuing influence in the Democratic Party. Twenty percent thought this was true of the Republican Party.

The group of social scientists concluded that there is reason to believe that religious beliefs lead many of Schwarz's followers to see communism as an earthly manifestation of the devil. As one Crusader expressed it: "I'm a Bible student and I am convinced that the Communist movement is Satanic in its origin, principles, and ultimate aims." The study also found that many of those questioned used communism as a convenient label for all works of the devil—political, economic, and even sexual—and that to them, the word communism embraced everything bad.

These citizens are not crackpots and malcontents, nor are they lonely, frustrated individuals looking to join just about anything that meets and screams. Because of their high educational and income status, most of them are active members of all kinds of church, civic, and veterans' organizations.

Sometimes one of the "schools" may produce a revealing incident. In January, 1962, a woman took up a stand on the front steps of the Oakland, California, auditorium where the Schwarz "school" was to be held. With an American flag beside her, she held up a sign that read "Remember Hungary!" Obviously trying to do her bit in the fight against communism, she was reminding "students" not to forget the Hungarian revolt of 1956. According to one observer, the Crusaders, presumably a well-educated crowd, seemed to have no idea what the lady was up to. They shouted, "Go back to Russia!" All were too engrossed to hear her plaintive cry, "But I'm on your side!" After a little while her gentle assurances seemed hopeless. She sighed and went home, trailing her sign dejectedly.

When it was announced that Dr. Schwarz would run one of his five-day anti-communism "schools" in Indianapolis, Indiana, the official organ of the Roman Catholic Archdiocese, *The Criterion* (October 25, 1963), published some sharp comments:

Dr. Fred C. Schwarz is coming to town Monday to save us from Communism again. He and his road show will be in Indianapolis just in time to compete with the goblins in making Halloween interesting.

Schwarz is the slickest of the far-rightists who have fatted themselves on the deep concern among Americans about Communism. . . .

One of the strange things about this alien who vigorously smears America's government and private institutions and tells its citizens how dumb they are is that he offers no solutions. He just says everything is a mess, collects a lot of money from the well-to-do, and hurries on to the next town.

This formula invariably leaves a ferment which local ultra-rightists of all descriptions attempt to turn into heady wine. Schwarz is nothing if he is not a potent force for community divisiveness, distrust and confusion. . . .

When Dr. Fred C. Schwarz hurries on to the next town, they too will find that he is a potent force in the collection of money.

The "schools" of anti-communism have been a major source of income for the Doctor's organization. Normally a Schwarz "school" is sponsored by a local citizens' committee, or by a Freedom Forum made up of leaders of local Right Wing organizations which co-operate with the Christian Anti-Communism Crusade—but it is the Crusade which receives the tuition checks, called "donations," for purposes of tax deductibility.

The Crusade has been a financial success, even though its income dropped from well over a million dollars in 1961, after the widespread criticism of the Radical Right. Nevertheless, the receipts were still substantial. In 1961 this tax-exempt corporation, which began on a shoestring, reported to the Internal Revenue Service an income for that year of $1,273,492 (in 1960 it had been only $364,535). In 1962 and in 1963 the total gross income dropped significantly, but Schwarz has collected more than $2,500,000 in the last few years.

The Attorney General of California once compiled and analyzed a list of materials Schwarz offered for sale to students of communism. He reckoned: "If an individual bought just one of each available tape and one each of each booklet, it would cost him $689.10." The Attorney General added: "No wonder this whole movement has been called 'Patriotism for Profit.'" (Schwarz declared this to be a slander.)

Tuition to Schwarz's classes is not called "tuition." Nor is there an admission charge, for that would involve paying a tax to the Government. Like his admission, the Doctor's tuition is a "donation," of $20. The "schools" will accept cut-rate donations from ministers, priests, rabbis, teachers, students, policemen, firemen, and servicemen. If a student does not want the whole five-day course, a $4 to $8 donation permits him, for one day, to learn how to save his country.

Attendance at the "schools" has varied from a low of only seventy-five in Philadelphia to several thousand in Miami. Sophisticated cities, such as San Francisco, Philadelphia, and New York, are not fertile fields for Schwarz to harvest; nevertheless, the most successful "school-rally" Schwarz ever held was in August, 1961, at the Los Angeles Sports Arena. The cash receipts were $311,253 and expenses only $96,516, leaving a nice, patriotic profit of $214,737 for the organization.

The most spectacular success of the Christian Anti-Communism Crusade illustrates how some of the money spent on extremist propaganda remains unreported because it is paid by a sponsor who deducts it as a business expense. In 1961, Schwarz held a rally in the Hollywood Bowl, this time using not only anti-communism as the drawing card, but also an impressive number of film and TV stars. A TV Special—composed of the rally and other seminars conducted by Schwarz in California—was put together. The New York *Daily News* devoted three hours of prime evening time to presenting this production—"Hollywood's Answer to Communism"—on its own station and publicized it as "a public service" program. Actually the time was paid for by the Schick Safety Razor Company and by Technicolor, Inc., which had paid for a thirty-three-station live telecast of the rally on the West Coast. The price paid to the stations, which certainly must be considered as part of the total cash outlay for propaganda, quite properly was not reported by the Crusade because the money did not go through its books.

Flushed with the success of the Hollywood Bowl affair, Schwarz decided to invade New York and hold an Anti-Communism Rally on June 28, 1962, in Madison Square Garden. When the Social Education and Action Committee of the Presbytery of New York heard of it, a memorandum was sent out to churchmen. It read in part:

"We support our government in its resistance to a Communist take-over in the free world, and we think that it should be spared the distraction at home of this lunacy of the extreme Right. . . . Hurling their unsubstantiated charges of disloyalty at leaders and institutions dedicated to building the free society that communism despises but can scarcely defeat, they are creating an anxiety neurosis in the nation. They are destroying the people's trust in their free churches, community, schools and elected governments. . . . Dr. Frederick Schwarz and his Christian Anti-Communism Crusade avoids the extremes, relatively speaking, of Welch and the Birchites. Nonetheless, there is a disturbing if unplanned relationship between these two . . ."

Members of Radical Right organizations volunteered to help make the Garden affair bigger and better than the Hollywood Bowl rally. Schwarz managed to get time on WOR-TV in the Metropolitan New York area, and was given a laudatory editorial by the New York *Daily News*. The publicity machine worked smoothly, but New York had heard too much criticism of Schwarz's operation. The rally was a failure. The Crusade lost an estimated $75,000.

In the broad breakdown of the million and a quarter the Crusade received in 1961, "schools and rallies" accounted for a high $462,000. "Meetings" brought in more than $245,000. The Crusade's report to the Internal Revenue Service offers no explanation of the difference between a meeting and a rally. "Banquets" accounted for $89,000, presumably from admissions and donations at graduation celebrations. "Brunches" produced $290,000. There was no explanation of what a brunch is in the spiritual and patriotic curriculum of the "schools."

Not listed as income by the Crusade are the large sums spent by corporations and wealthy individuals to buy television and radio time, newspaper advertisements, and reprints of Crusade literature for mass distribution. Schwarz has explained that the money does not pass through his organization's hands.

Nevertheless, the Doctor has had generous financial support. Some of the Crusade's biggest gifts have come through the Glenmede Trust Company of Philadelphia, which was the font of $40,000 between 1958 and 1960, of $45,000 in 1961, and some $40,000 in 1962. Glenmede has acted as trustee for a J. Howard Pew foundation. Other generous spenders for the Crusade were the Schick Safety Razor Company and its president, Patrick Frawley, Jr., The Rotary Club of Los Angeles, and the Richfield Oil Company. The Allen-Bradley Company of Milwaukee has paid for numerous Crusade reprints circulated around the country.

In the twelve years of his Crusade, Schwarz has poured sizeable amounts, presumably collected from Americans to save the United States, into various projects in foreign lands. Those who received these outlays are sometimes referred to as "certain parties."

The details of what was done with these thousands of dollars is not recorded in the annual reports to Internal Revenue. All the Crusade reports is that it has spent so much in this country or that. The Americans who gave Schwarz these thousands to "save America" have been given no proof that the sums went for education about communism. Schwarz told *The New York Times* that in 1961 the Crusade spent $234,560 in "foreign missionary work" which included $152,615 spent in India—$58,000 for a rotary press and a building to increase the distribution of *The Voice of Kerala,* a daily newspaper with a circulation of 29,000 which Schwarz said the Crusade has been subsidizing for nearly three years; $5,000 for an anti-Communist book distribution in Kerala; $10,000 to buy property for a home for orphan boys in Secunderabad, in Andhra State, and for the sustenance of fifty boys and their teachers.

To buy property anywhere for an orphanage is certainly a worthy undertaking, as is the feeding of orphans and those who teach them. But how and why the cash collected to "save America from the Communist threat" is spent in distant India to house and feed orphans is puzzling.

Neither in such newspaper interviews nor in the Crusade's annual reports to the Internal Revenue Service is Schwarz very specific about the sums spent abroad, such as $37,067 that had been laid out in British Guiana. What Schwarz did in other foreign countries with tax-exempt American money is also vague. Schwarz says, for example, that he gave "approximately" $25,000 to the Asian Institute of Research in Tokyo, and "approximately" $2,400 for a publication called *Our Africa* in Johannesburg, South Africa. Money spent in "saving" Spanish-speaking countries in the Western Hemisphere included the cost of printing a comic book widely distributed in Mexico. This contained color cartoons of Communist soldiers prodding a priest with a bayonet; a woman with a hammer and sickle on her uniform flourishing a whip threateningly over helpless little children; a group of slave laborers, one of whom was being lashed by a guard.

Horror comics for Mexican children—a strange "educational" enterprise for an organization which is, according to its articles of incorporation, "irrevocably dedicated to religious, charitable, or scientific purposes."

Dr. Frederick Charles Schwarz has spoken for himself in a number of interviews and perhaps it is best at this point to report on a few relevant matters in the Doctor's own words. Following are excerpts from significant questions and answers on the televison program, "Meet the Press," heard nationally on August 26, 1962:

JAMES WECHSLER *(New York Post):* Will you tell us, Dr. Schwarz . . . what your view of the John Birch Society is? I have read your comments and in many places, it seems to vary, depending on what city you are in. . . .

DR. SCHWARZ: . . . I don't feel competent to give an official judgment on the John Birch Society because I don't know too much about it. . . .

RICHARD CLURMAN (*Time* and *Life* magazines): Dr. Schwarz, as a teacher of anti-communism in the United States, are you at all concerned with the excesses on the right?

DR. SCHWARZ: No, I certainly am not. I think that this tremendous concern about the right is a hysterical escape from people who are not prepared to accept the magnitude of the Communist danger. . . .

MR. CLURMAN: May we talk for a moment again about the John Birch Society, which you alluded to a moment ago? . . . Robert Welch himself has said that former President Eisenhower was a Communist dupe, that Allen Dulles and the Secretary of State John Foster Dulles, were tools of the Communist conspiracy. . . . Surely as a teacher of how, effectively, to fight communism, you must have a clearer view of whether the John Birch Society is effective or not.

DR. SCHWARZ: . . . I do not sit in general judgement on other organizations or individuals. . . .

MR. CLURMAN: Don't you quite properly, sir, sit in judgement of organizations that you feel are Communist organizations?

DR. SCHWARZ: I feel our field is—we are specialists, if we are specialists in anything, in the field of communism, and I think when people get out of their field, their decisions and their influence is thereby weakened. . . .

MR. WECHSLER: . . . You have talked a good deal about the function of your movement in educating the country. Is it your view that the leadership of this country is inadequate to that role? . . .

DR. SCHWARZ: Yes . . . I think on the evidence it is quite clear that our past programs, whoever is responsible for them, have been inadequate.

In some questions and answers published in the Kansas City *Catholic Reporter,* Dr. Schwarz revealed a little more of himself:

Q: There is apparently some question as to whether you are an expert on communism, doctor. Just how would you define yourself?

A: I am a specialist in the popularization of Marxist-Leninism. You can't fight communism unless you understand it. And knowledge is power.

Q: To whom are your books and rallies and schools directed?

A: To every voter and potential voter in the United States. They're a grass-roots education designed for everyone, not just an educated elite.

Q: Do they represent your most mature thoughts on the subject?

A: Yes, among my books, *You Can Trust the Communists* is my fullest treatment. . . .

Q: Do you recommend books by anyone other than yourself, your speakers, and J. Edgar Hoover?

A: No.

Q: Why not?

A: Because there are so many books on communism and I would have to list them all. If I left some out, the authors would be saying I was slighting them.

Q: What do you think our universities are doing to instruct the young on communism?

A: I can't say. I wouldn't know.

Q: What makes you think Americans don't know enough about communism?

A: My observations, statements I hear, things I read. . . .

[In his opening address at the Omaha School, Dr. Schwarz described in gruesome detail what life under Communist rule is like and predicted the same treatment for Americans if they do not do something about it right now.]

Q: Do you think the people of Poland and Hungary still look to the West for liberation?

A: I wouldn't know anything about the people over there. I've never been in either country.

Q: Have you ever been to Russia?

A: No, I haven't. People are always asking me that and I tell them that it's not neecssary to go to Russia to understand how the Communists treat the people under them.

Dr. Schwarz, as already indicated, does not always hesitate to criticize United States policies. He has even implied that recent leaders of this country, both Republicans and Democrats, are not quite right in the head. In 1957 testimony as a "specialist" on communism before the House Committee on Un-American Activities, Schwarz was asked if he believed it possible to negotiate with the Soviets. He said: "To negotiate true peace with people who are utterly dedicated to the concept of the historical inevitability of class war and their victory is impossible. To think that we can do it is to indicate a failure to understand communism so completely that it approaches mental illness. . . ."

In lectures at his "schools" and in interviews given to reporters, the Australian has often become involved in comment on his host country's internal affairs. He does not, for instance, like the way the Voice of America does things: "If we were urging them to revolt against their masters, that would be one thing," he told an audience in New Orleans, "but when we keep reminding them they are in jail, I can't see what good that does." In Philadelphia, he told an audience that American support for a coalition government in Laos "will be playing the Communist game"—thus creating doubts in the minds of his listeners about the integrity and patriotism of the late President Kennedy and of State Department officials.

Schwarz has not hesitated to attack organized labor, the film and television industries, American universities, liberals, intellectuals— or any other group or institution which does not see things as he sees them. When it is suggested to him that as an alien he is meddling in our internal affairs, he quickly tells his audience, as he did in Seattle: "Our purpose is not to create distrust or to pit neighbor against neighbor. We are out to look at the truth and to examine it." When the Alameda County, California, AFL-CIO Labor Council passed a resolution opposing his Crusade scheduled for Oakland, Schwarz promptly compared the Labor Council to the Central Committee of the Communist Party in Russia. "It's the same method the Communists use," he said.

In an interview with a Miami newspaper, Schwarz criticized the Kennedy Administration. "I don't think the Kennedy Administration is making any difference" in slowing the Red advance, he said. "A year ago Kennedy was saying, 'the presence of Communism in the western hemisphere is not negotiable.' Now we are negotiating. Does that sound like progress to you?"

On June 26, 1963, at the Long Beach, California, Women's Club, Schwarz further involved himself in American domestic politics. During his talk a man in the audience arose and suggested throwing out of office all those liberal intellectuals so bitterly denounced by the Doctor. "We need to elect a different President!" the man shouted. "A President like Barry Goldwater!" At this the audience broke into loud applause, whistling and shouting its approval.

Schwarz held his hands high and in a voice that could be heard above the uproar shouted, "I would say Amen! Amen! Amen!"

Exercising some political influence of the more hysterical sort,

Dr. Fred Schwarz remains one of the significant voices in the halls of the Radical Right. Although that shrill voice, with its Cockney flavor, is a bit quieter than it has been in the recent past—and although it now stimulates a somewhat smaller return in the ever-present collection basket—Schwarz is still an important "advance man" for the country's powerful extremists of the Right. His generalizations and glib, horrifying hyperboles are still frightening those people who are understandably concerned about communism.

If Schwarz had just once used his alleged "expert" knowledge of communism to lessen the atmosphere of fright that hangs about his own followers, then one might have been ready to accept the loud protests that he is a moderate. But he has only thickened that atmosphere. He continues preaching for pay fear and pessimism. And those who are softened up in the one-day rallies, one-night stands, "schools," and brunches of the Christian Anti-Communism Crusade, are prime recruits for the Birchers and the other political extremists who move in after the Australian medicine man leaves town.

4

The Christian Crusade
— Reverend Billy James Hargis

"People distrust a politician trying to get elected, but listen to a preacher," Dr. Billy James Hargis once told a reporter. "They figure he has no gimmicks. I don't have a gimmick."

If people really figure that—they don't know Dr. Hargis.

As Dr. Schwarz pleads for funds to "educate" Americans about the evils of communism, the Reverend Dr. Billy James Hargis, obviously banking on the fear that communism will destroy organized religion, sends the hat around for contributions to save the church—more especially his own branch of the Disciples of Christ. The two Crusaders use different pitches, with neither showing the same major interest in building membership at the grass-roots level in the manner of the John Birch Society. Of all American evangelists propagandizing for the Radical Right, Hargis is the most zealous and energetic and perhaps leaves the greatest impact. His "religious" vehicle is the Christian Crusade—the popular name of the Christian Echoes National Ministry, Inc., a tax-exempt corporation which, for all practical purposes, is the Reverend Dr. Hargis.

This pudgy, prosperous evangelist has turned Radical Right propaganda into big business, directing it from the four-story building his Christian Crusade occupied in 1962 in Tulsa. From here his radio broadcasts reach great numbers of listeners. From here he writes weekly newspaper columns, magazine articles, religious sermons, books, tracts, and pamphlets. From here he makes tape recordings and publishes two magazines, one of which has a claimed circulation of 130,000 and may well be seen by twice as many readers.

A veritable Niagara of propaganda has flooded the Southwest and other parts of the country from this Tulsa building. All of it carries forward the wild Radical Right assertion that there is treason in high office in the United States and that Communists are everywhere. With Hargis, such exaggerations are usually followed by eloquent pleas for more money to enable the Reverend Doctor to intensify his warnings to America of the dire peril it faces. The method works, because so many middle-aged and elderly Americans, unduly frightened by what they hear from him, send Hargis lots of money in order that he and his Crusade may save our nation. The total is close to a million dollars a year, mostly in contributions in the $1 to $5 category; this is because the overwhelming majority of his followers are well along in years, and many of their dollars come out of meager savings or social security checks. From such funds Reverend Billy James Hargis takes a salary of $500 a week. The tax-exempt religious organization which he dominates bought a $44,000 home for his comfort, and they call it the "parsonage" though the Reverend has not ministered a church in fourteen years —even his own sect long ago stopped carrying Billy James's name in its yearbook list of clergymen.

In 1958, Reverend Hargis' nonprofit Christian Crusade dipped into its till of charitable contributions, originally given to "save America," for the purchase of a $6,000 Lincoln automobile, and in 1961, the organization used $7,500 of its alms for an even fancier car. Upkeep for the vehicles is borne by the Christian Crusade with money sent by Americans whom Hargis has frightened with tales of imminent catastrophe. On top of all this, Billy James, his wife and his father, as trustees of the nonprofit institution, voted $200 a week for housemaids and other domestic help for the "parsonage."

Perhaps it is because he is an ordained minister that Billy James's listeners believe he tells them only the truth. What he says makes a deadly impact. Billy James admits frankly that he seldom preaches on religion now; the concentration is on communism and how it has boldly infiltrated all aspects of American life. An enthusiastic supporter of the John Birch Society, and one of the

Society's official Endorsers, the Reverend goes out of his way to praise Founder Welch and his organization.

Radical Right listeners seem rarely to ask for proof of the charges made by their leaders. For instance, in January, 1964, Dr. Hargis spoke under the sponsorship of the Central Christian Church at Ft. Lauderdale, Florida, on the theme, as usual, of communism. He gave the congregation the "lowdown" on the assassination of President Kennedy. The murder was, he said, an example of the Communist use of terror. (This was, of course, also the Birch Society explanation. But neither the FBI nor the Dallas police found any evidence whatsoever of a Red plot. To listen to Hargis and Welch, such unanimity of opinion among these agencies should not fool anyone at all.) Hargis "revealed" further that the killing of Lee Harvey Oswald, the President's alleged assassin, had been carried out in collusion with gangsters of Murder, Inc., and of the Mafia.

Hargis did not explain just how the Reds and the Black Hand had become partners. He did have, however, a fund of information, including the fact that this country was steeped in socialist groups only one step removed from communism. He named these: the American Civil Liberties Union, the National Council of Churches, the National Association for the Advancement of Colored People. He also assured his open-mouthed listeners that the American Nazi Party was tied up with the Communists.

To make these charges, he must have assumed that no one would ask him for substantiation. He was right; no one did.

Although the Christian Crusade is granted a tax-exempt status as a religious body by the Internal Revenue Service, much of the evangelist's talk on this occasion, as on most others, was politically partisan. Its main burden was the boosting of Senator Barry Goldwater for President. At the conclusion, Hargis made his inevitable appeal for donations, explaining that he had just written another book and needed $7,500 to have it published. Ushers went through the audience passing out charity envelopes as Hargis called for $100 checks. Each donor would get $100 worth of copies of the new tome, Billy James said.

Billy James is about forty. Jiggling a wide double chin when publicly pleading with the Almighty to bestow generosity upon his hearers, Billy James has been variously described as portly, stocky, beefy, or just fat. Les Dunnavant, a faithful follower who chauffeured Hargis' luxurious Greyhound "home and office on wheels," once told a reporter: "We can't keep any sweets around. If it's in here Billy will run to the refrigerator like a kid. We try to keep him on lean meat. He's a connoisseur of food—the consumption of it." Hargis expressed it differently: "I can't drink Metrecal and speak every night. I carry a tremendous schedule." In short, he indicated, he simply had to eat.

The Reverend Dr. Billy James Hargis delivers his nightly speeches in a moderate, conversational tone—up to a point of emphasis, and then his arms wave and a pudgy finger jabs the air as he reaches a fire-and-brimstone pitch. If only by sheer contrast to his quiet voice at the opening of his remarks, his thundering brings listeners to the edges of their seats. The speeches are peppered with a touch of cracker-barrel humor. When a phrase finds favor with an audience, he adds it to his permanent presentation. Once when he referred to the Union Theological Seminary as the "Union Theological Cemetery," the audience laughed. Now it is a standard line with Billy James.

Hargis moved toward his lucrative brand of envangelism when he was quite young. As a student he had been shy and quiet. His family was of moderate means, yet he seldom had spending money, rarely dated girls or went to parties. Scholastically, he had just made it with a C average until about midway through the eleventh grade. At that point he changed as though he had been touched by a good fairy, and his personality blossomed and his tongue unlatched. Almost overnight he became a polished speaker. Simultaneously, his scholastic ratings jumped mostly to A's. But his conversation was not of religion; it was chiefly of politics and government.

Billy James graduated from Texarkana High School and enrolled in Ozark Bible College at Bentonville, Arkansas, an institution with only twenty students. After attending this academy about a year, he was ordained at eighteen as a minister in the Disciples of Christ Church, a denomination which merged some years ago with the Christian Church. There seems to be good reason for his being dropped from his church's yearbook. "He is now engaged in a private enterprise which has no connection whatsoever with the Christian Churches (Disciples of Christ)," a church leader said.

Hargis' first pastorates were in small towns in Oklahoma and Missouri. He settled finally in Sapulpa, Oklahoma, when offered the pulpit of the First Christian Church there. The turning point in his life, Hargis says, came when he was twenty and was visiting with a minister to whom he expressed the fear that Communistic influences might be taking control of Christianity in this country. The minister's "So what?" so infuriated young Billy James that he then vowed, he says, to dedicate himself to stop the growth of communism. He persuaded his church to pay for a "religious" radio broadcast, and the response from listeners was a revelation of the numbers he could reach through this means. As an energetic young man of twenty-five, he quickly found his small-town pastorate unsatisfying. In 1950, he resigned to launch the campaign to save America from Communists and Liberals.

Within a year Billy James incorporated as a "religious, non-profit making body" called the Christian Echoes Ministry, Inc.—later, the Christian Echoes National Ministry. The bylaws of the corporation are not on file with the Oklahoma Secretary of State.

Before long, Hargis was broadcasting across a wide swath of America's heartland—from Roaring Spring, Pennsylvania, south to Eufala, Alabama; from a South Dakota station (with the call letters KORN) to the people in Thief River Falls, Minnesota, and in Muleshoe, Texas. Hargis was a man of the cloth, and his impassioned warnings of the horrendous domestic Red Plot impressed or frightened many people. They responded generously to his pleas for money to support and expand the Crusade. In 1952, his first full year of "saving America," Billy James took in over $70,000 through contributions, the sale of publications, and profits from a hotel and recreation camp for his followers. At the year's end the corporation had a nice surplus of $33,000.

As a religious preacher, Hargis intensified his theme that treason is everywhere and that communism is about to seize the country and destroy its churches. He rapidly built up a following estimated to number 75,000. In this he has been aided for almost ten years by L. E. ("Pete") White, a shrewd public relations man who earlier, in just a few years of intensive promotion, had turned the famed faith-healing preacher, Oral Roberts, into a national personality and a million-dollar enterprise.

It did not take Billy James very long to perfect his technique of raising money. Always conscious that people will tend to believe ministers, he devised a unique ritual of backwoods, fundamentalist exhortation and loud prayers to the Lord to open the eyes, hearts, and wallets of his listeners. The night he raised $38,870 to pay for twenty-six half-hour talks on a national radio hookup will illustrate the effective devices he employs:

The scene was the Third Annual Convention of the Christian Crusade. Some seven hundred Crusaders were in the audience. Hargis told them there was good news that day. He had a chance to go on the Mutual Network for six months at a special low rate— "for only $38,870," as the evangelist put it. Hargis then launched what a *New York Times* reporter described as a "prayer auction" to raise money. Using alternate appeals to God and to the seven hundred persons present, Hargis began by crying out:

"I pray to God for one man to sponsor this program for six months. I know that man exists in this audience. Will he stand up?"

No one stood.

"All right, then, we will divide this burden. I need four men who will accept God's challenge and give ten thousand dollars each to sponsor this program."

Two men stood up.

"Give us four, Oh, God, who would give five thousand dollars each. Quickly! . . . Two thousand?"

One man stood.

"One thousand dollars?"

Three men stood up.

And that's how it went, down from $500 to $100. When Hargis had finished, seventy-nine men and women had pledged a total of $38,870—the exact amount needed to put the Tulsa evangelist on the air.

The entire proceeding was, in short, an auction by a skilled performer who was selling God, religion, the church, and the preservation of the United States while he held the Bible in one hand and a cash register in the other.

No one in the Radical Right compares with Billy James Hargis in the effectiveness of appeals for contributions, and he is just as competent in his written pleas as in his personal appearances. The printed requests are frequently works of art, and there is a solicitation in almost every piece of mail that goes out of the Crusade's headquarters. Each sounds a heart-tugging note—from a simple cry that this is "An Emergency Appeal!" to a melancholy moan that if sympathizers do not send money in a hurry, the Christian Crusade will be washed up. In such heart-rending appeals, Hargis sometimes writes messages across the top of the letter in his own handwriting, like "Shall I quit now?"

The reader is often prodded to make his contribution for specific projects, and Billy James has many projects. Sometimes Betty Jane, his wife, is able to touch the hesitant heart. In July, 1962, a letter reproduced from her handwriting in a personalized communication from her to the formidable Crusade mailing list of a few hundred thousand souls, read:

Dear Christian Crusade Friends. . . . I have always tried to keep the children mindful of their Daddy . . . proud of him and the work he is doing. Only recently we have felt the need to tell them why he is not liked by everyone. This is hard to explain to little ones but . . . I thought they should be prepared if they should hear something unfavorable about their Daddy at school or at play.

I have prayed that some article in some magazine or newspaper might note that Billy is a father of four children who love him very much . . . he [Billy] is pictured by the liberal press as heartless and greedy, "out" for money and publicity and doing our country more harm than good.

Following this wifely and homey confidence came the pitch:

Recently, because of illness, I have not been able to visit the office as often as I like, but I know the work is in great financial need right now. I can sincerely say that Billy's every thought is on Christian Crusade. He is always thinking what else can be done to get the message out, at the same time working day and night to provide the "ways and means."

Won't each of you help to relieve some of this pressure by your contributions? He will return to his desk next week after a speaking tour to 13 towns . . . He will be tired but a wonderful response from you, his friends, could lift a great burden from him. I pray the Lord will use me through this letter to help Christian Crusade, for I want so much to do my part during these critical days. . . .

P.S. The office informs me that Billy has written a brand new booklet called "American Socialism—Moving America Downhill!" His staff tells me this is the best thing he ever wrote exposing all American Liberals. Also, if you would like one, I would like to send a snapshot of Billy and the children.

Billy James Hargis is more frankly and more specifically political than is Dr. Schwarz, even though once accredited as a minister of God.

At the end of November, 1963, Hargis addressed three hundred influential citizens in Borger, Texas, who came from several nearby communities. The subject was "America, Back to God and Constitutional Government." When Borger's mayor introduced him, Hargis urged his fascinated listeners to return the United States to a form of government which emphasized individual freedom and free enterprise. He said that while different philosophies are espoused by the two major parties, Democrats such as Strom Thurmond and Harry Byrd have the same political views as Republican Barry Goldwater. According to the local newspaper, Hargis worked himself to a fire-and-brimstone stage, shouting:

"The healthiest thing would be to get these conservatives out of both parties and start a conservative party!"

The audience cried, "Amen!"

"Take a second look at the civil rights legislation," Hargis continued. "If you want to serve nobody but a blue eyed German at your place of business, that is your right."

He tore unmercifully into the United Nations, calling it "that traitorous outfit in New York City." He warned his credulous audience of the dangers of a Red take-over because of liberal influences, a take-over so near that he apparently thought it justified this anguished cry:

"This coming Thanksgiving may be the last legal one we Americans will celebrate!"

Having frightened the audience thoroughly, he jabbed a forefinger at them and yelled, "What are you sitting around for— waiting for a tornado? When are you going to do something to bring truth to the American people?"

If such talk does not clearly establish that the Christian Crusade uses religious trappings as a screen behind which to disseminate pseudo-political propaganda, a study of Billy James's newspaper, *The Weekly Crusader,* will do so. The following cover titles on recent issues of the official publication indicate the interest of the Reverend Doctor in the things that are Caesar's:

> "The Communications Media: Aiding the Kremlin"
> "The World Court: Threat to American Sovereignty"
> "The Story Behind Birch Society Attacks"
> "Mr. Kennedy, Whose Side Are You On?"
> "The 'Liberal' Threat"
> "Subversive Forces Influence 1962 Elections"
> "Washington, D. C.—Uncertainty, Dishonor, and Failure"

Hargis knows that blatant political activities would endanger his coveted tax-exempt status. When he called what Treasury Department officials might have regarded as a political conference, designed to persuade a number of Radical Right and fellow-traveler organizations to co-ordinate their activities, he emphasized that he and Betty Jane were personally paying for the meeting hall. Christian Crusade funds, he said, were not being used for this meeting, which was held on the night of March 20, 1962, and turned out to be an important, closed-door affair. About one hundred top-level delegates from approximately seventy five Right Wing groups met at the Washington Hotel in the nation's capital in response to the personal invitation Hargis sent out. The invitation read in part:

> Dear Fellow Country savers: I do not have to tell you that our country is in jeopardy. . . . I feel that there is a growing need for greater coordination of the efforts of the anti-communist and conservative movements of America.
>
> Last summer, while in Washington, D. C., a congressman friend, who must remain nameless at this time, suggested that we have a monthly or a quarterly meeting of the leaders of the grass-roots anti-communist movements in Washington with the conservative congressmen from both political parties. . . .
>
> It is not a fund-raising affair and at this writing, I feel that no press representatives should be allowed. We are not going to Washington to make news, but we are going to Washington to listen to some great patriotic anti-communist leaders brief us on pending legislation that needs the support of the conservative masses.
>
> Organizations that are anti-Catholic, anti-Jew, anti-Protestant, anti-Negro are not welcome at this meeting. This meeting is for those responsible, reputable anti-communist groups that are concerned with the growth of communism internally and want to do something about it. This is not an effort to unite all these movements into one organization, either. We are not interested in a unity, but in cooperation.
>
> Mrs. Hargis and I will pay the cost of the auditorium. There will be no contributions taken, pledges solicited, or books sold. . . .

The conference decided "to actively support, when the organization's structure permits, conservatives running on either political ticket." The formation of a third party was discouraged. Instead, it was suggested that Conservatives should go to work on the precinct level, backing and encouraging others to back the Conservative candidates.

In a later report, Hargis informed his followers that Congressman E. Y. Berry had asked the delegates "to sound out their congressional candidates on their liberal tendencies, and cast the vote for only those who are unalterably opposed to liberalism." Congressman John Rousselot, he stated, had accused the "political liberals" in Washington of attempting to "socialize the nation one step at a time." The congressman, an avowed Bircher, demanded that President Kennedy "get tough with liberals and communists before our nation is wrecked."

The Washington conference ended with those present agreeing to meet periodically to determine specific areas in which they could co-operate and to devise tactics which would influence, if not actually capture, one or both of the major political parties. It was an ambitious goal and a revealing one.

There was something in the political meeting convened in Washington by Dr. Hargis that smacked of the conspiratorial attitude which the evangelist attributes to his enemies. Also present in this gathering of "loyal Americans" were certain specific influences darkly corrosive of American democracy.

Admission was by invitation only, and a thorough security check was made at the door to make sure that only those with such invitations were admitted. Newsmen were not welcome. Some reporters who had learned of the Far-Rightist gathering waited outside and were able to identify quite a few who attended. Among those recognized were representatives of the Daughters of the American Revolution, the John Birch Society, the National Indignation Convention, We, The People! (of which Hargis was national chairman), the Right To Work National Committee, Young Americans for Freedom, the American Society of Physicians and Surgeons, the American Coalition of Patriotic Societies, the Citizens Foreign Aid Committee, Liberty Lobby, the American Free Enterprise Association, and The Manion Forum. There were also two representatives from outfits whose major activity is to spread anti-Semitism.

Hargis has consistently said he wants no part of anti-Semitism and nothing to do with anti-Semites such as Gerald Smith. Yet, Smith's long-time professional associate, Mrs. Opal Tanner White, arrived for the conference and was able to pass through the security check. Present, too, was a youngish man who said he represented the Nationalist Party of New York, a gutter-type anti-Semitic group. Just how these anti-Semites came to be present, while their likes were at least publicly rejected, was never explained.

Despite the participation of these particular delegates, identified with anti-Semitism, Hargis insists that the Christian Crusade is not anti-Semitic. Actually, neither Hargis nor Christian Crusade has disseminated anti-Semitism. Yet, even aside from the Washington conference, some of Billy James Hargis' closest associates have been identified with anti-Semitic causes and activities.

When Hargis originally decided on his save-the-country campaign, one of the first persons to whom he turned for guidance was the late Reverend Gerald B. Winrod, a propagandist so notorious for his pro-Nazism and anti-Semitism in the 1930's and 1940's that he became known as the "Jayhawk Nazi."

Billy James can call himself "Doctor" because of an honorary Doctor of Divinity degree given him in 1954 by The Defender Seminary in Puerto Rico, an enterprise set up by the Reverend Winrod. The degree is unusual because it was given to Hargis before he got his Bachelor of Arts in 1956 from the Burton College and Seminary of Manitou Springs, Colorado. Two years later the same institution gave him a Bachelor of Theology degree. (The Department of Health, Education and Welfare says Burton College is a "degree mill," which it defines as "an organization that awards degrees without requiring its students to meet educational standards for such degrees established and traditionally followed by reputable educational institutions.")

In 1957, Dr. Hargis was given an honorary Doctor of Laws degree by Belin Memorial University, then located at Chillicothe, Missouri. This university, too, is listed as a "degree mill" by the United States Government. Dr. Clyde Belin, president of the University, was indicted by a Federal grand jury in Kansas City on June 25, 1959, on six counts of using the mails to defraud, offered no defense, and was sentenced to a year in prison.

Not only did Hargis go to Winrod for professional guidance, but he also wrote articles and letters for Winrod's *Defender,* once a major anti-Semitic publication on the American scene. Hargis also co-operated with the late Reverend E. F. Webber, former pastor of the Calvary Tabernacle in Oklahoma City. Webber conducted the "Southwest Radio Church of the Air" and issued a magazine called *Truth,* which published articles by such notorious anti-Semites as Don Bell, George Deatherage, and the Reverend Bob Shuler, Sr. In 1958, Hargis and Webber joined forces for a series of one-day Crusades in six Texas cities, billing them as "The Texas Tour for Christian Americanism."

After the *American Mercury,* a once truly great magazine, had deteriorated into an organ for blatant anti-Semitism, Hargis actively promoted it among his followers, making an arrangement with its publisher to exchange articles and to offer special joint subscription rates for the *Mercury* and his own Christian Crusade magazine. In urging this package deal, Hargis praised the anti-Semitic publication as ". . . far and away the most courageous and authentic patriotic publication in America today. . . . Published by fearless Christian Americans, the *Mercury* brings TRUTH and HUMAN INTERESTS into *our* home each month . . . and I think you'd like it in *yours,* too." (The *Mercury* has since changed ownership and now reflects a fundamentalist and ultra-Rightist viewpoint, but no longer disseminates anti-Semitism.)

Ed Hill of Tulsa, Oklahoma, who contributed money to Gerald Smith's organization, is a trustee of the Christian Crusade. The late W. L. Foster of Tulsa, also a financial contributor to Gerald Smith's outfit, was Hargis' business advisor. Lieutenant General (Ret.) Pedro A. del Valle, a vice-president of the late Merwin K. Hart's National Economic Council, and himself an anti-Semite, was once listed as a member of Hargis' national advisory committee.

Allen Zoll, a notorious anti-Semite who in the 1940's headed the American Patriots, Inc., an organization listed as subversive by the United States Attorney General, was on the staff of the Christian Crusade in 1961. He joined after he had made a deal to sell Hargis the "priceless" files he had collected. (Among Hargis' endless appeals for money was one for $2,400 to pay the shipping costs of these files which, Crusaders were assured, contained the "names of thousands of clergymen and educators who had chosen to affiliate with communist front organizations over the years.")

Willis Carto, who was present at the political meeting called by Hargis at Washington, D. C., in 1962, is an official of the Radical Right body in Washington called "Liberty Lobby." He was a featured speaker at a major Christian Crusade convention in Tulsa. From 1955 to 1960, Carto was executive secretary of a San Francisco organization called Liberty and Property, which published the periodical called *Right.* This publication not only disseminated blatant anti-Semitism, but was a clearing house for news and information about anti-Semitic activities.

Wickliffe Vennard, manager of an insurance company in Houston, Texas, believes that the Federal Reserve System causes most of the evils not only in the United States but across the world. His "revelations" about the Federal Reserve System are generously salted with charges of an openly anti-Semitic nature. Vennard also distributes documents spiced with euphemistic references to a "small minority" which "financed the Russian revolution" and which "furnished advisors to our Presidents." His material states that "our enemy was and is within—the International Zionists who steered our ships of state from Wall Street by means of money control." In August, 1957, Hargis praised Vennard's book on the

Federal Reserve System (*The Federal Reserve Corporation*) and offered it as a free gift to potential contributors.

Besides worrying about what he sees as the imminent Communist take-over of the United States, Hargis is also troubled about young people. If the young could be properly trained (for a reasonable price), they could develop into effective anti-Communist "leaders." The evangelist decided to found a college which would concentrate on anti-communism, at the same time serving as a hotel where scholars could live while studying, and which, between semesters, could operate as a lucrative summer resort. Hargis bought the sixty-eight-room Grand View Hotel in Manitou Springs, Colorado, and broadcast plans to establish an institution of learning:

"For over one year now, I have been aware of the fact that the conservatives of America are not reaching America's youth as we should. Most of our Christian Crusade rallies are attended by middle-aged couples and older folks, but very few young people of high school and college age attend. . . . We need to reach these youths. We are all aware of the liberal poison being spread in our high schools, especially in the metropolitan areas, by the National Education Association."

Describing the new college as "our greatest project," Hargis happily announced the purchase of the hotel at the foot of Pike's Peak, and said that at the outset it would house the Christian Crusade's Summer Youth Anti-Communist University. "Every two weeks," he explained, "we will train 150 students who will return to their high school and college campuses to fight communism." (The Colorado community did not turn joyous handsprings over their new neighbor. When told of Hargis' plans to make Manitou Springs a college town for eager young Radical Rightists, Reverend Warren Hile, pastor of the First Christian Church of Colorado Springs, and one of the most respected ministers in the area, commented: "The nation is full of these radio preachers who prey on old people and collect millions.")

Interested observers of Hargis' activities and techniques are not certain whether he is trying to alert people to what he sees as Left Wing dangers or whether he simply uses superpatriotism as an attention-getting gimmick to attract crowds in order to sell his neatly packaged propaganda products. One such observer who has studied various Hargis rallies and activities noted that for years Oklahoma had been the happy hunting ground of the itinerant medicine man. Traveling in a covered wagon and calling himself "Doctor" or "Professor," the fast-moving pitchman attracted a crowd by putting on quite a show, and then peddled snake oil or some other nostrum guaranteed to cure what ailed the customers. Hargis, said this observer, is today's version of the snake oil peddler. He has the cure for whatever ails America.

As did the smarter medicine man, Hargis, using every conceivable means to draw money for his Crusade from viewers, listeners, and readers, has annually increased his gross receipts as he has expanded his "ministry." In 1961, he took in some $816,000. His expenses, which he listed as "religious promotion," included $293,000 for radio time, $118,000 for printing, $28,000 for travel, and $12,000 for speaking tours. It was to aid him in his travels that the Crusade leased the sleek Greyhound bus and reconditioned it at a reported cost of $50,000. The land-cruiser was given wheel-to-wheel mustard-color carpeting, orange upholstery, a desk, a stainless steel kitchen with refrigerator, a bathroom with shower, a mobile telephone, radio broadcasting facilities, and comfortable sleeping accommodations for five. Billy James rode in $50,000 worth of kingly comfort when called away from his $44,000 "parsonage" and in need of more space than is afforded by his $7,500 automobile.

"I couldn't build a movement sitting in my office," said Hargis. "I believe in personal contact. You've got to get out and shake hands. My creed, too, is follow-up."

As a traveling minister of the gospel, Billy James is always on tour, declaiming that treason is everywhere and that the nation is in mortal danger. Frightened Americans go on pouring a river of gold into his lap so that he may go on "saving" the country and its churches from the Reds. The unmistakable rise in the total wage he pays to his office staff—girls who open with care the envelopes containing checks and cash in mail which arrives by the sackful, girls who warmly acknowledge contributions, girls who meticulously fill out cards for future money pleas and do other such office work—indicates how Hargis' movement has grown. The weekly wage for clerical help has climbed from a few dollars to over $1,500.

When in 1961 and 1962, national condemnation of the Birch Society snowballed, Hargis was caught in the resulting criticism of the whole Radical Right and suffered a severe setback. He had expected his 1962 income to reach $1,250,000, but it added up to about $775,000—not, however, an untidy sum.

Before the temporary adverse reaction to the Radical Right became evident, a banner year seemed to be in the offing for the fast-moving evangelist. A Tulsa public relations firm that Hargis had hired almost ten years before turned up with a proposal for an "Anti-Communist Leadership School" to train leaders to fight the Red evil—at $100 for five days.

The Hargis School attracted national attention of sorts, perhaps because of nimble public relations footwork. It opened at the Mayo Hotel in Tulsa in January, 1962, under the warm glow of television lights. National magazine writers and newspaper reporters swarmed over the hotel rooms that were converted to academic purposes. A quick check showed that there were 179 students from twenty-three states—men of the cloth, business people, housewives—a cross section of Americans truly troubled by the shrill Hargis alarms that Reds are under our very beds and that the big take-over has been set, so to speak, for the day after tomorrow.

The students were to be the first of the new apostles who, after hurried studies, would go out to carry the Hargis message throughout the land. Each earnest, well-meaning pupil listened attentively to interminable tape recordings and to dull talks by teachers who were presented to them as experts. For the $17,900 the students paid, they heard how an awesome number of native Communists, Left Wing sympathizers and fellow-traveling Liberals were successfully plotting to destroy the Republic.

From the most sincere of his adult students, Hargis selected those whom he flattered with the title "Associate Evangelist." He encouraged them to help sell Hargis books, Hargis pamphlets, Hargis films, Hargis records, Hargis songs, Hargis folksy sayings, and other Hargis products—and to send him the cash for the Crusade.

The second Leadership School, in 1963, was held in a motel outside of Tulsa, and its major theme was that American domestic reforms of the last thirty years were part of a Communist conspiracy. Julian Williams, director of research for the Christian Crusade, read from Communist writings to show that Left Wingers favored these reforms, as if that fact automatically rendered the reform bad. The intrinsic character of the proposed reform was apparently irrelevant.

To a reporter from the *St. Louis Post-Dispatch* who covered the second Hargis school, the money-conscious evangelist voiced his conviction that the clear drop in public attention and a consequent decline in contributions to his Crusade were due to the "liberal press—a biased, prejudiced press." The evangelist holds the opinion that Liberals are of more concern than Communists.

He is actually more afraid, he says, of the "economic, political and religious Liberals" than the Reds themselves.

Billy James is an Endorser of the John Birch Society and he regards Robert Welch as "a great American patriot."

Another Birch Society figure who has attracted Hargis is former Major General Edwin A. Walker. Walker had resigned his commission in 1961 after the discovery of his improper political activities, conducted while on duty in Europe, had led to disciplinary action. The General had gone on to become a hero of the Radical Right, a status he reinforced by appearing at the University of Mississippi, at Oxford, in September, 1962, at the time of the riots resulting from the registration of Negro student James Meredith. In 1963, with Walker as the drawing card, and with the help of his own public relations firm, Dr. Billy James Hargis organized a seventeen-state, twenty-seven-city, coast-to-coast series of rallies to save the country from Communists and Liberals.

The tour was called Operation Midnight Ride—a name obviously chosen to give it the appearance of a 1963 variation of Paul Revere's historic warning to his countrymen that the enemy was upon them.

In every city where Walker and Hargis were scheduled to speak, Radical Rightists and their fellow travelers ardently aided in promoting the superpatriotic meetings. Birch Society members were helpful, especially since the Founder had urged in his monthly Bulletin that they climb on board Billy James's "Ride." The smoothly directed campaign won maximum publicity for the national tour wherever it went. Since the Radical Rightists are often respected members of their community, they are easily able to establish personal contact with local newspaper editors and with managers of local radio stations to assure advance coverage of such doings. In one Southern city, word even went out from Ku Klux Klan leaders urging their hooded followers to be at the Hargis rally and to stir up attendance from among those they knew. In each city telephone squads were organized to spread word that today's Paul Reveres were on the way.

Hargis and Walker drew almost 40,000 persons at their twenty-seven rallies. Judging from these audiences, and from the amount of the collections and the extent of the sale of literature, the Midnight Ride was a very successful venture. Nowhere was the turnout greater than in Los Angeles, where, on the evening of April 3, 1963, the Preacher and the General completed their cross-country tour at the Shrine Auditorium before an audience of 4,500.

It was an exciting evening. Crowds happily waited more than an hour and a half in a gala atmosphere before the doors were opened. One enthusiastic woman gushed that it was "the biggest thrill of a lifetime." The waiting mass of people outside the great meeting hall swelled to unexpected proportions, and still they came —by car, by bus, and on foot. Vendors with feelings for patriotism and profit appeared, and they peddled with equal fervor little American flags and bags of peanuts. Other cheerful hawkers sold newspapers and pamphlets. Many had brought along their own copies of nationalist publications, including issues of *Common Sense,* the notorious anti-Semitic periodical printed in Union, New Jersey. (To those who did not have a copy, an elderly, sweet-smiling woman in a flowing, wide-brimmed hat peddled the hate sheet, extravagantly assuring all within earshot that *Common Sense* was "fine, patriotic literature.") Still others offered a selection of John Birch Society materials. One street peddler boldly waved postcards which advocated "A White Christian Party." The people bought literature, exchanged periodicals, and gossiped with noisy cheer. It was the county fair—with an ugly, pseudo-political attraction at its core.

Then the friendly mood of the 4,500 mostly middle-aged and elderly men and women suddenly changed. They became aware that sign-carrying pickets from the National Association for the Advancement of Colored People were marching among them. The carnival spirit vanished in an ominous silence. Men who had been jesting with one another turned grim faces to the pickets, faces that could fuse into an unreasoning mob. "Give me a machine gun and I'll mow those bastards down," said one rally-goer.

Three buses appeared, filled with Hargis people from the Central Baptist Church. The new arrivals began pounding their palms against the sides of their buses, shouting insulting comments at the NAACP marchers. Anticipating that their rally would be picketed, each busload had brought its own supply of placards, which were promptly passed out. Almost simultaneously a group of John Birch Society people appeared with their own signs, and the area before the Shrine Auditorium became a confused mass of pickets.

The doors finally opened and the people moved quickly into the arena to try for the best seats. A conflict was avoided because the "patriots" were more anxious to see and listen to, up close, the defenders of their churches and their country. In no city visited by the tour were these happy Rightists charged admission. Had they been so charged, the door receipts would have been subject to a Federal tax. Instead, they were politely asked for a donation of one dollar. No donation, no entry.

Hargis, an alert go-getter, had been aware that General Walker, his big drawing card, was not a good public speaker. The former military man had a tendency to become so incoherent at times that members of the audience simply had got up and walked out. Hence, the appeal for money was always made immediately after Billy James had finished speaking.

As always he handled the plea with skill. Before he asked for contributions, Hargis opened his heart to the audience in a gush of frankness. The purpose of the tour, he said, was not only to alert America but also to raise money to carry on the great work. Therefore, when "Christian patriots" went among them with buckets for the cash offerings, everyone should keep in mind that half of all funds collected would go to General Walker, who had voluntarily surrendered his Army pension. In city after city, when the collection buckets—and they really were buckets—were passed among the audience, they were filled with bills from $1 to $100.

At the time of the "Midnight Ride," the eminently respectable religious publication, *The Christian Century,* reacted strongly to the efforts of Hargis and Walker. It declared:

"These two men will in effect be crying to the American public, 'The Reds are coming; not by land or by sea, but from your schools and colleges, your churches, your textbooks, your libraries, your government.' Paul Revere, whom they aspire to imitate, alerted the nation to a real enemy and did it for nothing, save love of his country. This time, at much greater cost than money, in assaulted personalities and institutions, and in resultant dissension, the nation will be alerted to a domestic enemy which exists largely in the minds of the radical right."

The Christian Crusade itself had never convened a meeting that equaled the size or enthusiasm of the Shrine Auditorium rally. If criticism of the Radical Right for a time hurt the Hargis operation, and if members, radio ratings, and circulation of the Crusade's periodicals dropped off temporarily, the movement nevertheless remains strong and influential, and the appeal of Billy James Hargis himself—like the force of his noisy exhortations to God and to Mammon—remains undiminished.

Hargis crossed the Texas border to a radio station in Monterrey, a station which he says "contributed more to Christian Crusade's growth than any other single radio station." His Mexican broadcasts blanket the Southwest. The station he uses at San Diego covers all the Western states, the Southwest, part of the Midwest, Western Canada, and even Alaska. And he is now trying to extend his broadcasts to embrace the entire western hemisphere. He said that "whereas American radio stations are limited in power, and must 'protect' other American stations, Mexican stations, through a long-standing agreement with the American government, have the right to boom their broadcasts all over the hemisphere on . . . three frequencies, without interference."

Until 1962, Hargis' voice was heard regularly over some two hundred radio stations in forty-six states of the United States, and from some dozen television outlets in twenty states, costing about half a million dollars a year for broadcasting time. When the pinch was on in 1962 and 1963, Hargis retrenched to about fifty radio stations and a few scattered TV outlets.

Early in 1964, however, Hargis began a comeback that regained the lost ground—and then some. By July, he was able to announce that the Crusade's $300,000 deficit for 1963 had been cut in half during the first half of 1964.

Subscriptions to his magazine, which had totaled 100,000 and had dropped to 72,000 at the end of 1963, re-crossed the 100,000 mark to a claimed 130,000. His headquarters staff of fifty, cut in half during retrenchment, was back at fifty—although a 10 percent pay cut had not been fully restored to staff members. But far more important, Hargis had sharply boosted his radio outlets across the country. By summer, he was being heard on 400 stations daily. And he was ready, he said, to launch Crusade broadcasts in Spanish over 110 stations in Latin America.

Hargis credited Goldwater's quest for the Republican nomination for much of the 1964 spurt by the Crusade and other Right Wing groups. Other factors, he said, were the assassination of President Kennedy "by a Communist" and the nomination of a number of Conservatives in 1964 Congressional races.

Flushed by his comeback, Hargis continues to thunder the Radical Right gospel as he builds towards new peaks. He continues his midnight-riding, warning fearful Americans against those he claims would destroy America and Christianity.

And he continues to attract a lot of money.

5

The National Education Program

— Dr. George Benson

"The stakes are very high. If we fail it means a Communist world, a Godless world—the Dark Ages all over again. . . ."

This is the usual ingredient of fear in the writings of Dr. George S. Benson. But there's good American optimism, too:

"If we will build sterling Christian character we can have higher morality, greater moral strength . . . if we can immunize our people to Communist infiltration and propaganda, then productivity will go up 4 percent or more a year. . . ."

The man who attaches industrial productivity to Christian morality (he has done so under some understandably large grants from major American corporations) is a former Church of Christ missionary in China and a long-time anti-labor propagandist in the United States. He is now the president of a small college tucked away in the sleepy foothills of the Ozarks, a college recognized as the academic seat of America's Radical Right.

The town is Searcy, Arkansas—population 7,500.

The campus, which is now home to Dr. Benson, is that of Harding College, a coeducational institution affiliated with the Church of Christ. On this campus there is a tax-exempt organization, financed by a handful of big-business corporations, foundations, and wealthy individuals, which produces "educational" materials designed to counteract what the Far-Rightist mind sees as Communist and socialist propaganda.

The organization, known as the National Education Program, issues textbooks, pamphlets, school study outlines, and motion pictures—all such materials pointing to the advantages offered by the most rugged system of free enterprise, and to the evils of "socialism." (To those who operate the fountainhead at Searcy, the economic reforms of the past thirty years are but socialistic way stations on the road to communism.)

The NEP, as they usually call it, also issues newspaper columns which are distributed free to an estimated 3,600 weekly papers said to have a combined circulation in the millions. Once a month, a column is reprinted and shipped in bulk lots to approximately 600 business firms which distribute the material to employees and to 926 newspapers published by companies for their employees. Television and radio broadcasts are produced; for more than a decade the NEP's radio program, "Land of the Free," was carried on 368 stations. Its classroom movies have been shown in over three thousand schools in thirty-five states. From the Harding College campus, a lecture circuit covers most of the fifty states, and a "National Program Letter" goes out at a dollar a year to 30,000 "opinion molders" all over the nation.

The output is prodigious, well-financed, always ultra-Right.

Both Harding College and the NEP have grown to their present status through the efforts of the sixty-six-year-old Benson. After some ten years in China, George Stuart Benson was recalled by his church in 1936 to take over the presidency of a two-building, unaccredited institution of learning of which he himself was a graduate. Harding College had a student body of two hundred, a debt of $75,000, and a sense of despair. Benson found the United States a changed country. There had been a great Depression. But to a man who had come from a country of incredible poverty, where tens of thousands of human beings died of starvation, America was an unbelievable land of milk and honey. Federal Government efforts of the 1930's to counteract business stagnation and combat unemployment looked to the returned missionary like the beginnings of socialism or communism. Benson said he was "shocked and saddened at the lack of understanding and appreciation which most Americans seemed to have of their country and their heritage. They seemed beaten by adversity," he continued, "disillusioned with democracy, ready to give up a free enterprise system which, even in the depths of the depression, gave them a standard of living far beyond anything else in the world. They had lost their Christian convictions and their sense of moral purpose and were listening to all manner of false prophets." Good sense, most of this, but . . .

Shortly after he took over the presidency of the college, Benson began to explain his concept of Americanism to adults at gatherings in private homes and to youngsters in high schools. In nearby Batesville, Arkansas, the editor of the local paper heard him speak and invited him to do a weekly column. A radio station in Little Rock offered him air time once a week for a fifteen-minute broadcast. Both projects caught on. Other newspapers asked for the column, and other radio stations offered air time. Invitations to speak came from cities far from the Ozarks.

Benson first achieved widespread public attention in 1941, testifying before a congressional committee in favor of disbanding three New Deal agencies—the Works Progress Administration (WPA), the Civilian Conservation Corps (CCC), and the National Youth Administration (NYA). Later in 1941, he appeared before another congressional committee to urge lowering of personal income tax exemptions. He claimed that persons earning less than $1,800 a year, already taxed indirectly, would probably prefer to pay direct income taxes as a way of feeling that they were bearing their share of the nation's wartime defense expenditures.

At the end of 1941, Benson was among those honored by the rightist Tax Foundation for his efforts on behalf of national fiscal economy. Along with Senator Harry Byrd of Virginia, he was awarded the Foundation's silver medal. Benson's name was now on its way to its present eminence in the Far Right Wing Hall of Fame.

The economics-minded missionary, whose doctorate is honorary, presides today over a four-year college that offers courses in twenty-one subjects besides the Bible. Though much of the activity at the Searcy campus centers around NEP's propaganda operation, Harding regards itself primarily as a religious educational institution and is strict in what it demands of its students. Church attendance is compulsory—morning, evening, and Sunday. The campus atmosphere is one of religious righteousness and industrious zeal.

Not until Benson had successfully raised the college's scholastic standards did he seek to have it accredited. He was told he could have the accreditation if the college would separate itself from its

extracurricular activities, which meant its huge production of
Far-Rightist propaganda. NEP had been created in 1948 with
some $32,000 of Harding College funds, but to get the accredita-
tion Benson agreed to establish the National Education Program
as a separate, nonprofit, tax-free educational entity.

Although Harding's faculty is not pressured to hew to NEP's line,
many observers feel that the separation of the two institutions is
not quite complete.

George Benson is the president of both. The boards of trustees
are the same. NEP has a provision that if it is dissolved all property goes to Harding College. Benson sometimes answers mail
to NEP on Harding College stationery. NEP occupies rent-free
space on the campus and has full use of the college printing press.
Harding College officials and faculty members, like Dr. Clifton L.
Ganus and Dr. James Bales, participate in NEP-sponsored Freedom Forums and other Far-Rightist gatherings. Benson, nevertheless, states that "the National Education Program is not a part of
Harding College" and that "they are separate and distinct."

Under Benson's direction, two men not connected with the college supervise the actual NEP propaganda outflow. The first is
Howard Bennett, a retired General Electric executive, whose specialty is employee relations. When he was with the huge corporation he originated a plan to "teach the fundamental facts about
America's private enterprise system to G.E.'s 280,000 employees."
He traveled from plant to plant throughout the country to set up
educational programs.

The other is NEP's finance director, General W. P. Campbell,
former assistant chief of finance of the U.S. Army. The General
has a history of activity in Radical Right groups. He is a member
of the national advisory committee of Billy James Hargis' Christian Crusade, has served as a director at large of We, The People!
and is on the board of endorsers of Americans for National Security.

Naturally, much of the material poured out across the nation
from the National Education Program is practically indistinguish-
able from the propaganda outpourings of Hargis and others on the
Far Right Wing. From all of them come the themes that the moment of the planned Communist take-over is closer than most
Americans realize and that the Communist problem is more domestic than international.

Of the thirty-five films produced by NEP, perhaps the best-
known and most controversial is "Communism on the Map,"
which is said to have been seen by millions of Americans. The list

of civic, service, patriotic, and industrial organizations which have purchased it is impressive, and perhaps disquieting.

The writer of this film's script was Glenn Green, then an NEP vice-president as well as a member of the John Birch Society. When Green left the Searcy propaganda mills there were published reports that he would represent the Birch Society in the New York area, but he wound up as an executive in Washington for the National Right-to-Work Committee, a Right Wing lobbying group which seeks the passage of laws against what it considers "compulsory unionism." In creating the text of "Communism on the Map," Green appears to have drawn heavily on the preachments of Founder Welch of the Birch organization.

The picture of the world that is drawn in the film—of country after country in the grip of Communism—is that picture of the world drawn by Welch at the founding of the Birch Society in Indianapolis, since preserved for posterity in the *Blue Book*. The same picture is repeated annually by Welch in the summer "scoreboard" edition of the Birch Society's *American Opinion* magazine. In this annual inventory, each country of the world is listed according to the percentage of Communist control which the Birchers say it has undergone. (In July, 1964, the magazine's scoreboard found the United States 50 to 70 percent under Communist control, up from 20 to 40 percent in 1958.) In August, 1961, Welch claimed that Birch Society members were responsible for more presentations of "Communism on the Map" than all other groups and individuals put together.

Some of the other films turned out at Searcy are animated cartoons done by men who have had considerable experience in Hollywood. The NEP described one of them as follows:

"Dr. Utopia offers his patent medicine 'Dr. Utopia's Ism' for curing all political ills. Those who take it soon find themselves living under totalitarian government with troubles far worse than those they were trying to cure. Stresses the importance of preserving the free enterprise system and the American way of life."

A major motion picture company distributed these cartoons to some 15,000 commercial theaters where they were seen by millions of Americans. The audiences were not told that these were propaganda films made with money given by big business firms to influence America's political and economic thinking.

The Harding-NEP complex is itself big business, and it has required—and has received—sizeable financing from some sizeable interests.

Harding College owns a printing plant, a concrete block factory at Bald Knob, Arkansas, a laundry and dry-cleaning plant which services Searcy citizens as well as students, a camp (the Dr. George S. Benson Camp Tahkodah for Boys), a dairy, and two farms. One farm of 151 acres was partly a gift of the late Sterling Morton, a Chicago industrialist who until his death was a frequent contributor to Right Wing causes. In 1946, the college bought radio station WHBQ in Memphis for $300,000 and netted $80,000 in the very first year of operation. In 1954, it leased out WHBQ and WHBQ-TV for fifteen years and received $2,879,045.84 in the deal.

By 1948, Benson's promanagement activities had attracted the attention of industrialists, and they then contributed generously to his efforts. One of these benefactors was Alfred P. Sloan, Jr., then chairman of the board of General Motors Corporation, who had heard Benson warn that the free enterprise system would be lost if American industry did not sell the people, and especially its own employees, on their version of the American "way of life." Sloan asked how large numbers of Americans could be reached with this message, and was told that films were the best medium for mass education.

Some time thereafter, Benson received $300,000 from the tax-exempt Alfred P. Sloan Foundation. By 1951, grants from this foundation alone totaled almost $600,000, given to help produce motion pictures pushing Benson's views on "free enterprise" and warning that government economic action led to socialism and then to totalitarian communism. Sizeable contributions were made by other tax-exempt foundations, such as the Maurice and Laura Falk Foundation of Pittsburgh, which reportedly sent along $75,-000. With the original Sloan grant the college produced its semi-humorous film cartoons, selling for $100 each, which have been seen by an untold number of people.

The National Education Program operates on $200,000 a year. About half of this tax-exempt money is from contributions made by American corporations and individuals who feel that NEP's work is vital to the preservation of the American way—or at least to their view of it. The other half comes from the sale of NEP's enormous output of partisan propaganda materials.

Simply as a fund-raising operation, Dr. Benson's educational and propaganda complex has written a sensational record over the years, especially since the college enrollment even today numbers only 1,200. And it would appear that the millions of dollars poured into Searcy by private and corporate contributors has been attracted as much by the Far-Rightist philosophy expounded by Benson and the NEP as by the educational credentials of the college itself, because, until 1954, there was no organizational distinction between the two units headed by Benson. Contributions sent to Searcy prior to 1954 were, in a sense, for the overall Benson operation.

Even since the technical divorce of the NEP from the college, there have been some indications that in fund-raising, a clear line of demarcation between the educational and the propaganda institutions on the campus has not always been drawn. When a $2,000,-000 building program was launched by Benson for his Searcy complex a little over a year ago, $700,000 of the total was described in a fund-raising brochure as the cost of constructing a building to house NEP operations on the campus. The brochure, entitled "The American Heritage," bore the imprimatur "Harding College, Searcy, Arkansas," and solicited not only the $700,000 for the NEP building, which was called a "Continuing Education Center," but $1,000,000 for a new Harding College Science Building; $100,000 for a Library for the Graduate School of Bible and Religion; and $200,000 for two residence halls for the Bible school.

It seems clear, in any case, that Dr. Benson's educational and propaganda activities at Searcy have been the beneficiaries of a startlingly great amount of individual, corporate, and foundation largesse. Some idea of the kind of money that has poured into Benson's coffers in recent years can be gleaned from the following:

Among foundations, the Sloan Foundation has sent at least $600,000; Armco Steel Foundation, $67,500; Allen-Bradley Foundation, $60,000; the Donner Foundation (now called the Independence Foundation), $38,000; the Rosa Mary Foundation, $35,-000; the Texas Educational Association, $47,250; the Stockham Foundation, $25,000; the Houston Endowment, $20,000; and assorted other foundations a reported total of almost $175,000 over a period of years.

Among industrial corporations, Republic Steel sent $140,000 over a recent five-year period, U.S. Steel contributed $33,000, and the Cameron Iron Works in Houston ponied up $25,000. In the oil industry, Gulf Oil contributed $55,000; Esso, $10,000; and General Crude Oil, $5,000. Olin-Mathieson sent $57,000; Lone Star Cement, $10,000; Alcoa, $5,000; three utilities were good for a total of $20,000; five smaller firms contributed $30,000.

Wealthy individuals have also sent money to bolster the Benson propaganda plant. The largest known gift—corporate, foundation, or individual—was made by the late Harry R. Kendall of Evanston, Illinois, an insurance executive who received a doctor of laws degree from Harding. He made a bequest of stock valued at about $2,500,000. Two Wilmington, Delaware, individuals—Lammot DuPont Copeland and Jasper Crane, a retired DuPont executive, gave $36,000 in a recent five-year period, while Bernard Peyton of Princeton, New Jersey, who supports other Right Wing organizations, sent $33,500 in the same period.

All these contributions are only a part of the monies that have been poured into the campus in the Ozark foothills. But they indicate the cash value of education and propaganda for Benson's big-business version of the American way of life.

"Why Do So Many Success-Minded People Take the Dale Carnegie Course?" The question was asked in an advertisement in an Illinois newspaper. The answer was provided in the ad by Dr. George S. Benson, who was identified as "a prominent U.S. educator, author, lecturer and commentator."

Certainly Dr. Benson is, despite his missionary and academic background, very success-minded.

A pink-cheeked, silver-haired, immaculately dressed gentleman, Benson is the stereotype of a successful businessman or banker. And like the businessmen who back his operations, he is a man who stands hard and fast to his ideas. As a fundamentalist he will have nothing to do with modern doctrine—including Darwin's theory of evolution. Benson enjoys much prestige in Arkansas and he holds honorary degrees from several colleges. He is known throughout his state as the man who breathed life into a dying center of learning, the man who brought millions of dollars into the community from the thriving business of the NEP and from a $13,000,000 endowment fund for Harding College.

The large-scale propaganda center which Benson established at Searcy, and which spreads its output across the country to other Far-Rightist groups and to civic and business organizations as well, brought him into touch with other leaders of the Radical Right.

In 1946, Benson was a speaker at a Friends of Frank Fay rally in Madison Square Garden—a gathering organized ostensibly to support actor Frank Fay, who was having troubles with Actors Equity because he had raised serious questions about the participation of five fellow actors in a Left Wing meeting. The rally proved to be a *cause célèbre* for a wide variety of New York ultra-Rightists, anti-Semites, and former followers of the Reverend Charles E. Coughlin, and many of them were present at the Garden that night. Although Fay was a Catholic, as were a number of his supporters, the benediction at the end of the rally was pronounced by Reverend Carl McIntire, whose record of anti-Catholicism is well-known.*

McIntire was quoted at the time in newspaper reports as stating that he had attended a small luncheon hosted by the late Merwin K. Hart, at which plans for the Frank Fay rally were initiated. Hart was famous as an anti-Semitic propagandist.

Just how Benson came to participate in this extremist rally eighteen years ago is not known. His speech at the rally warned of the dangers of communism; it contained no anti-Semitism. In 1949, his name appeared again—as one of those who had been invited by Merwin Hart to attend a secret meeting in New York to form a postwar Rightist movement along the lines of the Depression-born Liberty League and the wartime America First Committee. When the press got wind of Hart's scheme, the secret conclave was hastily called off. Five years later, Benson was identified in news stories as a member of National Policy Committee of For America, a Radical Right organization formed in May, 1954, at a luncheon sponsored by the late Colonel Robert R. McCormick, publisher of the *Chicago Tribune*. Co-chairmen of For America were General Robert E. Wood, long a leader of the Far Right; and Clarence E. Manion, who has since formed the Manion Forum, a radio propaganda operation, and who is also a member of the John Birch Society's national council. The national policy committee of For America was almost a "Who's Who" of the American Far Right of ten years ago.

In 1957, Benson addressed the annual meeting of the Congress of Freedom, an extremist organization formed in the mid-1950's whose speakers, platforms and sponsorship have not always been free of anti-Semites, and at whose conventions anti-Semitic literature has been easily available.†

Benson's own thinking follows that of his associates on the Extreme Right. He spouts what might be called the Conspiracy Theory of Economics—believing as he does that America's traditional system is being destroyed by a pernicious fifth column of secret Communists who advocate, among other things, a shorter work week and higher wages. At the NEP's 25th Freedom Forum in February, 1964, he told 150 businessmen students that the Communist Party of the U.S.A. was behind efforts to increase

*See *The Troublemakers.*
†See *Cross-Currents.*

wages and shorten the work week so American industry would be less able to compete in the world market. As a peddler of such scary inside stuff, Benson is not quite in the Welch-Schwarz class, but he has often echoed some of the most extreme cries of the far outer fringes, such as the claim that the United States is practically isolated. "If the chips were all down we could probably count only on West Germany, Japan, the Philippine Islands standing by the United States," he has said. "England has too many labor unions headed by Communists; she will not fight the Communists. No hope at all of France or Italy doing it. Probably no hope in the Scandinavian countries. . . ."

Benson is convinced, along with the other spokesmen of the Radical Right, that America is threatened by "thousands of Communists . . . infiltrated into our American institutions and . . . seeking to undermine our way of life." He believes that since 1918 "the Communists have penetrated every important segment of American society . . . education, religion, labor, industry, government. . . ." Since the foregoing assertions could have been made by Robert Welch himself, George Benson has been asked on occasion if there were any connection between the John Birch Society and himself.

This question has always seemed to irritate him a good deal. But, in one of his own newspaper columns, "Looking Ahead," dated March 16, 1960, Benson had let his stamp of approval thump rather enthusiastically on the John Birch Society. In this column he described for his 20,000,000 (claimed) readers how twelve distinguished citizens of Searcy met in a private home one night, ". . . meeting to plan a month's work on behalf of their nation. They are dedicated to the cause of freedom."

He explained: "This was the regular monthly meeting of the John Birch Society in Searcy." And after stating the aims of Welch's organization, he concluded: "Any American who loves freedom and is willing to work, work, work to protect it can find intelligent direction and companionship in a John Birch Society group." He closed the column mentioning the Society's Belmont, Massachusetts, address for the information of any of his readers who might have wished to join it. Robert Welch reprinted Benson's piece in the next issue of the Society's Bulletin, adding some glowing praise of Benson and the National Education Program.

One day almost ten years ago, Benson stood on a platform before an audience composed mainly of business people and introduced Dr. Fred C. Schwarz, who was then just beginning his mission to save America.

The occasion was a five-day enterprise called a Freedom Forum. One of National Education Program's influential propaganda activities, the Freedom Forums were originally designed to teach business executives how to educate employees. Instituted in 1949, they were part of a joint campaign by the Association of National Advertisers and the American Association of Advertising Agencies "to improve knowledge of the [American economic] system at the plant and community levels." At these Forums, spokesmen for some big corporations would discuss the best ways to influence and change their employees' political and economic attitudes. But this approach gradually underwent change until the emphasis began to fall on the Communist menace and so-called socialistic trends.

With Benson's introduction of Dr. Schwarz, the Freedom Forums took on a wholly new look. Now they named communism as the cause of almost all of America's economic and political problems— not the communism in the Soviet Union (which, judging from the emphasis, the Forum thinks poses a comparatively smaller threat), but undercover communism in the United States, creeping swiftly and secretly toward 1973.

Since the Freedom Forums began on the Harding campus, management people from nearly 1,000 companies around the United States have attended. Faculty and administrative officials from 192 school systems and colleges have also come to learn about the secret Communist conspiracy which allegedly is behind government spending, high taxes, foreign aid, and similar measures. Each student pays $150 and each session has from 125 to 150 students. Besides the big shows at Searcy, there are some fifty or sixty local, one-day Freedom Forums held in different parts of the country each year—an average of about one a week. Sponsored by local organizations such as the Chamber of Commerce and the Farm Bureau Federation, these can be arranged through the NEP, which will supply speakers, materials and other help.

The type of lectures offered at a Freedom Forum can be judged by the identity of some of the speakers who have appeared in the past few years:

—Dr. Fred C. Schwarz, of course.

—William Grede, Clarence Manion, and Tom Anderson—all Birch Society national council members.

—Dr. Howard Kershner, head of the Christian Freedom Foundation, which equates Christianity with extreme *laissez-faire* economics.

—Edward Hunter, a respectable anti-Communist writer who says he invented the term "brain-washing" and who heads the

Anti-Communist Liaison Committee set up by Billy James Hargis to unify the splintered Far Right.

—Dr. Milton Lory, president of the American Coalition of Patriotic Societies, an organization of a hundred super-patriotic groups, some pronouncedly racist.

At a Freedom Forum held on February 4 and 5, 1964, in Little Rock, Arkansas, with about 150 students attending, one of the main speakers was William Grede of Milwaukee, Wisconsin, chairman of the Grede Foundries and a former president of the National Association of Manufacturers. Grede is also one of the guiding lights of the John Birch Society. His contribution was the forceful assertion that industry has a moral obligation to make as much profit as it possibly can, and that what industry does with its profit is a moral matter which cannot be legislated by the Government. Grede said since the adoption of the income tax in 1913, socialism had been gathering steam in the United States.

Benson's address on that occasion was a quiet assurance that knowledge and understanding are the answer to most of the country's economic ills. It was his view that "powerful sources" were advocating "wrong remedies."

Because the Radical Right has faced increasing criticism from the press, the clergy, educators, elected representatives, and civic leaders, Benson has tried to dispel the public image of Harding College as an academic spokesman for extremism. A few days before Christmas in 1963, he wrote to the *Denver Post* that "Harding College has taken care not to become affiliated with any of the extreme groups on either Right or Left." In offering this statement, he conveniently overlooked Grede, Billy James Hargis, Fred Schwarz, Clarence Manion, Glenn Green, and members of the John Birch Society or other Radical Right groups who have been linked to his organizational activities. Benson still gets repercussions from the column he wrote praising the Birch Society, and in his letter to the *Denver Post,* he explained that the Birch column had been written long before he learned of the Founder's "harsh criticism of President Eisenhower and before that criticism had received publicity." However, he reaffirmed his agreement with the basic, stated aims of Welch's organization.

Benson even adopted a Welchian defense. He claimed that criticism of Harding College had begun late in 1960 when Moscow issued orders to United States Communists to destroy all "anti-Communist" groups. Benson and Welch share the certainty that any criticism of their organizations and their activities is Communist-inspired.

Though much of Dr. Benson's propaganda was originally concerned with changing the views and mental attitudes of big industry's workers, he has expanded his efforts to include everyone he can reach. To the hundreds of thousands of partisans of the Far Right, however, the academic appeal is somewhat less magnetic than the frenzied, fire-and-brimstone appeal that is possible in the name of religion, even when it preaches the gospel of political extremism. What the cap and gown lends to the propaganda of George Stuart Benson is an aura much the same as that which attitudes of piety and authority lend to the Rightist preacher—a man such as the Reverend Carl McIntire, for example, the man who brought Dr. Fred Schwarz to America, and who now broadcasts five days a week over some five hundred radio stations throughout the United States, spreading fear in the name of faith.

6

The 20th Century Reformation Hour
— Reverend Carl McIntire

"You either agree with McIntire or the Devil. Take your choice."

The phenomenon that is the Reverend Carl McIntire was thus described by one of his loyal Collingswood, New Jersey, parishioners.

If you are a supporter of the National Council of Churches, as most of America's Protestants are—or, for that matter, if you are a Liberal, an integrationist, or a Roman Catholic—then you certainly are not *with* Carl McIntire. For the dominant factor in this preacher's life has been the certainty that his own very narrow view is the only correct one, and that any view that differs is indeed diabolical.

A fundamentalist, Dr. McIntire long ago rebelled against the philosophy and authority of the Presbyterian Church in the U.S.A. And he did so in such a way that in 1936 he was ousted from that church, first by a vote of the Synod, then by a vote of the General Assembly, which is the Supreme Court of the denomination. The Assembly accused McIntire of defaming the character of fellow Christians, breaking certain of the Ten Commandments, causing "dissension and strife," and engendering "suspicion and ill will." Once expelled, McIntire built his own house of worship. He also set up his own church federation, the American Council of Christian Churches. This offbeat association immediately began to wage war on the National Council of Churches, an affiliate of which had ousted McIntire from its clergy.

As the years passed, McIntire set up a number of other religious enterprises. In the course of such intensive organizational activities, he always found time to preach the destruction of all Communists and heathen, and to warn against the path to hell trod by the "liberals" in leading the nation to ruin.

Yet, from 1936 to 1960, with all this effort, with all his talks from the pulpit, and with all the myriad words in his own small newspaper, the *Christian Beacon,* Dr. Carl McIntire reached comparatively few people. By the early sixties, just before Radical Right organizations in the United States seemed suddenly to receive millions of dollars from important corporations and large business firms, the *Christian Beacon* had set up a subsidiary called the 20th Century Reformation Hour to broadcast McIntire's dissident views, which until then had been heard only over a small radio station in Chester, Pennsylvania.

The Reverend never explained why he decided to start large-scale broadcasting in 1958. Nor is there any evidence that he is one of those who has received sizeable contributions from industrialists financing the Radical Right's mushrooming propaganda mills. It is possible, however, that he has since been encouraged in his enterprise by the success of Dr. Fred Schwarz, whom he helped bring to the United States, and by the impressive rise of Billy James Hargis, whom he helped build into an international figure via a Bible balloon project aimed at countries behind the Iron Curtain. Whoever or whatever inspired him, Dr. McIntire now broadcasts five times a week over 577 radio stations, reaching a daily audience of millions, and presides over a rapidly growing propaganda operation.

As a religious organization, the 20th Century Reformation Hour has a tax-exempt status from the Internal Revenue Service. And though McIntire constantly attacks the NCC for the preaching of a "social gospel," his own broadcasts all too often are less concerned with religion than with politics and economics. McIntire's broadcasting approach is to rely upon his listeners' religious convictions, hoping their fervor will help persuade them to support Radical Right political concepts and programs designed to rewrite the American foreign and domestic policies of the last thirty years.

Because of his large audience, Dr. McIntire is one of the major influences currently trying to push America to the Right.

In his fervent exhortations, he has told pious listeners: "Freedom of religion must be preserved in the United States . . . and to do it the income tax must be abolished." Along with such tortured reasoning, he denounces many policies of the United States Government and almost all the policies of the National Council of Churches as pro-Communist. Of course, the careful scrutiny of the Internal Revenue Service does not escape his attention, perhaps because it sometimes looks into the hundreds of thousands of dollars the McIntire operations have received as tax-exempt money—money which is donated to be spent for religious activities. For example, in a 1962 pamphlet on the income tax, McIntire wrote:

"The spectacle of the Federal Government investigating individuals because of their religious contributions is also intolerable. . . . The use of the income tax to harass church and Christians is intolerable. As soon as an individual is investigated the implication generally accepted is that he has done something wrong, that he is not honest!"

McIntire once said that the phrase "common man" is "an innocent sounding term, but it is filled with all the tyranny of State control." He urged revision of labor laws which protect the right to hold union membership, favoring instead the so-called right-to-work laws being promoted by the Far Right.

The list of enlightened social measures Dr. McIntire opposes is long and sufficiently impressive for him to win substantial support from sources which traditionally finance tax-exempt groups engaged in formal campaigns to reverse the progressive political and economic attitudes of the American people. Other propaganda centers, such as Dr. Benson's Harding College and NEP, and the Manion Forum (to be considered in the next chapter), are being financed by interests seeking profoundly to change America's way of thinking. Most claim patriotism as their motivation. McIntire claims he is doing God's will.

There is no evidence that any of McIntire's enterprises received money specifically to inject religious influence into public discussion of civil rights or employer-employee relations. Yet as far back as 1949, the American Council of Christian Churches, not a rich organization by any means, paid for full-page newspaper ads in Ohio to tell readers that a proposed Fair Employment Practices Code in that state, designed to prevent discrimination in hiring because of race, creed, or national origin, would take away from man his God-given endowment of freedom of choice. It would also, the statement went on, encourage state socialism by placing Ohio in a field in which government does not belong, and endanger national security through infiltration into vital industries of Communists who supported FEPC legislation. "We believe," said the ad, "that an FEPC law in Ohio would set class against class and race against race . . . is Ohio ready for the 'police state'? FEPC is neither Christian nor American. . . ."

Over the years, a number of Radical Right organizations have been established as religious, educational, or charitable institutions. They applied for and were given Federal tax-exempt status and then proceeded to use their funds for purely political and economic propaganda. McIntire's organizations collect money as religious institutions but devote considerable effort to propaganda in behalf of Radical Right political and economic concepts. Citing Biblical authority, the American Council of Christian Churches, as far back as 1947, urged all deeply religious, God-fearing readers to oppose the trade-union closed shop; failure to oppose it would negate one's personal responsibility to God as well as to his American system of government. Said the ACCC:

"The closed shop violates freedom of conscience and the Eighth Commandment, 'Thou shalt not steal.' "

The fantastic argument: Untold numbers of Christians objected to joining unions and thus being "yoked together with unbelievers," destroying "the unity and oneness of our people in our democratic order."

In recent years most Protestant churches in America have shown a growing desire that racial discrimination in the United States be completely eliminated and that no one be denied his rights because of the pigment of his skin. McIntire and his ACCC are opposed to this concern for racial minorities, and have been all along. As far back as 1948, at an Atlanta, Georgia, meeting, McIntire's ACCC declared that the proposed national FEPC "promotes class consciousness and inspires hate between peoples" and that FEPC "is a vital part of the Communist program." Speakers there charged that FEPC legislation, which prohibits employers from discriminating against prospective workers because of color, race, or creed, is nothing but Socialism in disguise, and poses a great threat to national security.

The rock on which the McIntire operation was founded is the modest Bible Presbyterian Church in Collingswood, New Jersey, a small town of middle-income homeowners in the Philadelphia-

Camden area. McIntire built the church over a quarter of a century ago after his expulsion by the Presbyterian denomination. He had 1,500 members then—he has about 1,700 now. A complex of buildings, eighteenth-century English, houses his other operations. A few blocks away are the 20th Century Reformation Hour offices, quartered in a three-story former school building with the high ceilings and high windows common to the late 1890's. Research for the Reverend's radio programs is conducted in a "periodical room," one wall of which is lined with more than 150 publications, domestic and foreign, secular and religious. Several women scan the magazines in search of items on which the minister can base his broadcasts. Administrative detail and the huge mail from his many listeners are handled in this building, and here McIntire has his private office.

The daily incoming mail runs between two and four thousand letters and is worked over in a large, well-lighted room. A dozen greying ladies open the communications and set them in neat piles to be handled by the proper persons. Special attention is given to pink envelopes, for these contain the weekly tithe payments listeners send to help pay for radio time to carry on what the preacher calls the Lord's work.

The man responsible for all this activity is a well-built, athletic six-footer pushing sixty. A reporter who interviewed him wrote that Dr. McIntire has "a beauty of a handshake and a 'hello' as hearty as a breakfast cereal commercial." The voice is resonant and comforting, and because of his height the minister seems to bend protectively over those with whom he talks. As a preacher he is eloquent, and when called a modern Luther or Calvin he is visibly pleased. McIntire once described himself as "a tall, graying, lively-eyed man, consumed with a desire to do the Lord's work and to do it at any expense of his personal time and energy." His conversation and public talks are liberally sprinkled with phrases like "The Lord Jesus told me to do this."

Besides his role at the helm of the *Christian Beacon* and the 20th Century Reformation Hour, and as founder of the ACCC, McIntire is also a leader of the International Council of Christian Churches, which was created to oppose the World Council of Churches abroad just as the ACCC opposes the NCC at home. Likewise, McIntire helped in the formation of the Independent Board for Presbyterian Home Missions and the Independent Board for Presbyterian Foreign Missions, the latter chartered in 1934 to combat the "modernism" of the official Presbyterian missions. Both the Independent Boards have close ties to the Collingswood operations.

McIntire also plays a leading role in several fundamentalist educational institutions, serving as an official of Shelton College, Ringwood, New Jersey, Highland College in Pasadena, California, and Faith Theological Seminary in Elkins Park, Pennsylvania.

In 1963, McIntire added still another dimension to his overall operation with the purchase of a seaside hotel at Cape May, a New Jersey shore resort. The hotel was renamed The Christian Admiral and now serves as a center and meeting place for various conferences staged by McIntire, especially during the summer months.

The Christian Admiral, purchased for an estimated $300,000, with refurbishing estimated at an extra quarter of a million, offers rates to guests of about $45 to $85 a week. McIntire followers in the various states have undertaken the refurnishing of various rooms ($1,000 a room) for a Hall of the States on the third floor. One group from Virginia undertook a Patrick Henry Room, and McIntire's organization received contributions for a General Mac-Arthur Room and a John Birch Room. The library is decorated with portraits of McIntire, Major Edgar Bundy of the Right Wing Church League of America, and J. B. Matthews, the anti-Communist consultant whose public charges of Red infiltration in the Protestant clergy a decade ago have made him a hero to McIntire and other Radical Rightists, although they cost him his job with the late Senator McCarthy's investigating committee.

The weekly summer conferences at The Christian Admiral schedule leaders of the Right Wing fundamentalist movement as top speakers, along with such secular luminaries of the Far Right as General Walker, Birch Society National Council member Tom Anderson, and Senator Strom Thurmond of South Carolina.

As a clergyman, McIntire's concept of what Christ taught and what Christianity means for mankind is curious. McIntire apparently believes that when Jesus said, "Suffer the little children to come unto me," it meant white children only. The radio preacher drums into the ears of his listeners that those who support "racial brotherhood" teach a false concept of Christianity. Talk of racial brotherhood, he thunders, is just Communist propaganda designed to create "class and racial strife in which the Communists delight." McIntire and his dissident faction accuse as pro-Communist all those who favor laws putting Negroes, Orientals, Mexicans, and Indians on a footing equal with whites. They charge that the entire civil rights program is "serving the ends of radical powers who are working for a socialistic order in this free land."

In his virulent opposition to the major Protestant denominations, McIntire has even warned against helping the hungry, sick, and homeless overseas. After World War II, with the hearty endorsement of President Truman, leading clerics organized a humane effort, called One Great Hour of Sharing, to assist the stricken and needy in the war-devastated lands. McIntire denounced this as nothing more than part of a scheme to insinuate "modernism" into European churches and "to raise cash to purchase . . . socialistic propaganda."

He damns all United Nations activities, including the sale of UN Children's Fund greeting cards, the money from which is used to help the sick and hungry children. He cautions his followers to guard against the "terrific emotional appeal" of solicitations "in the name of suffering children," which he claims is only a cover-up for some insidious Red plot.

His attitude is puzzling until one listens to Dr. McIntire's view of things. "We live in a world of power," he tells his listeners. "Force rules. It always has, since the day that sin entered it, and it will continue to do so until the day Lord Jesus Christ Himself returns. . . . We should frankly concede that the vision of universal world peace is impossible of fulfillment with man's heart so wicked and so sinful."

McIntire's philosophy of force takes him beyond the concept that good Christians should smite unbelievers and destroy them with the wrath of the Lord. With man's technological advance, this destruction, he obviously believes, can be visited on the heathen by death striking from the skies in evidence of Divine Wrath. In 1944, McIntire's ACCC telegraphed President Roosevelt asking that the two Japanese State Shinto shrines be destroyed by bombs to shatter the Japanese belief in the "protective power of the divine emperor and his ancestors." In later years, the ACCC were all for a preventive war against the Communists. At their 1948 annual convention, the clerics in McIntire's ACCC pleaded:

"For us to have the atomic bomb and, in the name of a false morality born of a perverted sense of self-respect and pacifist propaganda, to await the hour when Russia has her bombs to precipitate an atomic war, is the height of insanity and will, when the fateful hour comes, be a just punishment upon us. It is a betrayal of Christian principles and common decency for us to sit up and permit such a revolutionary force to gain advantage for the enslavement of the world."

McIntire is adept at identifying himself and his various organizations, such as ACCC, with matters of public interest and controversy which give promise of making good newspaper copy and of keeping his causes in the public eye. When President Truman called columnist Drew Pearson an "S.O.B.," McIntire could not resist the temptation sanctimoniously to demand that the President apologize for this affront to religious Americans. McIntire, incidentally, had cleaner but more insulting words for the same writer.

On October 29, 1948, when it appeared that Governor Thomas E. Dewey might be the next President of the United States, the ACCC convention at Philadelphia adopted a resolution opposing the possible appointment of the late John Foster Dulles as Secretary of State or United States delegate to the United Nations. The resolution charged that Mr. Dulles had for fifteen years been "an effective tool" of "extremely radical and pacifist" churchmen associated with the National Council of Churches and the World Council of Churches, which were branded as "cooperating fronts for World Socialism."

Mr. Dulles, whose credentials as a pillar of the church and of the American system were hardly vulnerable to that kind of attack, went on to serve the Truman and Eisenhower administrations with distinction. But the 1948 ACCC blast, coming just before Election Day, was good for some garish headlines.

McIntire has kept in touch with other Far Right operators over the years. His appearance at the Madison Square Garden Friends of Frank Fay rally in 1946, where Benson was a speaker, has been mentioned, as has his role in helping to bring Dr. Fred C. Schwarz to the United States, and his promotion of Billy James Hargis to a headline personality (this promotion involved a scheme for floating Bibles over the Iron Curtain via balloons). A few years ago Hargis listed an encomium from McIntire in a promotional sheet titled "Commendations from Great Leaders."

But McIntire's roots in the Far Right go even deeper, and into even darker regions. He maintained a long-standing friendly contact with the late Merwin K. Hart, of the National Economic Council, who was a focal point for much of the Extreme Rightist activity of the 1940's and 1950's. Hart's reputation as an anti-Semite appears to have been no barrier to McIntire's friendship, which may not be surprising in view of McIntire's view of brotherhood as a fraudulent concept.

Another hate peddler with whom McIntire has maintained a friendly tie for some two decades is Harvey Springer,* an outspoken anti-Catholic bigot who has also dabbled in anti-Semitism. On a number of occasions McIntire and Springer have spoken from each other's pulpits. Springer's publication *Western Voice* has for years

* See *The Troublemakers*.

carried articles by and about McIntire. In 1960, Springer toured the country to fight the prospect of a Catholic President.

More recently, McIntire's name has appeared on the national advisory board of Young Americans for Freedom, the Right Wing youth group in which the minister's son is very active. He has a co-operative tie, as well, with the Right Wing Church League of America, and with Edgar Bundy, its executive official.

Nor has McIntire shunned the John Birch Society. The *San Francisco Chronicle* of April 4, 1961, reported that he had endorsed the Society, which was then the target of nation-wide condemnation, declaring that a lot of people were going to be sorry for the things they had said about the John Birch Society. He was quoted as calling the Society "a good, patriotic American organization," and as stating that "America needs many of the policies they support."

When he discusses other leaders in the movement, his talk can be more about the difference in technique than in the nature of the propaganda itself. Sometimes the green glow of envy almost shows as he speaks of the big contributions other Radical Right organizations get from foundations, corporations, and wealthy individuals. In commenting on Dr. Schwarz, he said:

"I differ from him in my anti-Communist approach. His emphasis is on the scientific and mine on the religious indictment of Communism. Perhaps that is the reason industrialists are more inclined to contribute to his movement than to mine; they feel more at home with economic arguments. I stick to my approach, which is that our prosperous society is based on a solid Christian foundation. Billy Hargis has a somewhat religious approach and seems to get some large backers, but not so many. My operation is much larger than his. Benson at Harding College, though a preacher, makes a straight businessman's approach and over the years has received some of the biggest contributions."

McIntire has thus aligned himself—as a bigger and busier (but financially poorer) brother—to all the leading lights of today's Radical Right.

Carl McIntire is one of the major anti-Catholic propagandists in America. His views on Catholicism were embodied in a statement made on November 2, 1951:

"The strengthening of the Roman Catholic Church throughout the world only involves the fostering of a false religion which enslaves human souls in darkness and superstition, and from which the Protestant Reformation of the 16th Century delivered us. . . . Rome will sell her secret confessional system for political world power. But actually the Roman Catholic Church becomes a 'spy system' through the priests, with the priests' loyalty first to the Vatican. If that obtains in other countries, it obtains, too, in our country. . . . Are not the Roman Catholics in the United States committed to a foreign power and do they not owe 'obedience and submission' to its head, the Pope? . . . If the priest inside the Iron Curtain countries is a 'spy' for the Vatican state, why is not a priest in the U.S.A. the same?"

In 1960, when the late President Kennedy sought the nation's highest office, the American Council of Christian Churches was active and vociferous in its opposition to a Catholic candidate for President.

Both in his sermons and in his newspaper McIntire made it clear that he opposed the then-Senator Kennedy precisely because the senator was a Catholic. The ACCC passed a resolution to this effect in 1959—before the active campaigning of 1960 began. The resolution said Senator Kennedy's nomination would precipitate a major religious conflict. After Mr. Kennedy's nomination, the Democratic Party published a pamphlet against religious bigotry which categorized McIntire as one of five "major anti-Catholic extremists operating in the current political campaign." Senator Henry L. Jackson explained that the memorandum was distributed to give "full ventilation to the hate mail being widely disseminated throughout the country." Senator Jackson finally asked Dr. McIntire pointblank, "Are you opposing Senator Kennedy because of his religion?" McIntire asked evasively whether or not they were going to get an apology. Jackson replied, "No apology and no withdrawal." McIntire then concluded with the weak rejoinder that he was opposing Mr. Kennedy "because I do not believe in his views on the extreme left and have serious doubts as to his consistency on the separation of church and state."

Throughout President Kennedy's years in the White House, McIntire emphasized aspects of the President's personality and policies distasteful to McIntire followers: repeated mention of the President's Catholicism, his efforts at accommodation with Russia, his pressure for social legislation, and lastly his scheduled appearance at the National Council of Churches' rally, planned for December 3, 1963, in Philadelphia.

In line with his constant policy of setting up rival, hostile demonstrations whenever and wherever the NCC was holding a convention, McIntire announced a monster counterdemonstration to be held in Independence Square on the same night.

The assassination of the President on November 22 led him to cancel it. And in a subsequent release, McIntire admonished the

American people "to return to the infallible word of God for comfort and guidance." He also warned Americans that Reds would blame the Right Wing for creating the atmosphere which brought about the assassination. About Jack Ruby he commented: "He was a Jew, a Kennedy supporter. . . . The American people must blame the Marxian philosophy and the Communists for this deed and there is no possible association between the assassination and the loyalty of the right wing to their country and to their God, and the determination of the conservative to resist Communism. . . ."

And like so many other Radical Right organization leaders who exaggerate the imminent threat of domestic communism and frighten Americans into extremist views on economic and political issues, McIntire has created his own investigative structure.

His purpose here is to keep an eye on clergymen whom he considers subversive or dangerous dupes. To this end he maintains a sharp lookout for ministers of every denomination who might be leftist, liberal, or involved in organizations which he believes tainted with modernism. It is the Reverend's ready boast that he has the most extensive files, except for the FBI, on Communists and fellow travelers in the churches.

The unceasing search for Communists and Communist sympathizers, carried out under McIntire's personal supervision, is directed by Dr. Clyde Kennedy, whose right arm in this intelligence operation is the Reverend W. O. H. Garman, pastor of a church in Altoona, Pennsylvania, and a former president of the American Council of Christian Churches. Garman considers his own preaching of the word of God to be a sideline; his full time is given to tracking down purported Communists, "modernists," and "revisionists." (He once wrote of some leaders in the National Council of Churches that they had "denied the fundamental, cardinal tenets of the historic Christian faith as taught by Christ and the Apostles," and branded them as "traitors to the Lord Jesus Christ. . . .")

McIntire himself repeatedly charges that the National Council, with its 40,600,000 members, is pockmarked with Communists. These allegations evidently have made some impact in various parts of the country although they have no genuine substance. McIntire is proud that ACCC material about alleged Reds in the Protestant clergy was included in an Air Force Manual which caused a furor in 1960. Significantly, when the Defense Department's attention was called to the unsubstantiated charges in the Manual, the Department ordered distribution of the document stopped and formally apologized to the National Council of Churches.

McIntire disapproves of almost everything the NCC does. When

the National Council applauded Freedom Riders who went South
to demonstrate their support for Negro efforts to win equality,
McIntire attacked the National Council for defying the law. He
charged that the huge religious organization was "becoming a com-
panion of riotous men and a shame to Christianity." He remembered to add: "At the root of all this trouble is nothing more than
Communist agitation, Communist fomentation. . . ."

McIntire's greatest impact on the American scene is from his
20th Century Reformation Hour broadcasts, sponsored by the
Christian Beacon, a small, eight-page weekly with an estimated
circulation of 45,000, and tax-exempt as a religious newspaper.
Of the *Christian Beacon*, the Protestant Episcopal Church's National
Council wrote:
"[It] has been circulated through the mails on a second-class
mailing permit, obviously by thousands of copies, but it would be
difficult to find a minister or an elder who has paid any kind of
subscription himself. . . . Other church publications have considered
The Beacon to be almost constantly in violation of accepted ethical
standards. It has not hesitated to pirate copyrighted materials of
any sort. It photographically reproduces all kinds of articles without permission. And it sometimes reproduces them in distorted
form."
How many members McIntire has in his organization can only
be guessed. His own claims vary widely from time to time. He
has claimed 200,000 or 300,000, sometimes 400,000 and, when
he is so minded, "nearly 500,000." Some years back, the National
Council of Churches appraised McIntire's membership as follows:
"The American Council has not been willing to publish any
statistics of its membership by denominations, so the total membership of the 15 bodies belonging to it is not known. But such information as is available indicates that the total membership of the
15 bodies is not more than 200,000, probably much less. . . . The
total membership of the denominations included in the American
Council is perhaps one-half of one per cent of American Protestantism."
McIntire keeps a large wall map of the United States with pins
stuck into it to mark the cities where he has radio outlets. The
pins show that he has 577 stations. He added some 250 stations
in 1963 alone. Many of the outlets are in the Bible Belts of the
South and the Midwest, and the map shows a noticeable sparseness
of outlets in the North and the East. Connecticut has two, Massachusetts three, and New York State only four (all in small towns,

with the exception of Buffalo). States having the largest number of McIntire outlets are: Texas 27, Florida 26, Pennsylvania 24, California 23, Alabama 20, Mississippi and Georgia 19 each, and South Carolina 17. There are none in New York City, Chicago, Philadelphia, or Boston. Apparently, McIntire cannot get a following in sophisticated big cities.

McIntire has his own studio in Collingswood where he records his daily broadcasts every morning from Monday through Friday. The recording is played back to his critical ears, then edited and telephoned to his station in Chester, Pennsylvania, which relays it to all the others. McIntire's radio attacks are directed against the National Council of Churches, the World Council of Churches, the Roman Catholic Church, the Revised Bible, the United Nations, United States "give-away" policies, a "planned society," medical care, civil rights programs, the income tax, and American social, economic, and political policy of the last thirty years.

During McIntire's radio broadcasts, Dr. Charles Richter, the assistant pastor of the Bible Presbyterian Church of Collingswood, usually sits near the microphone and, at the proper moments, cries "Amen!" *The Christian Century* commented:

"McIntire's 'Reformation' program generally begins with a highly slanted Biblical interpretation: e.g., the Book of Jeremiah denounces Communists in general and Khrushchev in particular. This is followed by 'documented' exposés of Communist conspiracy in high places of church and state. Customarily, McIntire concludes with an appeal to the American people to wake up—and to write for his 'documentation' and to contribute money so that more radio stations will transmit his broadcasts. McIntire's pronouncements are punctuated by the remarks from Charles Richter (better known as 'Amen Charlie'), whose job it is to inject Amen or Yes or No at appropriate intervals. . . ."

Despite widespread criticism of McIntire for inaccuracy, exaggeration, and what sometimes seems to be deliberate distortion, his followers fanatically support him. When ministers in Warren, Ohio, during the winter of 1962-63 tried to secure a cancellation of his broadcasts because the program was creating ill will in the community, his loyal listeners turned out in sub-zero weather to a protest meeting. The audience, counted at 2,350, jammed Warren's Packard Music Hall. Hundreds came in chartered buses from communities across the state and from adjoining Pennsylvania. The stage was bedecked with fifty-nine flags (courtesy of the Sons of the American Revolution), and the program included hymns and patriotic songs and Scripture readings. McIntire himself was welcomed by Mayor Robert Dunstan, who told the people that the preacher, like Noah of old, was "a man raised up by God in a time of travail." The hall echoed with "Amens!" and when he appealed for money for his radio broadcasts, McIntire collected over $4,000 in checks and pledges in addition to some very substantial cash offerings.

It costs from $1,000 to $3,000 to test the effectiveness of a radio station for six to eight weeks. McIntire operates on the hard business idea that each voice along the network must show a profit or at least maintain itself; if it cannot, it is dropped. Like other Radical Right fundamentalist preachers, he constantly solicits seed money to buy time on more stations. His fund-raising technique is similar to the old camp-meeting exhortation for funds for the Lord's work. When a solicitation produces a contribution, he follows it up with a "victory letter." This excerpt, written in 1962, indicates the impressive success which sometimes results from his appeals:

> We are over the top! God has given us the answer to our constant prayer that we should have 300 stations. Yes, it is actually 301. We have just come from the studio in which we reported to all of our listeners the magnificent, yes, the magnificent victory which God has given us! Thank God!
>
> Yesterday was the day. As the mail was being opened we had two additional contributions of $1,000 which put us over the top. We had to stop everything around here and our entire staff gathered in a large upstairs room where the mail is opened and we sang *Praise God*. We prayed and then testimony after testimony was given as to how God had led, blessed, undertaken, and now given us this victory. . . .
>
> We are now asking the Lord to give us an additional 300. He has done it for us once; He can do it for us again, and this is our request. . . .

On March 4, 1964, after a trip around the world with his wife, he wrote another letter to his contributors:

> What a blessed anniversary this is! The Monday after the first Sunday in March, 1955, when we had our annual Every Member Canvass here in the church, 'Amen Charlie' and I sat down at the microphone and started talking. . . . Now we have moved up to 577 radio stations. It seems utterly fantastic. It is nothing but a miracle, and our blessed theme text, 'For with God nothing shall be impossible,' I am sure, applies to what God is doing for us. . . .

For McIntire to spread his Radical Right propaganda via print and the airwaves costs perhaps $1,000,000 a year, and as the Reverend told an interviewer, "We have no fat cats. Our money comes from the faithful, and in small bills, but it keeps coming. It keeps coming."

Indeed, it keeps coming. To Carl McIntire it keeps coming from the "faithful" who have chosen McIntire over the Devil, as well as over Rome, Washington, and the NCC. To other propagandists of the Radical Right it keeps coming from the "fat cats" that McIntire denies knowing—from the corporations and foundations that would pay any price in an effort to change America's thinking into channels of fearful reaction.

Clarence Manion, to whom we now turn, is like Dr. McIntire in that he is a Far Right Wing voice heard on hundreds of radio stations. But, unlike the New Jersey preacher, this former law school dean has "fat cats" behind him. And he serves them well.

7

The Manion Forum
— Dean Clarence Manion

"Fear is essential to the salvation of the American Republic." So says Dean Clarence Manion, radio voice and high official of the John Birch Society, in a frank assessment of fright-peddling as a weapon of the Reactionary Right.

The story of the Manion Forum and its Far Right political propaganda properly begins with the story of Leo F. Reardon.

In the years just before World War II, one of the openly anti-Semitic and pro-Nazi periodicals published in the United States was *Social Justice,* a weekly newspaper published by Father Charles E. Coughlin of Royal Oak, Michigan. In three or four years, through this publication and by regular weekly radio broadcasts, the clergyman built up a following estimated at several million Americans, but the United States Government and Coughlin's own ecclesiastical superiors eventually put an end to his poison. Leo F. Reardon was confidential advisor to Father Coughlin and his personal representative in political affairs. His official role at *Social Justice* was that of a contest editor.

The Forum story—not at all one of anti-Semitism or pro-Nazism

—begins here because Leo F. Reardon is now the business manager of Clarence Manion's nation-wide propaganda mill in South Bend, Indiana, a complex operation with techniques of fund-raising (from corporations and wealthy businessmen) that must tax even Reardon's experienced mind. This experience included, besides the job with Coughlin, fund-raising and promotional work for other rather notorious extremist operations.

Reardon usually worked for a salary plus a percentage of the money he collected. During hearings before the House Subcommittee on Lobbying Activities in 1950, a 1947 office memo from Merwin Hart was read into the record. Hart, the anti-Semitic president of the National Economic Council, was protesting the integrity of his organization:

"We have never paid any commission on money raised except to the rather limited extent, and over a limited period of time, to Reardon. And we inherited Reardon." (There was no explanation of what Hart meant in saying he "inherited Reardon.")

When the United States entered World War II, Federal and church officials put an end to Father Coughlin's political activities; the days of a newspaper that spoke well of Hitler and spread dissension had passed. Leo F. Reardon eventually became a fund raiser for another anti-Semitic propagandist named Upton Close, publisher of a venomous newsletter, "Closer-Ups." Close climaxed a checkered career with a national radio network broadcast sponsored by Merwin Hart. The broadcasts terminated abruptly when Close and Hart fought over the spoils—the approximately $235,000 that had been raised to "save" America. It may be that Hart "inherited" Reardon at that point.

After being disinherited by Hart, Reardon apparently decided to strike out on his own. He created the American Education Association, and advertised his new venture in a Detroit newspaper with almost foolhardy frankness:

"This enterprise was started with the purpose of aiding in the important fight against Communist infiltration to the United States. It is not a non-profit organization for the very good reason that everybody associated with it believes in the profit system and American private enterprise. However, the greater part of any profit which might accrue from a national contest is immediately 'plowed back' into another pro-American competition or into a campaign to increase the national circulation of the Association's twice-a-month comment letter *Cross-Roads.* . . ."

Reardon's educational technique to stop Communist infiltration was, as might have been expected, the contest. All a contestant had to do was write a suitable caption for a picture and send in the caption along with from $2 to $5, depending on the picture and the contest. Built into the contest was a carnival barker's guarantee. The contestant who did not win did not lose his money. He was given, free of charge, a book called *Cartoon Contests—How To Solve Them* which might help in the next contest. Apparently the public did not consider the offer irresistible and the project failed.

Thus, we have an insight into the background of L. F. Reardon, the man hired to run the business end of a political propaganda organization that today utilizes the vast resources of radio and TV, and distributes millions of pieces of printed material annually across the nation.

And the setup of the operation in South Bend has been an appropriate challenge to Reardon's talents.

Under Indiana law a nonprofit corporation must file annual reports with the Secretary of State, listing its officers and stating how much money it received and how it was spent. Such reports are open to the public and the state has the power to ascertain the corporation's sources of income. From the day in 1956 when the Manion Forum was incorporated in Indiana, it ignored the required forms the Secretary of State sent for completion. No reports were filed. In 1959, after almost four years of neglecting the state law requirement, the corporation became dormant.

With no halt in its flow of propaganda, the Manion Forum became a trust—a legal entity which, in Indiana, is not required to report how much it collects or to open its books to the state except by court order. Moreover, contributions made to the Manion Forum Trust are not tax-deductible, so that the trust does not have to file the Form 990-A which the Internal Revenue Service requires of tax-exempt bodies.

The Manion Forum thus became, in a sense, a very private enterprise, financed largely by certain business firms and business leaders, to persuade Americans to accept the special political and economic viewpoints held by a Far Right Extremist segment of the business community. There is no way of telling how gifts to such a trust are recorded in the income tax returns of the contributors. But some political propaganda organizations which do not enjoy tax exemption do suggest in their solicitations that corporate contributors can charge such monies off as deductible business expenses. In any case, it's probably all quite legal, and shocking—as later details will show.

The day-to-day job of directing this highly financed effort to swing America to the Far Right is handled by Leo F. Reardon, who is now vice-president of the Manion Forum Trust.

Clarence Manion, the head of the organization, looked so prom-
ising in the 1930's as Democratic candidate timber in Indiana that
his name was frequently mentioned in newspaper reports as a possibility for elective office. In 1930, for instance, he was an active
candidate for a nomination to Congress, but was persuaded by the
local Democratic organization to withdraw in favor of another hopeful, who was elected. Newspaper reports said that in return for
this sacrifice, the local organization had promised to sponsor him
for appointment to an appellate court judgeship, but the appointment never materialized and Manion broke with the local organization.

He nevertheless remained important enough as an up-and-coming
young Democrat to be named as keynote speaker at the state convention in 1932. There he delivered a scathing attack on the
incumbent Hoover Administration in Washington, and the incumbent Republican administration in the Indiana State House.
He said the call of that hour was "for democracy or demoralization"
and he invoked the spirit of Jefferson and Jackson to inspire Indiana
Democrats for the campaign of 1932 that swept Franklin Roosevelt
into the White House.

In reporting the selection of the young Notre Dame law professor
as state keynoter, the *South Bend Tribune* of May 25, 1932, reported that Manion's "whole life seems devoted to a future in
politics and his principles are clear and forcibly put. He has spoken
out," the paper's report said, "against the growth of chain business
and the gradual decline of individual ownership which deprives
men of their property rights."

In 1935, with the New Deal in power two years, Manion received an appointment from Washington as Indiana director of the
National Emergency Council. And by 1938, he was being boomed
for the Democratic nomination to the Senate as a possible compromise candidate in a state convention deadlock then believed
developing between the incumbent governor and the incumbent
senator who were battling each other for the nomination. Manion's
contacts in the ranks of organized labor were good enough to produce newspaper reports that he stood a good chance of receiving
the support of the local AFL and CIO unions.

Manion did not get the 1938 senatorial nomination. In 1940, his
importance as a Democrat in the Hoosier State's political picture
was again underscored when he was asked by the Democratic
national chairman to resign from his Federal position, to which

President Roosevelt had appointed him in 1935, so he would be free to participate in the 1940 campaign.

A year later, in 1941, with much of the European continent under the jackboots of the advancing Nazis, Manion became a member of the national committee of the America First Committee, led by General Robert E. Wood, then chairman of Sears, Roebuck. This foremost isolationist organization of that period was eventually shown to have been infiltrated by elements opposed to American efforts to stop Hitler's march in Europe. (When Manion first joined it, America First was arguing that the war in Europe was none of America's business, that the United States should turn its back on Europe's problems and sit out the bloodshed. Such an attitude made it obvious that pro-Nazis would quickly try to insinuate themselves into the organization and, in retrospect, it is incomprehensible that the sincere isolationists didn't do more to prevent the infiltration.) Pearl Harbor rendered the America First program academic.

In January, 1943, with the forces of freedom heavily engaged around the globe and American GIs fighting on far-off battlefields, Manion delivered a public speech in which he lashed out at the "super-duper planners of what they call 'the brave new world,' " declaring that "only in America do we find people who are anxious to give away their country in exchange for the blurred blueprint of a nebulous super-state." Two years earlier, just before he joined the America First Committee, he had declared that "the last objective of the interventionist program is the establishment of a world state."

With the end of the Second World War, the views of the Notre Dame Law School dean who had once championed the rights of individual businessmen against the giant chains hardened even further. In 1952, he supported the late Senator Robert A. Taft in his bid for the Republican Presidential nomination, but when Taft lost the nomination to General Dwight Eisenhower, Manion bolted the Democratic Party to campaign for the Republican ticket under the banner of "Democrats for Eisenhower." When Eisenhower won the 1952 election, Manion was reportedly recommended by Senator Taft for the post of Secretary of Labor in the new Republican administration. Instead, however, the new President named Manion as Chairman of the Commission on Inter-Governmental Relations. Its task was to study Federal and state functions and overlapping jurisdictions, and to recommend ways to eliminate duplicative governmental activities.

It was not long, however, before the former law professor became politically embarrassing to President Eisenhower because of his

extreme views. In public speeches, he advocated sale of the Tennessee Valley Authority to private business and vigorously supported the proposed Bricker Amendment to the Constitution, which
would have limited the President's treaty-making powers, and which
the Eisenhower Administration strenuously opposed.

So, after less than a year in the Eisenhower Administration,
Manion resigned in February, 1954, and newspaper reports indicated that the resignation had been requested by the White House.
Some even said that Manion had been "ousted," and Manion himself was reported to have felt that he had talked himself out of
his job. Other reports said the White House felt Manion spent too
much time making speeches at the expense of his responsibilities
in Washington and that it was also unhappy with what he had
said on TVA and the Bricker Amendment.

In 1953 and 1954, the Bricker Amendment was a favorite project
and propaganda theme of the American Far Right. Moreover, dis-
illusion with the Eisenhower Administration was already beginning
to set in, especially among the Right Wing elements of the GOP
who had worked devotedly for Taft.

It was at this juncture in 1954 that the top leadership of the
long discredited America First Committee came together to form
a new organization to deal with the situation. The organization
that emerged was, like its ideological parent, dubbed with a patri-
otic-sounding name—For America. Its formation was announced
at a dinner in Chicago hosted by the late Colonel Robert R.
McCormick, the Far Right publisher of *The Chicago Tribune*.
Named as co-chairmen of For America were General Wood, who
had headed America First, and Manion. The national policy committee of For America included most of the leading extreme Right-
Wingers of that time and was loaded with extremely conservative
leaders of business and the professions.

The new group applied for, and received, tax-exempt status from
the Internal Revenue Service as an educational organization. (Later,
the IRS ruled that while For America's income was tax-exempt,
contributions to it were not.) An objective of For America was
to build support for Far Right political principles and Far Right
political candidates, regardless of their party affiliations.

And so it was that Manion, who had broken with the Democratic
Party after many years in its ranks, and who had been ousted by
a Republican administration for his extreme views, at long last
came to rest in the Radical Right.

Since then, Dean Manion's name has been associated with a

number of other organizations of the Radical Right. He is a member of the national council of the John Birch Society, and he is on the editorial advisory committee of the Society's monthly magazine, *American Opinion.* He is a member of the national advisory committee of the Hargis Christian Crusade. Since 1958, he has been legal counsel to the Citizens Foreign Aid Committee, a Far Right lobbying group which boasts that it is the "only national organization" devoted to the single objective of ending all foreign aid except that which would "strengthen our strategic fighting forces."

He served as a member of the national advisory council of the now-defunct Campaign for the 48 States, which was organized in 1955 to stop "inflation, socialism or collectivism." In 1955, also, he was listed as a member of another Far Right group, the Committee of Endorsers. In 1956 he played a leading role in the third party movement seeking the election of former United States Commissioner of Internal Revenue T. Coleman Andrews as President of the United States. (Andrews has since joined with Manion on the national council of the Birch Society.) In 1957, Manion was listed as head of the Interim Committee for Independent Political Action, another rump political movement. In 1959, he was a member of the Committee Against Summit Entanglements, an early Birch front organization set up after the Birch Society was formed. In 1961, Manion's name appeared as a member of the American Committee for Aid to Katanga Freedom Fighters and as an advisor of the Right Wing Intercollegiate Society of Individualists.

Manion made numerous speeches in the month following the formation of For America, and with his exceptional skill as an orator, laid down some major themes of the American Far Right, some of which are still echoed today, a decade later. In one such speech he declared that eight of the ten commandments in the *Communist Manifesto* had been adopted, "in whole or in part," by the United States Government. In another, he urged that the United States sever diplomatic relations with every Communist and Communist-influenced country. He even assailed the proposed United Nations pact against genocide.

One such Manion speech was sponsored by For America, and was carried over a nation-wide network of 472 radio stations on June 16, 1954.

Whether that was the germ of the idea for the Manion Forum radio broadcasts cannot be ascertained. But a few months later, in August, 1954, the Manion Forum of Opinion was organized to sponsor the ex-Notre Dame Law School dean in a nation-wide weekly series of radio broadcasts. The *South Bend Tribune* of

August 4, 1954, reported that "Manion had been offered commercial sponsorship," but that he had chosen instead "to set up a forum backed by bankers, industrialists and businessmen."

Telegrams were sent out to 340 prominent leaders of business and industry throughout the country, outlining plans for the broadcasts and soliciting financial support; it was said that by the organizational technique to be employed, the "confining influences of commercial sponsorship" would be "averted." The telegram added: "Voice of Manion, week after week, will alert millions to efforts of those who would perpetuate American involvement foreign wars and entanglement international schemes [sic] while our own country rots within from one-worldism, socialism and communism." Plans were also announced for a solicitation to 50,000 industrial, business, and professional men in all states as soon as the broadcasts actually began. Recipients of the wires were asked to send $250 to $5,000 or more, personal or corporate, to this "non-profit, educational effort."

Trustees of the new Forum were B. K. Patterson (now deceased but at that time president of the St. Joseph County Bank and Trust Company); R. E. Snoberger, a Chicago industrialist; Ray L. Lamb, a Cleveland lawyer and a partner in the brokerage firm of Merrill Lynch, Pierce, Fenner & Beane; and Manion himself.

The *Chicago Tribune* reported that E. Ross Humphrey, the agent handling the proposed Manion broadcasts, was already negotiating for station outlets. Manion wrote the first of a series of alarmist personal letters to industrialists and businessmen, explaining that many who had heard his speeches had urged him to go on the radio. His opening letter read in part:

"The growing concentration of absolute power in the Federal Executive branch of our Government is destroying personal liberty, private property and private enterprise. This destruction is being accomplished through a spreading maze of unfathomable federal regulations and unlimited confiscatory taxes on all persons, all property and every business enterprise. These liberty-destroying forces are effectively screened by the wasteful, frantic foreign policy that now dominates both of our political parties. We debauch our dollar and dissipate our resources in fruitless, deadly, Communist-inspired military diversions all over the world, thus weakening ourselves at home for the planned Communist kill-from-the-inside.

"These are the alarming conditions upon which the imminent destruction of America is now predicated."

Manion was soon on the air, thundering just such fear propaganda as this over twenty-nine stations of the Mutual Network. His first broadcast was carried on October 3, 1954. Two years later, the Manion Forum was chartered as an Indiana "not-for-profit" corporation. In a promotional folder it issued a few years ago, the Forum described in capsule form what it opposed and what it favored. Among those things it opposed:

"The murderously oppressive Marxist Federal Income Tax; gigantic and unnecessary subsidies of tax money for fantastic highway and housing projects; Federal aid to education which would inevitably be followed by Federal Socialist control; tyrannical control of American workers by politically and ruthlessly ambitious union czars; appeasing and fraternizing with Communist mass murderers, thugs and slave masters."

The Forum favored:

"Leaving education to the states; restoration of states' rights as provided by the Constitution; anti-trust legislation governing the unions and Right-to-Work laws; unification of the American people and a rebirth of patriotism by emphatic assertion of the power and determination of this Nation and its allies to 'bury' Communism throughout the world."

Manion frequently declares that there is a critical need for the hard, clear voice of freedom for the United States and liberation for the oppressed nations who languish in Communist slavery. But Manion's major efforts and those of his organization seem most aimed at liberating the oppressed people of the United States from the slavery imposed on them by the domestic and foreign policies of the Roosevelt, Truman, and Eisenhower administrations. His own statements are more extreme than the program of the Manion Forum itself.

In 1954, for instance, Manion denounced social security, calling it "a palpable fraud" as insurance. In 1956, when he opposed both Eisenhower and Stevenson for President and supported T. Coleman Andrews on a third party ticket, Manion declared:

"Since the carbon copy candidates [of both political parties] endorse the confiscatory taxation of Americans for world wide giveaways, then the American people must and will challenge the immoral discriminatory Federal Income tax and wipe it out of existence."

On spending, he wrote in a January, 1961, Manion Forum Letter:

"We simply cannot have wasteful 'foreign aid,' 100% parity subsidies to farmers, hospitalization for all over 65, gigantic internal spending for unneeded schools—all of this Socialistic nonsense—and maintain the value of the American dollar . . . ."

The Supreme Court is a major target for Manion:

"Everyone except the United States Supreme Court knows that Communism has infiltrated into every facet of our society and that the tempo of its march toward the achievement of its goal is rapidly increasing in this nation.

"Yet, the majority members continue to treat it as a belief, an association, an ideology, perfectly harmless, incapable of wrong and therefore entitled to the protection of our Constitution. . . ." And again: "The record reveals that the chief, if not the only beneficiary of the Warren Court's Constitutional constructions have been convicted criminals, Communists, atheists and clients of the NAACP."

Though the Manion Forum does not disseminate fear as melodramatically as do Schwarz and Hargis, it nevertheless does disseminate it. From his own speeches and printed materials issued in South Bend come such quotations as these:

—"Sovereignty of the 48 states is the only remaining dike holding the Communist front from America."

—"American industry and personal freedom are at the barricades. Unless our people impel Congress to save this nation, the end of liberty is in sight."

—"Unless we can here and now crystallize ways and means to revive popular respect and enforcement of the constitutional rights of the states, communism will soon take over this country from the inside and without firing a shot."

—"Our worst danger is not Moscow. It's in Washington. There's where the Devil's brew is being stirred by a group of addle-pated 'Liberal' Internationalists, steering us down the river to 'One-Worldism' and slavery."

Attending a 1961 Crusade for America rally in Garden City, New York, a reporter for the Long Island *Newsday* wrote:

"Clarence Manion, key figure in the ultra-Conservative John Birch Society, brought his 'gospel' to Long Island last night, calling for a nuclear war in preference to 'surrendering to Communism.'

" 'I am tired,' Manion said, 'of hearing an old man like Linus Pauling (the Nobel Prize winning scientist who opposes nuclear testing) cry his fear of death in a nuclear war. . . . How long does he want to live anyway? If we must fall to communism, I would rather it be over the remains of 10,000,000 charred bodies of which I would be proud to be one.' "

"Pat," as Manion is known to his friends, was born July 7, 1896, in Henderson, Kentucky, received an excellent education and has several degrees. He taught American history, government, and constitutional law at Notre Dame, and from 1941 to 1952 was dean of its Law School. Former students unanimously agree that Manion was an authority on the history of the period in which the Constitution was drawn up and on the individuals who wrote it, and that he was delightful in his classroom lectures.

Despite his long career as a public speaker and political figure, Manion is essentially a reserved man. Besides its knowledge of his academic and political activities, South Bend seems to know little except that he is a member of the legal firm of Doran, Manion, Boynton and Kamm. In town, however, Manion is not considered an active practicing lawyer.

More heard about than heard from in his own neighborhood, Manion lives with his wife on a forty-five acre estate outside of South Bend where he breeds Arabian horses. There are five Manion children in their twenties and late teens. The family is closely knit. In 1956, when Manion led the third party movement in Indiana, Mrs. Manion was at a table in the Pick-Oliver Hotel lobby seeking signatures for the Constitution Party petition. Marilyn, their older daughter, works on the TV phase of the Manion Forum, occasionally appearing with her father on camera.

Manion has published at least seven books, the best known being *The Key to Peace—A Formula for the Perpetuation of Real Americanism*. In it he attacks social legislation as "socialistic" and advances the argument that "each responsible human being has both a natural right and natural duty to acquire and hold private property."

A *Chicago Tribune* reviewer said: "This book should be read by everyone who loves his church and his country. It is the finest political-spiritual study of America I know." *Human Events*, a publication which today serves as a philosophic guide to the Radical Right and its fellow travelers, reported that the book ranks with the Gettysburg Address and the Declaration of Independence. But a critic for *The New York Times* received it differently: "This book is fundamentally at war with American tradition as this reviewer understands the ideas and forces that have made America great and its people free—with rationalism, with liberalism, with the belief that people can put their talents and abilities to work and through individual and collective efforts establish a just and rewarding social order."

In February, 1964, when the Manion Forum launched its intensive Far Right propaganda to condition America for the November elections, the *Indianapolis Times* wondered who was putting up the money. As mentioned previously, Indiana law specifies that a non-profit corporation must file an annual financial report with its Secretary of State. The newspaper sought to inspect the reports for their news value. There were none. The Secretary of State assured the *Times* that the necessary forms had been sent every year to C. M. Boynton, Manion's law partner and the Manion Forum's agent of record, and that Boynton had apparently ignored them. The Secretary of State also assured the *Times* that the Manion Forum would be instructed to submit the delinquent reports. The *Times* published the story about the nonexistent annual reports and editorialized that "Clarence Manion, the New Dealer-turned-Bircher, spent much of his life molding the minds of the young.

"That's one reason it's so discouraging to see the Manion Forum, a not-for-profit corporation chartered in 1956, flout its legal obligation to file annual reports with the Indiana Secretary of State."

The Manion Forum then filed the delinquent reports. And in March, 1964, after the critical press statements, the former dean wrote to the *Indianapolis Times*:

"The fact is that the Manion Forum ceased to operate as a corporation in 1959 when all of its corporate assets were turned over to trustees. Since that time the Forum has been conducted as a private, not-for-profit trust fund, using the agency of the St. Joseph Bank and Trust Company of South Bend as the sole recipient and disburser of all its funds. . . ."

The reports, finally submitted, showed that between June, 1956, and December 31, 1959, the organization had received and spent more than one million dollars, and that almost all its money came from contributions. The reports did not identify the donors or the individual gifts.

When the Forum changed its legal status, it had 5,100 members and a debt of $23,000. It had been spending $92,000 a year in salaries and commissions, $38,000 for printing, and $172,000 for air time. A Manion Forum pamphlet published in 1962 indicated that a number of the broadcasts were paid for directly by local sponsors "dedicated to free enterprise, and the belief that the Forum's Conservative viewpoint should be brought to the attention of every American family. . . ."

Although the Forum altered its corporate character, Manion did not stop broadcasting. Now his organization is the Manion Forum Trust. It is an elusive legal entity, operated by trustees, which seeks to mold the views and attitudes of millions of Americans. It claims to be motivated by patriotism but seems to prefer that its finances and its expenditures be kept from the public records.

In any event, the required reports which Manion Forum, Inc., tardily filed early in 1964 showed that in 1956 its gross income was over $141,000; in 1957 it passed $293,000; in 1958 it was over $305,000; and in 1959 it jumped to over $387,000.

In 1960, Manion told his supporters that he was spending over $8,000 a week for air time and to distribute his radio speeches, or about $400,000 a year. In 1962, the Forum's pamphlet "Seven Years of Progress" stated:

"It now costs more than $10,000 a week to maintain the radio program and . . . to distribute bales of Conservative literature, besides overhead expenses. Among supporters are many of the nation's largest corporations, hundreds of medium and small companies, and thousands of patriotic individuals who send $5 to $50 every few weeks."

Since the Manion Forum now has over three hundred radio and television outlets, the cost of this propaganda deluge must have risen. It is quite likely that today, the Forum and those of its supporters who pay stations directly for air time are expending between $500,000 and $750,000 a year to bring the Far Right message to an audience of many millions.

In 1962, the Manion Forum told its readers:

"More than 700 leading industrialists and businessmen of the United States have aided financing by writing 'covering letters' to their suppliers, corporate executives and patriotic individuals in their respective communities, urging financial support of the Manion Forum."

The pressure of a big subscriber's covering letter to a supplier is obvious. The supplier is apparently afraid that if he does not contribute, the solicitor (the purchaser of his product) will find another supplier from whom to buy.

Nor does the Manion Forum ignore the printed word:

"Its dissemination of Conservative, anti-Socialist, anti-Communist literature has seldom been equaled in American History. . . .

"Daily the Forum is deluged with requests for material. Millions of copies of the weekly radio speeches have been purchased by corporations and patriotic individuals for distribution to business associates, employees, teachers, clergymen, college and high school students. Many stirring addresses are reprinted in hundreds of daily and weekly newspapers across the nation.

"More than 10,000,000 individual printed pieces have been distributed by the Forum in the last seven years . . . broadcast tapes are rerun by literally thousands of civic, church, youth and Conservative organizations in all sections of the country."

At the beginning of 1963, the Manion Forum expanded its operations for the first time into the field of television, supplementing its radio programs which were then being heard over 276 stations in 42 states. The TV operation was launched over 36 stations in California, Oregon, Washington, Idaho, Nevada, Montana, and Arizona.

A promotional letter, signed by Reardon in December, 1962, announced the new TV venture and declared that it would increase the Manion Forum's listening audience by at least a million. "Henceforth," Reardon wrote, "we can give the Liberals, International-Socialists, Pinkos, 'Welfare Staters' and Communists 'both barrels.' "

The TV venture, he added, was "due to the patriotic cooperation of Mr. D. B. Lewis, President of the Lewis Food Company, of Los Angeles, which is sponsoring our TV program in the above seven Western states, paying the heavy costs of station time, provided we can help finance the incidental expense of production, advertising and dissemination of literature."

Reardon's letter said that in its first stages, the TV broadcasts would be used to show that "Conservatism scored a distinct victory" in the 1962 congressional elections. They would also be used to alert millions of Americans to support the coalition of Northern Republicans and Southern Democrats (as well as Southern Republicans) so that the "Socialist 'Welfare State' nostrums in the 88th Congress will be snowed under. . . ." Finally, the TV programs were to be used to bring to the viewing audience members of Congress "who will demand a full-dress Congressional investigation of the State Department, the Defense Department and the Central Intelligence Agency to find out who are the men who induced President Kennedy to deliver Cuba and expose Central and South America to Khrushchev and International Communism."

Reardon's letter, of course, ended with a plea for financial contributions to help meet a $45,000 operating deficit, to meet current expenses of $10,000 a week, and to implement Lewis' generosity. To do all that, Reardon wrote, $100,000 was needed in the ensuing six weeks. Since the Manion Forum has continued operations and has expanded even further, the money undoubtedly was forthcoming.

At the start of 1964, the Forum announced that "our 36-station television network will be expended." There was another plea for funds to do the job—and more. For 1964 was, of course, an election year. The letter also told what was to be done in the 1964 political campaigns. It was sent out in January, 1964, by Herbert V. Kohler of the Kohler Company, Kohler, Wisconsin:

"Newspaper ads, direct mail, posters, bumper stickers and telephone calls! All will play an important role in our campaign. Billboards—one of the oldest, most successful mediums of advertising —used heretofore to publicize bourbon, beer and Burma Shave, will be utilized to define Conservatism, to promote free enterprise and to 'sell' Americanism. Local sponsors—or national—will be used wherever possible. Where sponsorship cannot be obtained, we must purchase the time ourselves. Television time is being cleared. Program production is underway. Tie-in advertising copy and mats are in the 'works.' Contracts must be signed. Production costs must be met. Yes, it will take money—big money! No, we do not have it. We have faith. We have hope. We have determination."

To get money from industrialists and businessmen and to persuade listeners, viewers and readers to support its Radical Right objectives, the Manion Forum spreads the usual fear propaganda. A back-page ad of one reprint of a Manion broadcast reads:

"If this speech by Dean Manion fails to revive your patriotism and make you 'boiling mad' you are all set, body and soul, for the Communist take-over."

It then adds: "After reading it we ask you to do two things now:

"1. Order printed copies in quantities for general distribution— so that the dying spark of love-of-country can be revived in others.

"2. Unless you are a supporter of the Manion Forum, become one today. Your check, or that of your company, of from $25 to $1000 will help to continue and expand a great patriotic network which has enabled the American people by the tens of millions to hear addresses such as this every week for close to seven years."

Sometimes the Forum's appeals for money can scarcely be distinguished from the embarrassingly obvious tactics used by people like the Reverend Billy James Hargis. In 1963, it will be recalled, Hargis told an audience that it might well be their last "legal Thanksgiving." The Manion Forum tells industrialists:

"Your check for $50 to $500 or more will help us to move more quickly to offset the now frantic determination of the Liberals to give us another brace of 'me too' candidates in 1964. It gives us no comfort to remember their financial resources are unlimited. We are sure you realize that time is short. Remember, 1964 may well be our last chance for a choice."

Such appeals to fear are not particularly surprising when it is recalled that Manion has been quoted as saying that "fear is essential to the salvation of the American Republic." While he has publicly backed away from Robert Welch's accusation that President Eisenhower and other great Americans of recent years were tools of communism, Manion believes that both major political parties are suffused with "left-wing international Socialism." He has perhaps paraphrased Welch's charges, declaring that "some contend that an anonymous third force captured General Eisenhower in a plot to kill the Republican Party."

One of the ways in which the Manion Forum seeks to infiuence American political life is by encouraging the formation of local Conservative Clubs around the country, which it services with its Newsletter and other printed materials. It claims that there are at least eight hundred such clubs in operation and that "the rebirth of Conservatism didn't just *happen*." The Forum claims that it "paved the way" for much of the conservative movement of today in the United States and that "many of the Forum's earliest friends and supporters are now active in various Conservative endeavors."

The Forum guides and instructs the members of these clubs, although each club itself is distinct, local, and individual. The local officers set its specific tasks—distributing literature, protesting "Socialist" legislation, and screening congressional candidates to determine whether they deserve the support of the good little Rightists who belong to the clubs. The Forum itself stands ready to help in the formation of new clubs and to supply them with "ammunition" when they are organized.

A number of important Radical Right and fellow-traveling organizations have launched drives to win the American college student. In 1963, the Manion Forum, encouraged by its success, informed its contributors that it had "added to its intensive program a new and energetic 'accent on youth.' "

College radio stations now carry Manion weekly radio programs; large numbers of high school and college libraries throughout the country are supplied with the Manion Forum Year Book and other such materials, and the Forum gladly helps students in their classroom work and in research. Appeals are addressed both to students and alumni to "help make Manion broadcasts the new campus craze." A sample back-page ad on a printed broadcast reads:

"From all parts of the country, our student mail carries the same message: 'Where can I get the facts and material compiled from the Conservative point of view?' College students repeatedly tell us that they are subjected to a preponderance of Liberal views and opinions from professors, textbooks and visiting lecturers. They feel that Conservatism deserves equal time.

"Now available to these college students is a program designed to present the Conservative view. The weekly broadcasts of the Manion Forum are being offered, *free of charge,* to the student radio stations on the campuses of the Nation's colleges and universities. . . ."

There, the young leaders—or more likely, followers—of tomorrow's Radical Right will be found. And Dean Clarence Manion, who has called himself "an unreconstructed McCarthyite," will have contributed his share to their "education"—a barrage of well-financed propaganda carrying an impact of fear for the future of America.

The unreconstructed McCarthyism of Manion—or of Dan Smoot, another broadcaster who carries the frightening message to millions of Americans—would create that future out of a national retreat into the past.

8

Life Line Foundation, Inc.
The "Dan Smoot Report"
— Dan Smoot

Because he is color-blind and has fallen arches, Dan Smoot of Dallas, Texas, was rejected for military service during World War II. He applied to the FBI for a job, was accepted and assigned (so he tells us) to a subversive activities squad.

That's how Dan Smoot's career as a "saver" of America began. After nine years in the Justice Department, he resigned in 1951 and undertook the more profitable vocation of being a private political vigilante. Today he employs a staff of fifteen to aid in his sizeable operations. Smoot now broadcasts weekly over a hundred radio and TV stations with an audience that has been estimated in seven figures. He publishes a newsletter and is in great demand as a public speaker at $750 a speech. In all of these enterprises Smoot's message is the same: the Communists, the Socialists, and the Liberals are burrowing in, softening up the United States for the final Red take-over.

As a former Government man, Smoot offers himself as an expert on communism and subversion. His claim, however, may perhaps be judged in the light of his belief that "as philosophies of government, modern liberalism, communism, and fascism are all essentially the same."

Smoot's propaganda hews to the regular Radical Right line. In April, 1962, in a fiery talk in Orlando, Florida, delivered before an American Legion Post and carried on local television, Smoot denounced "liberalism," which he said could lead to the demise of America and to a one-world socialistic-Communistic system. He called for the impeachment of Chief Justice Earl Warren, and urged that the United States immediately "hit Cuba with overwhelming military force." A local television outlet, WLOF-TV, broadcast an editorial a day or so later and commented on the evening's events:

"Typical of the speakers brought in by extremists, Mr. Smoot, a so-called expert in Communist infiltration, pointed his finger at such supposed Communistic dangers as . . . the Kennedy Administration, the United Nations, Mrs. Roosevelt, Ed Murrow, Walter Reuther, Secretary of Labor Goldberg, the income tax, and even fluoridated water. This was his contribution to the exposure of the giant Communist Conspiracy. . . .

"Also attracted on this nut-gathering occasion were two Storm Troopers wearing olive-green uniforms and arm-band insignias with a big 'W' inside the band. They said they were members of the 190-strong organization known as 'White Americans.' They took pride in distributing the most vicious, deceitful race and color hate propaganda we have ever seen."

Smoot and the Legion officials denied any association with the fanatics in uniform, but such are the dangers and the attractions inherent in extremism, and such are the strange forces often found in patriotic guise as camp followers of those who preach the doctrine of the Extreme Right.

Dan Smoot is a well-built, handsome man with a rugged face and a persuasive platform manner. Born in Missouri in 1913, the son of a tenant farmer, he was orphaned by the time he was eleven. According to his own accounts, he did all kinds of manual work to survive, much of it as a migratory field hand who followed the harvests in the Midwest. At eighteen he arrived in Dallas and got a job with a produce firm for which he worked for the next nine years, during which time he also acquired a B.A. and an M.A. from Southern Methodist University. He then went to Harvard University as a Teaching Fellow in English and did graduate work for a doctorate in American Civilization. It is this brief stay at Harvard which leads overzealous publicity men to advertise him as "a former Harvard professor." In response to a query, Harvard University wrote:

"Dan Smoot was appointed Teaching Fellow in English for one year at Harvard, beginning September 1, 1941. However, he resigned as Teaching Fellow April 6, 1942. Our records do not indicate that Mr. Smoot was ever a professor here."

From Harvard he went to the Federal Bureau of Investigation and eventually was assigned to the Cleveland, Ohio, field office, where for three years, according to his own biography, he was part of a special squad investigating Communists. From there he was transferred to FBI headquarters in Washington, D. C., where, his newsletter used to claim, he was "administrative assistant to J. Edgar Hoover." Mr. Hoover himself says:

"I wish to advise that there is no position in the FBI entitled 'Administrative Assistant to the Director'; however, Mr. Smoot was an Agent of this Bureau from March 23, 1942 to June 15, 1951, when he voluntarily submitted his resignation. . . ." (Smoot no longer claims he was administrative assistant to Mr. Hoover.)

After two years in Washington, Smoot received a transfer to the FBI Dallas office, where he served an additional two years. In Dallas he met oilman Haroldson Lafayette Hunt, one of the richest men in the world, who was bent on saving America in his own way. Hunt's idea of an ideal government was spelled out in a book called *Alpaca,* which bears his name. In it he declared that a perfect government is one where "the more taxes you pay, the more votes you get . . . [and] if you accept State aid because you are poor or sick, you cannot vote at all, and you are denied an old age pension." *Alpaca* was privately printed in 1960, and Hunt still sends copies (sometimes in batches of 100) free of charge without even being asked. Recipients include colleges and universities.

Out of an income estimated at nearly $1,000,000 a week, Hunt for several years had been financing a widespread campaign to change America's views to conform to his own. Dan Smoot resigned from the FBI and went to work for Facts Forum, Hunt's political propaganda operation. Smoot once told why he left the FBI and went to work for the wealthy oilman:

"I wondered, when I was a member of the FBI Commie Squad, why those who oppose Communism were vilified and slandered. I learned the reason. It was because people were blindly following the philosophy of the New Deal, which stands for the total transfer of power from the individual to the Federal Government under the claim of using the power beneficently. This is the same philosophy of the Fair Deal, the New Frontier, and Modern Republicanism. . . . It is also the basic philosophy of Communism, Fascism and Nazism."

Facts Forum offered an elaborate package of radio and TV programs, a monthy magazine called "Facts Forum News," pamphlets, and the services of a free circulating library studded with the works of men like the late Senator Joseph McCarthy, a particular favorite of Hunt's. Smoot became radio and television commentator for Facts Forum and gave weekly thirty-minute broadcasts over 350 radio and eighty TV stations with a combined listening and viewing audience estimated in the millions.

When Smoot first went on Hunt's payroll he apparently did not know what his new boss thought of a democracy which gave to a grimy employee in the oil fields exactly the same political voting power a billionaire had, even though the billionaire pays more taxes. Smoot had thought that democracy was the greatest form of government ever devised. "Democracy," he said in one of his Facts Forum broadcasts, "is a political outgrowth of the teachings of Jesus Christ . . . Christianity was essential to the creation of our Democracy." And again: "We in Facts Forum know that American Democracy . . . is still the most nearly perfect expression ever made by man in legal and political terms of a basic ideal of Christianity." Just about then, someone apparently explained to Smoot that democracy is really a terrible way to live. Dan Smoot evidently saw the logic of the assertion and became convinced that democracy was a concoction probably devised by the devil himself. Not long after he had voiced enthusiasm about democracy as a political outgrowth of the teachings of Jesus, he told a Canadian audience:

"One of the best indications of how far we in the United States have slipped is the wide contemporary use by practically all our intellectual and political leaders of the word 'Democracy' to designate our system. . . . The Founding Fathers knew, and Jefferson said in specific terms, that a Democracy is the most evil kind of government possible."

In subsequent talks throughout the United States, Smoot continued his assault on America's faith in its democratic system of government. In an October, 1961, speech before the extremist and Far Right National Indignation Convention in Houston, Smoot declared:

"Democracy always degenerates into tyranny. The majority is not blessed with morality or wisdom. The Founding Fathers knew this. They knew that a dictatorship of the majority is not Constitutional Government. . . ."

Whether Smoot, like H. L. Hunt, feels that rich men are blessed with morality and wisdom and should have more votes than their less affluent fellow citizens cannot be said. But on the subject of democracy, Smoot had certainly come around to the boss's way of thinking.

The man who hired Smoot for the staff of Facts Forum, and who feels that big taxpayers should have more votes than small taxpayers, is considered somewhat eccentric. His financial worth is estimated at about $3,000,000,000 and his annual income at about $50,000,000. Despite this, he uses tax-exempt organizations in his effort to influence Americans in favor of his bizzare political and economic concepts, while at the same time bending every effort to make these outfits as self-supporting as possible.

When H. L. Hunt formed Life Line Foundation, Inc., in 1958, the new organization sought and received a postal subsidy as a religious organization, a subsidy which was later revoked. For other reasons, Life Line Foundation retains its tax-exemption.

But while the Foundation receives some tax-free contributions, most of its income is derived from the sale of Life Line radio and TV tapes, and its publication, "Life Lines." Hunt has insisted that the only way to finance a winning propaganda campaign is through the use of advertising funds and commercial sponsorship. In short, by contrast with the earlier Facts Forum (largely dependent on contributions), the activities of Life Line Foundation are kept as self-sustaining as possible.

The Foundation is Hunt's major propaganda medium, established in September, 1958, in the period when the "new" Radical Right was just beginning to spring up and to generate activity across the country. Life Line Foundation, Inc., was created by amending the corporate charter of Hunt's earlier Facts Forum.

Perhaps the reason for amending Facts Forum out of existence was the widespread attack upon it as a Radical Right propaganda medium. When it was converted to Life Line, the Internal Revenue Service did not require a new application for tax-exemption, although almost everything was changed—the name of the organization, personnel, the nature of the program—everything except the one man who conceived and controlled both setups.

Today a smoothly operating organization devoted essentially to spreading Hunt's own personal propaganda line, Life Line reaches its audiences via the spoken and the printed word. The thrust of the Hunt propaganda operations, despite his somewhat novel viewpoints, is essentially the same as the thrust of other Radical-Rightist propaganda in the United States. Hunt's particular idiosyncrasy is to refer to those with whom he disagrees, and to all who disagree with him, as the "Mistaken"—with a capital M. An April, 1962,

Life Line release declared that "MISTAKEN is the title which Life Line has fixed in the public mind as a specific, but nonlibelous designation for all enemies of Freedom—Communists, Fellow Travelers, etc., leaving them to classify themselves." (How to call a man a Communist nonlibelously.)

In the eyes of H. L. Hunt and Life Line, the country is and has long been in the grip of an internal conspiracy of the Mistaken. The internal conspiracy is viewed as deadly and dangerous and its success as imminent. Its manifestations on the domestic front are the income tax, proposals for Medicare, programs for Federal aid to education, mental health, the Federal farm program, as well as Government expenditures for highways, urban renewal, and other services.

The American foreign aid program is viewed as "subsidizing socialism in many countries," and the UN as having been planned by the Soviets "to suit their future plans." The world organization, Life Line tells its audiences, is being used by the Soviets "as an instrument by which they intend to rule the world."

Unlike Facts Forum, which made a pretense, in its broadcasts and printed matter, of presenting both sides of an issue, Life Line propaganda makes no such effort. The line is dished up straight and unadulterated—though often with subtlety—over more than three hundred radio stations and almost fifty TV outlets which cover more than forty states. The radio program is daily, and Life Line TV is a five-day-a-week television program. "Life Lines" is a four-page political commentary published three times a week; Life Line Links, a book service which furnishes members with Rightist books and printed materials. And in addition there are Life Line Seminars and a Life Line Essay Contest.

While Life Line claims it does not deal with racial questions, does not criticize minorities or church groups by name, and does not charge the existence of communism in various walks of life, the fact is that these propaganda points are subtly made. "Life Lines," for instance, criticizes the United States Supreme Court "since 1954" —when the now-famous school desegregation decision was handed down. It alleges that the Communists have benefited from "support gained from church circles in the United States." The idea is planted that professors and educators "may be peddling" the "smooth line of socialism" and doing so "behind the cloak of professional respectability and academic freedom."

Despite denials, Life Line's fear-mongering shows.

By 1955, there were reports that H. L. Hunt was trimming his financial support of Facts Forum and that Dan Smoot, along with other staff employees, had left. Smoot claims he resigned to start his own operation. In any event, shortly after leaving Hunt, he went into business for himself with a newsletter called "Dan Smoot Speaks" which later became the "Dan Smoot Report."

Radio broadcasts made his name well known to millions of Americans and he hoped to find subscribers—at $10 a year—to his publication, and advertising sponsors for radio and television appearances. Within six months he was on stations KTAN and KPRB in Sherman, Texas, sponsored by one Harold W. Totten, who identified himself as general manager of the Washington Iron Works in Sherman, although he owned the business. (In his own community Totten is known as a "character" who lives in an atmosphere of constant and imminent peril. It is said that Totten believes in a two-gun policy—one gun on his person and another on top of his desk where anyone who calls on him can see that it is within easy reach. He has been an active distributor of anti-Jewish literature. The "Dan Smoot Report" of June 29, 1956, quoted a letter from Totten to Smoot: "For America's sake keep up your fine courageous work. You may be assured we intend to sponsor your type of reporting until this fight is won.")

Almost as soon as he had gone into business for himself, Smoot began to link up with other elements of the Radical Right. In September, 1955, he addressed the national convention of We, The People! in Chicago and was elected a director-at-large. (Attending that gathering were the late anti-Semite, Merwin K. Hart; Bertrand Comparet, attorney for Gerald Smith's Christian Nationalist Crusade; and Bryant Bowles, a leader of a violently racist and anti-Jewish organization called the National Association for the Advancement of White People, who was later sent to a Texas prison for killing his brother-in-law.)

At about the same time, Smoot was listed as a member of the National Advisory Council of the Campaign for the 48 States, now defunct, but the predecessor organization of one currently active Right Wing movement—Americans for Constitutional Action.

In November, 1955, Smoot was elected co-chairman of For America, and on Washington's Birthday in 1956 he shared the speakers' platform at New York's Carnegie Hall at a big For America rally, where he declared that "modern liberalism and Communism are the same" and that "the income tax amendment of 1913 removed the one limitation which made socialism impossible."

During 1956, Smoot spoke at the convention of the Congress of Freedom, an Extreme Right Wing group whose meetings have been marked by the presence of known Extremists and bigots. Smoot was elected to the Board of Directors of this group shortly thereafter.

Although he was becoming a leading figure in Radical-Rightist circles by this time, Smoot was still far from prosperous. Headquarters for the "Dan Smoot Report" was the dining-room table of the apartment where he and his wife, Mabeth, lived. But there are elements of the Horatio Alger story in Smoot's rise. Gradually, subscriptions came in. The business operations of the ex-FBI agent, purporting to be an expert on communism but who fails to distinguish between liberalism and communism, soon overflowed from the dining-room table into the Smoot bedroom.

The big break which took Smoot out of the minor leagues came late in 1956—just about a year after he had opened his own propaganda shop. Mrs. Smoot was handling the office routine at home while Smoot himself traveled around the country, speaking as an expert on communism, and taking a leadership role in the third party movement for T. Coleman Andrews for President of the United States. One of Smoot's speeches, in October, 1956, was scheduled at the Freedom Club of the First Congregational Church of Los Angeles, a Rightist forum operated by the minister of the church, Reverend James W. Fifield. In the audience sat D. B. Lewis—the same Dallas Bedford Lewis who was the millionaire president of the Lewis Food Company, and who was later to put up the money to launch the Manion Forum in television programing. Lewis, who manufactures and markets Dr. Ross and Skippy brand pet foods, was then president of the Far Right group known as ORFIT, the Organization to Repeal Federal Income Taxes, and had been characterized by *Fortune* magazine as "vehemently anti-union."

Just as meeting H. L. Hunt had once changed Smoot's life, his meeting with Lewis wrought yet another big change.

Before he met Lewis, Smoot says, the big networks had bluntly rejected his programs. But Lewis changed all that. Enchanted by Smoot's ideas and personality, Lewis agreed to sponsor Smoot on radio and television. He bought weekly time on independent radio and TV stations throughout his company's marketing area, especially in Hawaii, California, Oregon, Washington, Idaho, Utah, Nevada, and Arizona. Within half a year the Smoot program was being carried by sixty-two stations. Today, more than half of the Smoot broadcasts on 110 radio and TV outlets are sponsored by Dr. Ross brand pet foods; the other sponsors are businessmen in the communities where the stations are located. D. B. Lewis sometimes gets lyrical about the Smoot broadcasts:

"We've sponsored everything from Hopalong Cassidy to Tarzan

but Dan is far and away the best seller. I'm getting more for my advertising dollar than any businessman in America. People get so excited over Dan's show, they'd feed the dog food to people, if we let them."

Lewis uses economic pressure on both radio stations and newspapers when they oppose his views. A California newspaper which defended the United Nations, supported President Kennedy's social programs, and criticized the Radical Right and its fellow travelers, had its Lewis Food Company advertisements canceled with the explanation: "Mr. Lewis is spending so much money promoting Conservative causes that he doesn't want to dilute his efforts."

And for Mr. Lewis, Dan Smoot seldom dilutes his extremism.

In its fright-peddling about the advanced stages which Communist penetration has reached in the United States, the Radical Right often seizes on grossly false rumors (which can easily be checked but which instead the Right spreads around the country like a dry grass fire) and builds these rumors into hysteria.

One such rumor (in which Smoot was not involved) picked up and spread on the winds of the propaganda network, pertained to Operation Water Moccasin, the counterguerrilla training operation mentioned earlier in this book that involved some troops of the United States Army and some from various foreign but friendly countries. In a very short time, the training operation was painted by crackpots and Radical Rightists (plus some respectable Right-Wingers, including a member of Congress) into some sort of secret and subversive plot for a take-over of the United States by the foreign troops involved in the exercise. As an added fillip, there were accompanying rumors which purported to indicate that hundreds of thousands of Chinese Communist troops were poised in Mexico for an imminent invasion of the United States across our Southwestern border.

A few years before the Operation Water Moccasin scare, however, there was a brouhaha stirred up by the Radical Right over the so-called Alaska Mental Health Bill in which Smoot played a role. This was a proposal to give Alaska, still a Territory, the authority it lacked to care for its mentally ill who needed hospitalization and to create community health services for early diagnosis and treatment. To the Extremists on the American scene in 1956, the Alaska Mental Health Bill was a Communist plot to set up a huge concentration camp in Alaska—a "Siberia, U.S.A.," as they called it—to which anti-Communists and those intent on exposing Communist plotting and infiltration in the United States Government would be railroaded.

Dan Smoot was one of the rumormongers who poured out the fantastic charges via the printed word and over the air waves. He explained why he and others were warning that the Alaska Mental Health Bill was the start of an American Siberia:

"We are well aware of the use of drugs and isolation by Communist Governments to produce brainwashing on political prisoners. Could it happen here?" Smoot added: "I do not doubt that the Alaska Mental Health Act was written by sincere, well intentioned men. Nonetheless, it fits into a sinister pattern which has been forming ever since the United Nations was organized."

It seems almost impossible that a man who had once passed rigid FBI tests could accept this sort of hogwash without at least suspecting its fraudulent character. But Smoot appears to make mistakes like this. On another occasion, in the course of a 1961 Savannah, Georgia, television appearance, Smoot attacked the Methodist Church as riddled with Communists. People in Savannah were confused and troubled. The Methodist Ministers Association of the city saw the need to issue a six-page leaflet called "The Methodist Church Fights Communism" to explain what the Methodist Church really stands for. The leaflet stated:

"When critics of Communism use the very same methods that Communists use, they become friends, not the enemies, of Communism. . . . We wish to name some of these out-of-town critics that sincere people may be on guard against their tactics of mixing truth with distortion and falsehood. Among them are . . . Dan Smoot, Dallas, Texas. . . ."

Within the first year of issuing the "Dan Smoot Report" its author was denouncing integration as "an American tragedy" created by Communist infiltration below the Mason-Dixon line. This infiltration, he wrote, is part of a divide-and-conquer plan by American Reds who are aided in the plot by the "notorious National Association for the Advancement of Colored People." Smoot also attacked the Supreme Court and advocated that the entire Court be impeached.

When the *Dallas News,* in 1959, assailed "the professionals for profit who have found a remunerative field" in opposition to communism, Smoot accused the newspaper of favoring such opposition by ignorant amateurs only. The *News* replied:

"Patriotism is a justly venerated human quality. Patriotism for profit is just suspect. . . . If Mr. Smoot has not been around long enough to encounter it, the *News* has. When your daily mail includes such tripe as defining Communism as a Jewish conspiracy, a Catholic conspiracy, and an NAACP conspiracy, you can discern the hand of the patrioteer for profit. He exists. . . . The whole question is whether a man is out to make a fast buck or to serve the country."

Subscribers to the "Dan Smoot Report" include innumerable congressmen and senators. Because he feels it is important that congressmen know what is really "going on," a congressional subscription automatically gets a special 25 percent discount.

Mrs. Smoot feels that the number of subscribers (about 22,000) does not accurately indicate the impact of the "Dan Smoot Report" on America. She is undoubtedly correct, for the Smoots ship out about 1,300,000 copies a year which are paid for by supporters and business firms as gift subscriptions to employees, students, ministers, and others.

Smoot's radio and TV broadcasts are condensations of what appears in his "Report." With his published material selling well, Smoot decided in 1963 to expand his operations and sell tapes for home, church, and civic groups, in the manner of Dr. Schwarz and the Reverend Hargis.

And in the manner of Schwarz and Hargis, Dan Smoot purveys distrust and suspicion, though his is a more insidious kind. Because of his FBI background, Smoot's listeners and readers tend to believe that he is revealing matters of an important, confidential character which the average citizen does not know. In 1962, he published *The Invisible Government,** a 250-page book with the premise that the eminently respectable Council on Foreign Relations, together with a number of other civic and educational organizations, really constitute the "invisible government" of the United States. Smoot says that this invisible power exercises a controlling influence on the Federal Government's major policies and on officials who implement these policies. By skillful propaganda this alleged invisible government compels Congress and the public to support its policies with the ultimate objective, says Smoot, of converting America into a socialistic state, and then to make it part of a one-world socialistic system.

The John Birch Society Bulletin urged its readers to buy and read Smoot's *The Invisible Government* for revelations on the forces which are supposedly communizing America. "Walking Together," a weekly published by the Religion and Labor Council of America, analyzed both the "Dan Smoot Report" and the book:

"Smoot's technique . . . is a fact-larded, intellectual-sounding ap-

---

* Not to be confused with *The Invisible Government* by David Wise and Thomas B. Ross (New York: Random House, Inc., 1964), which is concerned with the CIA.

proach whose effectiveness lies in subtleties of assumption and innuendos more often than in blazing frontal attacks. There is an air of logic in his writings, a controlled emotionalism which tends to disarm the uncritical."

Dan Smoot is, nonetheless, an unbending Rightist of the more radical variety, and so the air of logic sometimes blows away. He has told his breathless audiences that a truly responsible Congress would impeach Earl Warren, end foreign aid, cast aside President Kennedy's disarmament plan, withdraw from the United Nations, and repeal the income tax. At one 1961 meeting in Houston, he called for "a wave of indignation" to oust the "spineless and treasonable characters we've got in Washington."

In the "Dan Smoot Report" he once suggested the election of a Congress that would "bring a bill of impeachment against John F. Kennedy."

Dan Smoot brings this radical gospel to millions. His counterspy background, like that insight into the ways of Divinity claimed by Dr. Hargis and Dr. McIntire, makes him a political "expert" in the eyes of those followers of the Far Right who always seem so willing to be told what to think, as well as what to be frightened of next.

9

Church League of America
— Edgar Bundy

Not all influential Radical Right organizations have audiences in the many millions or annual incomes in the hundreds of thousands of dollars. Of the several hundred organizations which have mushroomed in the past few years, most are local groups that make only a local noise. Perhaps a half dozen have some regional impact, or a national impact in some particular field.

In the field of religion, no Far-Rightist group has exercised greater influence among clergymen themselves than has the Church League of America.

From the time former New York Representative Hamilton Fish headed the first congressional committee to investigate subversive activities in 1930, a Chicago advertising man named George Washington Robnett kept track of the findings. As House, Senate, and various state legislative bodies authorized their own committees to investigate subversion, Robnett collected their published reports. He also accumulated a large library of Leftist publications—or those he considered to be Leftist.

Early in 1937, when Hitler was building his war machine and had already marched into the Rhineland, Robnett and two other men concluded that the Communist movement in the United States was a perilous threat to American security. The other two men were Henry P. Crowell, the head of Quaker Oats, and Frank J. Loesch, an important corporation lawyer in Chicago who once headed the Chicago Crime Commission which had made war on Al Capone.

Robnett, Loesch, and Crowell called a meeting of leading Protestant laymen on March 24, 1937, at which Robnett explained that his studies in the field of subversion and his analysis of the reports he had collected convinced him that Communists had infiltrated the Protestant churches. He believed that his information and material could be helpful to the clergy and suggested that a National Laymen's Council be established to keep a continuing eye on subversion within the churches. He told his guests:

"A part of the program proposed for this organization, which it is suggested that we create, is to publish and distribute to ministers and lay people regular bulletins in which would be described certain political movements which might have direct or indirect effects upon the churches or their work, or the future of religious movements. . . ."

That afternoon the National Laymen's Council of the Church League of America was founded, a private intelligence service which still today sells information to subscribers about alleged Communists, Socialists, Liberals, trade unionists, civil libertarians, and others whose views and activities do not meet Church League standards of patriotic purity. To "rekindle the spirit of valiant Christian Americanism" and to oppose "the challange of destructive, organized radicalism" were the announced aims. In the view of the Church League, such radicalism took the form of "a desire to centralize and expand Federal authority" which "must inevitably eventuate into some form of collectivism. . . ."

Within a short period of time, the Church League had more than 6,000 clergymen of all denominations and more than 50,000 lay members supporting its work and receiving its official publication, "News and Views."

How much of the Church League's activity is purely religious and how much, from the very beginning, was intended to be political, has never really been established. It is significant that the League's founding meeting in 1937 came at a time when President Franklin Roosevelt's plan to enlarge the membership of the Supreme Court was the top national political issue, and that both Frank Loesch and the League had taken a stand against the plan. It is probably significant, too, that in 1940 the Church League openly campaigned against President Roosevelt's bid for a third term in the White House.

In June, 1942, the League received tax-exempt status from the Treasury Department as an educational organization. Robnett guided its fortunes for almost twenty years, and toward the end of his regime, the League was operating on an annual budget of between $20,000 and $35,000. In 1956, when Robnett was succeeded by one Edgar C. Bundy, the income, expenditures, and activities began to boom. Headquarters were moved in the same year from Chicago to Wheaton, Illinois, and the League in a short time graduated from the ranks of the multitudinous extremist groups to become an influential force on the emerging Radical Right.

Although Bundy was ordained a Baptist minister in the Southern Baptist Convention in 1942, while on active military service in World War II, he has never held a pastorate, and his main qualifications for his post at the helm of the Church League do not appear to be primarily religious in nature.

Bundy served six years in Air Force Intelligence, rising from private to major, and served in every theater of war. In 1948, he returned to the United States from postwar duty in Alaska and became city editor of the Wheaton (Illinois) *Daily Journal*. A year later, Bundy achieved considerable publicity when he was invited by the U. S. Senate Appropriations Committee to testify on the deteriorating Far Eastern situation. He predicted the Communist attack on South Korea and warned of the impending fall of China. The publicity led to scores of invitations to speak before leading civic organizations, conventions, forums, patriotic societies, and political groups—and Bundy's career as an expert on communism was well on its way.

Church League publicity advertises Bundy as a soldier, journalist, and evangelist, and in his lectures under League auspices, his service as an Air Force Intelligence officer helps give him the aura of authority on communism and international affairs. He offers what appears to be inside stuff on intrigues between Protestant church leaders and Communists, and—like Hargis and McIntire—holds that "modernism" is a subtle tactic devised by Communists to undermine the United States.

Before assuming leadership of the Church League, Bundy was a dominant figure in the American Legion in Illinois and was president of the Abraham Lincoln National Republican Club, a Far Right group which had no official connection with the Republican Party and which publicly declared that it was "engaged in political action on the Right."

About two years before he succeeded Robnett as the executive chief of the League, Bundy was accused by the *Chicago Sun-Times* of strange political activity when he distributed a "smear" pamphlet against Senator Paul Douglas. The paper said the pamphlet had been obtained by Bundy from Harry A. Jung, a celebrated Chicago propagandist (Bundy denied having anything to do with Jung's material). At about the same time, Bundy played a leading role in condemnation by the American Legion in Illinois of the Girl Scout Handbook, which was alleged to contain material viewed by the Legionnaires as "un-American."

Bundy's organization says its objectives are "to distribute literature to ministers, to the extent of financial ability, giving them a picture of the dangers to them in our trend toward national Socialism . . . to try to influence these ministers and educate them to the point where they will, through the vast numbers they in turn reach, extend this influence and education and help to build a great national bulwark opposed to radical schemes and totalitarian trends; gradually to coordinate the voices of sound thinking ministers into a powerful voice that can mean something when great national questions and issues arise. . . ."

The League is thus a quasi-educational agency teaching the clergy to use its considerable influence with its congregations to oppose what the League believes to be dangerous tendencies in the Protestant churches.

A major part of its work is the sale of information about "subversives." With Robnett's collection of materials as the foundation, and with its own continuing research, the Church League says it now has "five tons of files" and "over 1,000,000 3x5 cross-referenced index cards on individuals, organizations and publications which have served the Communist cause in the United States. . . ." This data, the League says, falls into three categories: Communist Party members; fellow travelers, party sympathizers, or front-joiners; and mere Communist "dupes."

The League says that when it sells the information it is not "name-calling" but simply supplying "evidence" collected by Government agencies as well as by itself. Bundy assures those who buy information from him that his organization has one of the ten best files, other than the FBI's, on Communist activities in the United States. These files are offered to prospective buyers as *"insurance* because it makes those who read it more vigilant and more resistant to radical infiltration." The special background report service about available to those who contribute $10 a year or more. There are an individual (scheduled, perhaps, to address a church group) is limitations on the extent of this service, based on the amount of the

annual contribution. The more money, the more service—and that's
free enterprise.

The Church League also has a valuable library on Leftist organizations. One entire section is stacked with outright Communist
publications, some of which date back to the time in 1919 when the
Communist Party was first established in the United States. It
includes complete sets of the *Daily Worker, New Masses, People's
World,* and similar Communist periodicals. The files contain original
documents and Leftist propaganda issued by such organizations as
the American League for Peace and Democracy, catalogued in the
records as "the first Communist front organization in the United
States." But the inclusion in the library's section on communism of
data about Americans for Democratic Action and the American
Civil Liberties Union reveals the kind of confusion about subversion
that creates doubt about the possible value of any of it. (And the credentials of the Church League as a competent source of information
about communism are not enhanced by the fact that another section
of the library is devoted entirely to John Dewey, the educator whose
philosophy, says the Church League with a straight face, "softens
many intellectuals in America for the acceptance of Communism.")

Another unit of the league library concerns religion. It contains reports of hearings held by Government committees of one
kind or another on alleged subversion among the clergy, and on
the "un-American" character of ministers' sermons, books, and
pamphlets. So much for religion.

The League's "News and Views," a four-to-six-page newsletter,
is issued once a month along with other special reports and books.
"News and Views," edited by Major Bundy, is "a reporting service
for those who support the Church League work—and also to serve
itself as a source of income for that program." The monthly newsletter gives its readers a running picture of the Leftist movement in
the United States (as the League sees it) and emphasizes the great
benefits contributors can derive from its confidential files.

Circulation figures for the sheet are a prized secret, except for
the knowledge that it goes to anyone who contributes $5 or more
a year. (As third-class mail, the publisher is not obligated to supply
the postal authorities with an annual statement as to ownership or
actual circulation.) All ministers are placed on the mailing list as
soon as their names are sent in, whether or not accompanied by a
contribution. This, says the League, is made possible by lay contributors.

Special reports include reprints from newspapers, magazines, and
pamphlets issued by other organizations as well as by the League

itself. League supporters have been offered no fewer than 120 special reports, including pamphlets and full-length books such as Bundy's *Collectivism in the Churches* (recommended by the John Birch Society), *The Record of Certain Activities of 1014 Congregational Clergymen,* by J. B. Matthews, and similar fare. To this flow of propaganda, add a fifteen-minute broadcast each week over seventeen stations in eight states—with heaviest concentration in Florida and in California—plus a variety of tape recordings, films, and film strips which warn of the well-advanced Communist penetration of religion.

Almost daily, somewhere in the United States, the League is sponsoring local "counter-subversive seminars" or speeches by Bundy and assorted Radical Right speakers.

A seminar, which lasts from two to four days, is held when a local group requests it, but on condition that there be at least fifty customers at $10 a head. (Students are told that the $10 tuition is tax-deductible.) Before they ante up, the prospective customers are assured that "the instructors will be the highest qualified men in the nation." For those who cannot raise the minimum for a seminar, the Church League now offers a do-it-yourself kit of tape recordings at $75 a set, or $50 for rental. Lacking the $500 minimum, the student gets his education from a kit, "an economical plan which does not necessitate paying travel expenses and honorariums to the speakers." Illustrative titles of Bundy's recorded talks in the do-it-yourself kit are: "The Communists Are After Your Churches," "The Perils of the Social Gospel," "The Perversion of the Bible."

Six years after Edgar C. Bundy took over, when the League moved into a new $225,000 building in Wheaton, a week-long dedication ceremony brought together a number of Radical Right figures, including Reverend Carl McIntire, to whom Bundy and the Church League are ideologically close, and Milton Lory, another Extreme Rightist leader.

The new headquarters, a spacious Colonial building in a beautifully landscaped setting, has the appearance of a residential mansion instead of an office building. Here, the organization employs about twenty persons and operates on an annual budget of about $200,000. As did that of almost all Radical Right groups, the League's income jumped enormously in 1960—the Presidential election year—when it reached $78,000. It jumped to $196,000 in 1961, and in 1962 it passed $200,000.

The income of the Church League is chiefly from regular contributors—including such big corporations as Abbott Laboratories,

Armour and Company, the Greyhound Corporation, Monsanto Chemical Company, Borg-Warner Corporation, and the Celanese Foundation. The interest shown by these contributors in religious matters would not tend to raise the eyebrows, were the Church League not so boldly and frankly devoted to extremist politics.

Early in 1964, the League wrote its friends that it had "grown and grown," and renewed the appeal for contributions. "The budget has been almost doubling every year," the appeal said. "Our research files have expanded so that we are going to have to build again to accommodate this expansion and to keep our high rate of efficiency in processing the thousands of requests for information and Special Reports which pour in from every corner of our nation."

Apparently, while some of the large Radical Right groups have suffered at least some temporary setbacks, the Church League of America has expanded at an amazing rate in order to fill some people's need for fear and suspicion by supplying them with basketfuls of satisfying propaganda.

10

Conservative Society of America
— Kent and Phoebe Courtney

"We are proud to be considered members of the Far Right," Phoebe Courtney has said, "which we believe is much to be preferred to being members of the 'Far Wrong.'"

The peppery Phoebe and her husband Kent, who live and work in New Orleans, are up to their necks in the lucrative business of "saving" America. The Courtneys would "save" America from communism, socialism, Democrats, Republicans, Liberals, integration, income taxes, labor unions, public works programs, the Supreme Court, the NAACP—you name it; they'll save us.

The solution proposed by Kent and Phoebe Courtney, through their Conservative Society of America and their "Independent American" periodicals and broadcasts, is to organize a Rightist third political party, an aim shared by many other Radicals of the Right. The Courtneys hope that such a political alignment would also attract moderate Conservatives, and that it would be able to capture a goodly proportion of congressional seats, if not the White House itself. Third party aspirations aside, the Courtney's stated principles and objectives are, despite the "conservative" banner they fly, Radical Right in the most fiery sense of the word.

Kent Courtney is a forty-six-year-old, 230-pound, boundlessly energetic redhead with a round face, two chins, and a Falstaffian paunch. He is skillful and persuasive as a talker both on the platform and off. One of his favorite tactics, to win his audience, is to urge them to exhibit their sentiment by booing, hissing, or cheering. He warms them up by calling off names such as: "Mrs. Roosevelt" (boo!); "Barry Goldwater" (yeah! yeah!); "Ike" (hiss!).

Born in St. Paul, Minnesota, Courtney moved with his parents to New Orleans, where he attended the public schools. Later he studied at Tulane's School of Business Administration and then for three years taught economics, banking, and marketing at the University. In World War II he served in the United States Navy. When he returned to civilian life he worked as an airline pilot for Pan American World Airways, and after that he was employed as a commercial officer with the British Consulate in New Orleans, served on the staff of the Chamber of Commerce, was assistant to the president of a fruit shipping company, and worked as a public relations man. When asked about his experience, he speaks mainly of being a public relations man. Why he plays down the other jobs is not known.

Courtney got into Right Wing activity in 1954, when he served as chairman of the New Orleans branch of Ten Million Americans Mobilizing for Justice (for Senator Joseph McCarthy), a nationwide movement of Extreme Rightists which circulated petitions opposing the censure by the United States Senate of the late junior senator from Wisconsin.

In 1954, also, Courtney was an unsuccessful candidate for the New Orleans City Council. Following this, his wife and he launched their publication, *Free Men Speak* (later renamed the *Independent American*), and for two years published it on a part-time basis. Phoebe did the editing while Kent traveled widely addressing extreme Right Wing groups and segregationist outfits such as the White Citizens Councils. In that two-year period, Kent made his own name and that of the newspaper fairly well known in Right circles. In 1961, their political action operation, the Conservative Society of America, was formed—a kind of action-oriented, poor man's Birch Society. Courtney once explained that the CSA "picks up where the John Birch Society leaves off."

The national advisory board of the Conservative Society, moreover, is well stocked with supporters of the Birch Society, of which Kent and Phoebe Courtney are also members.

Phoebe, now forty-five, is an impressive woman with greying hair set into a winding braid on top of her head. In the days when the late Senator McCarthy shook the country with his Red hunt, the distaff side of the Courtney team first saw the need for —and the possibilities in—Right Wing propaganda activity. Today, as her husband explains cheerfully, "Phoebe is so far Right the only thing beyond is outer space."

An ebullient, fast-talking woman, she often uses colorful slang. She tells interviewers that the way the world is going has her in a constant "ever-lovin' tizzy." At one time she gushed that she had "adored" Roosevelt but Truman was from "No-Goodnickville." It has been recorded that when she orders steak for dinner she wants it "Communist blood red."

The husband-and-wife team who reportedly started operations with $18 in capital are not in the million-dollar-a-year income class. But they aren't doing badly. The money they take in for their organized assault on the American political mind is the result of contributions, the sale of publications, and membership dues. In 1960, their operations grossed about $135,000. In 1961, their gross was $180,000, and in 1962, around the $200,000 mark. Today, their Radical Right complex of publishing, broadcasting, and political action is in the quarter-of-a-million-dollar class, which is not bad for an ambitious couple who started out on a shoestring.

They employ some fifteen helpers, claim a payroll of about $3,600 a month, and sometimes run monthly phone bills of $500 or $700, which eats into the gross of about $4,000 a week, along with costs for postage, travel, gasoline, and all the other necessaries of a bustling propaganda operation.

Today, with Phoebe doing a large share of the editing, the couple writes and prints the newspaper and a torrent of pamphlets and books which, in shrill language, proclaim the standard way-out dogmas—that the Government in Washington and both major political parties are overrun with Communists and traitors, that the Communist take-over is well advanced in the United States, and that unless patriotic Americans act now to carry out the drastic and radical surgery advocated by the Right, the country will be lost beyond rescue. This message is banged home in hundreds of thousands of pieces of literature the Courtneys hammer out in an average year, as they extoll such heroes of the Radical Right as General Edwin Walker, Senator Strom Thurmond, and Senator Barry Goldwater.

Goldwater has not always enjoyed the Courtneys' full pleasure and approval. The main problem they have had with the senator from Arizona is that he insists on being a Republican, while the Courtneys have worked for years for a new party of the Far Right. In 1961, Phoebe Courtney urged Senator Goldwater to quit the Republican Party and campaign for the Presidency "as an independent Conservative!" She added that "the election of Barry Goldwater—as a Republican—in 1964 would be a disaster!"

The Courtneys' radical line and the senator's conservative line collided in the 1962 congressional election campaign, when Senator Goldwater declared that if he lived in New York he would support the candidacies of Governor Nelson Rockefeller and Senator Jacob K. Javits for re-election. To the Courtneys—especially to shrill and voluble Phoebe—that was just too much. To her, Governor Rockefeller and Senator Javits epitomize the enemy— the liberal enemy, whether Republican or Democrat. (One issue of the Courtneys' pamphlet series called "Tax Fax" bore the title "Nelson Rockefeller, the International Socialist," and carried the Courtney double by-line.)

Although the Courtneys had sponsored a Goldwater for President rally in July, 1960 (with Birch Society Founder Robert Welch as a speaker), at the time of the Republican National Convention, the first disillusionment set in when Goldwater supported Richard Nixon for the Presidency. With machine-gun rapidity, the Courtneys issued several editions of "Tax Fax" blasting Democratic candidates John F. Kennedy and Lyndon B. Johnson, and advocating support of "Thurmond for President."

In 1961, a New Party rally staged by the Courtneys in Chicago was the occasion for a statement by Kent Courtney that Goldwater had been "tainted by socialism" and might become useless to the conservative movement because he was too prone to compromise with the Rockefelller wing of the GOP.

The coolness to Goldwater persisted for the better part of three years. But by January, 1964, when Goldwater announced he would seek the Presidency, the Courtneys were willing to view the senator's wanderings away from the true faith, as preached by the Courtneys, as "water under the bridge." They welcomed his stated intention to seek the Presidency and not to compromise his principles or his beliefs. Phoebe revealed in a Goldwater for President mailing, dated January 7, 1964, that this interpretation of "Goldwater's new stand" was "based on first-hand experience." She said that Kent had flown to Phoenix to attend the news conference where the senator announced his candidacy.

"Afterwards," Phoebe wrote, "he had a little chat with Goldwater (Barry asked: 'How's Phoebe?'—so you see he isn't 'mad at me' for all those rather sharp editorials I've written during the past couple of years begging him not to compromise!).

"Kent told Goldwater that on the basis of the strong anti-Communist position contained in his opening announcement, that the *Independent American* would support him," Phoebe trilled on, adding: "Goldwater seemed very pleased. In answer to a question from Kent, Goldwater said that as he campaigned for the nomination, he would also be campaigning to elect anti-Communist Conservatives to Congress—which, though expected, is good news."

The principles upon which the Courtneys founded their Conservative Society of America are fifteen standard slogans of the Radical Right:

—Reappraise United States political and military doctrines; abrogate relations with governments that are openly "creatures" of the Communist Party; withdraw from all projects looking toward the establishment of world government; break off negotiations for suspension of nuclear testing and resume a "rational" program of testing; liberate Cuba, capture Chinese and Russian Communists in Cuba and hold them as hostages pending release of Americans from Russia and Red China; end programs of foreign aid to nations which don't support the United States in the struggle against communism; end government programs in domestic agriculture; return our immigration regulations to the "original legislative concept of preserving the American cultural heritage of freedom"; eliminate business and industrial operations of the Federal Government; protect the right to work without payment of union dues or joining of any organization; cut the size of the Federal bureaucracy; repeal the Sixteenth (income tax) Amendment to the United States Constitution; revamp the internal security system "to free the government of infiltration by subversive agents"; restore, by constitutional means, the "dignity of the Supreme Court . . . which has by its pro-Communist decisions set the Communist conspiracy free to destroy the sovereignty of our Republic"; and restore the two-party system by establishing a new conservative political party.

The aim of the CSA was to weld Radical Rightists and Conservatives throughout the country into a political force, though how many Conservatives would be attracted to so radical a program as CSA's is anybody's guess. The indications are that in the three years of CSA's existence, Courtney—for all his fast-talking salesmanship and boundless energy—did not exactly start a national groundswell.

Courtney has claimed members in forty-six states, but it is doubtful if more than a few thousand Americans paid the $20 annual dues (in advance) or signed up for the togetherness package for husband and wife of $30 a year (also in advance). Besides payment in advance, the Courtneys also have insisted that each new member sign a statement declaring opposition to all forms of totalitarianism, including communism, fascism, and socialism, before the member receives the specially designed lapel pin for those who have joined the CSA.

In 1961, the Courtneys, both of whom are members of the John Birch Society, joined the Society's drive to impeach the Chief Justice of the United States. Kent Courtney wrote:

"In view of the Communist-inspired attack on the John Birch Society, Phoebe and I are prouder than ever that we are both members of the John Birch Society. As a matter of fact, I am a chapter leader of the JBS here in New Orleans."

A large map in the Courtney print shop has pins placed in the areas where the CSA claims special membership strength; the pins show its greatest following to be in California. Courtney once commented jovially: "Political fads have a good history in that state."

In 1960, Courtney announced that he intended to be a candidate for governor of Louisiana on a States' Rights Party ticket. He laughingly told interviewers, "one is a nobody in Louisiana politics until he has been beaten two or three times running for Governor!" (He ran and won less than 3 percent of the total vote.) As a gubernatorial candidate, however, he was news, and the publicity made him better known and brought a lot of free advertising for his various promotions.

At his desk in the rear of the building Courtney writes the scripts for his weekly radio talks, broadcast over thirty-seven stations in thirty-six cities in nineteen states. He acts as radio commentator for the *Independent American,* and his broadcasts are basically abbreviated versions of issues of that periodical. The radicalism of the Courtneys' paper can perhaps be gathered from some samples:

"The New Frontier has written an ugly record of appeasement, withdrawal and betrayal across the face of the globe. . . . The really tragic betrayal is the betrayal of American interests. The retreat ordered by the Kennedy Administration is turning into a rout. It is bringing terrible danger to the American people; the Administration must be held responsible."

Again, on the Kennedy Administration, the Courtneys reprinted an editorial they attributed to *The Chicago Tribune,* which said in part:

"We sometimes wonder whether the Kennedy Administration is committed to national suicide or whether it is conducting a planned drive into surrender to Communism. . . . Mr. Kennedy would risk the existence of the United States on the flip of a two-headed coin."

In 1960, *Independent American* reprinted an article from the often anti-Semitic publication of the late Merwin K. Hart's National Economic Council, the "Economic Council Letter." The article bore the title "Is the State Department Selling America Down the River?" and the gist of the article answered, Yes.

On the United Nations, *Independent American* has declared: ". . . the UN's special agencies drain our resources to build Socialism, not Capitalism. The first big step on the road to peace will be passage of Congressman Utt's bill . . . to get the US out of the UN." As to UNICEF (the UN Children's Fund), the Courtneys urge their readers not to support it: ". . . when UNICEF money is sent to a Communist country . . . the money is distributed by Communist officials for Communist objectives."

NATO is called a "New Front for World Government."

Not only have Communists burrowed into the Government and other facets of American life according to the Courtneys, but they are even in the Girl Scouts and are practically running the YMCAs and the YWCAs. The *Independent American* has unabashedly charged that the YMCA and the YWCA have been infiltrated at all levels—local, national, and international—by Reds.

Nor are American leaders spared from the extremist and radical venom of the New Orleans husband-and-wife propaganda team. Former President Eisenhower was branded as "our surrender-obsessed President." Before Richard Nixon ran for President, Phoebe Courtney wrote in May, 1959: "Nixon . . . joined hands with the internationalists, the One Worlders—those whose aim is to destroy the national sovereignty of the United States by plunging this country into the fatal whirlpool of World Government."

And again, in the 1960 campaign: "Both parties are moving toward an all-powerful international Socialist dictatorship . . . Nixon and Kennedy are . . . riding the Socialist wave as far as it will take them . . . Nixon and Kennedy stand for the same thing."

The Courtneys' newspaper reaches a lot more Americans than its paid subscription list would indicate. A few years ago, for instance, 209,000 copies were distributed although the subscribers numbered only 11,500.

Besides their newspaper and radio propaganda, the Courtneys have authored, published, and distributed a number of books, including *The Conservative Political Action Handbook, The CSA Voting Index, America's Unelected Rulers, Disarmament: A Blueprint for Surrender,* and *The Case of General Edwin A. Walker.* The last defended Walker and contained what was described as "a documented expose of how the appeasers proposed to substitute surrender for victory." Courtney claimed the book, which sold some 15,000 copies at $2 each, was an important factor in mobilizing public opinion which resulted in the Senate hearings on "muzzling of the military." (Walker may have appreciated the effort, but he showed up badly in the hearings.)

The *Conservative Political Action Handbook,* also priced at $2, contains instructions on political campaign techniques—how to hold meetings and rallies, how to write letters to congressmen and to editors of newspapers, and general tactics to achieve political advantages. An example of the kind of "political action" material the Courtneys issue is the *CSA Voting Index,* at $4 a copy. *Human Events* and Americans for Constitutional Action, two Rightist forces, have received enormous publicity and substantial income from the sale of a congressional voting index, and the Courtneys decided to publish one of their own. The Courtney version was designed "to make available to Conservatives throughout the nation a voting index that is inexpensive, reliable, easily understood, non-partisan, and which gives a full picture as to how each Congressman voted on a wide range of important issues dealing with the general subject of the national economy, big spending, growing Federal control, foreign policy, appeasement, etc."

In a May, 1962, analysis of the Courtney *CSA Voting Index,* Drew Pearson wrote that it "asks in lurid red letters on its cover, 'How Soft on Communism Is Your Congressman?' The confused reader gets the impression that anyone who votes the 'Liberal-Socialist' line is 'soft on Communism.' " Pearson further noted that the *CSA Voting Index* had drawn "the amazing conclusion" that the late Congressman Francis Walter of Pennsylvania, chairman of the House Committee on Un-American Activities, who had "spent years fighting Communism," had "a 100% Liberal-Socialist voting record which, according to Courtney standards, makes him soft on Communism."

Pearson gave a few more examples from the *CSA Voting Index:*

"Speaker John McCormack of Boston, who in the 1930's headed the first committee to investigate Communism, is also branded by the Courtneys as having a 100% Liberal-Socialist voting record.

"The Courtneys add more confusion by claiming that GOP Congressman Walter Judd, who was once a prisoner of the Chinese Communists, votes the soft-on-Communism line 74% of the time.

"Even Congressman Charlie Halleck of Indiana, hard-boiled, Conservative leader of the House Republicans, may be a dangerous Red, according to Courtney standards, for he voted the Liberal-Socialist line 68% of the time."

The most popular publications which the Courtneys issue, and which they say have sold in the millions, are small pamphlets called "Tax Fax." These are attacks on Government programs and policies or on politically prominent individuals. By 1964, the *Independent American* had issued some fifty "Tax Fax" pamphlets (25 cents each). The following titles illustrate the subjects covered by "Tax Fax" and suggest the tone and approach the Courtneys take in their propaganda.

—"On Whose Side Is The U.S. Supreme Court?," which bore the subtitle "Pro-Red 'Batting Averages' of Members of the Supreme Court."

—"How Can The South Support Lyndon Johnson for President?" This attack on Mr. Johnson contained such subheadings as: "Johnson's Left-Wing Voting Record," "Extreme Left-Wingers Praise Lyndon," and "Johnson's Liberal, Anti-South Voting Record."

—"Kennedy: Profile of a Liberal-Socialist," with the subtitle "Is Kennedy 'Soft on Communism'?"

—"Medicare: A Socialist Fraud," which urged action against the late President Kennedy's Medicare program if readers wished "to prevent the Liberal-Socialists from increasing your Social Security taxes up to 10% of your salary in order to finance Socialized Medicine."

—"Civil Rights: Planned Dictatorship," which described proposed civil rights legislation as a power grab for Federal control of private property, business establishments, and education.

—"Communist Agitation and Racial Turmoil," which outlines what is branded as "the Communist plan to use the civil rights movement as a vehicle for revolution in the United States." The Courtney pamphlet demands a full congressional investigation of the extent of alleged Communist infiltration of civil rights organizations such as the NAACP, the Southern Christian Leadership Conference, and the Congress of Racial Equality.

From the time the Courtneys launched their propaganda mill, Kent Courtney has never lost sight of his political dream—the establishment of a more Rightist political party. Whenever he arrives in a town to deliver a talk, the private meetings in his hotel suites deal with uniting the various Rightist groups. Shortly after the *Independent American* was established, he went to New York City, rented a suite at the famous Astor Hotel, and made a series of appointments with Far Right leaders who were converging on the city to attend a For America meeting. Courtney was intent on drumming up attendance for a Third Party rally he himself was promoting the following night. It was there he cautioned his audience:

"Don't call it a Third Party. That would be unlucky. What we are doing is forming a coalition of Right Wing Republicans and Democrats. In the South we can count on partisans of segregation from both parties. We oppose Federal meddling in the schools and that should win us support from Catholics generally. We are now getting into the money. A businessman I talked to at the meeting last night is coming in with $35,000 today. We are finding other substantial money backers here in New York City."

Courtney passes up few chances to attract attention and win friends in high places. For the 1960 Republican Convention in Chicago his print shop prepared Goldwater for President signs. He organized a brigade of followers and gave each a placard, and at a given signal they went tearing down the aisles with the Goldwater for President signs. Courtney laughed happily in telling about it: "I told them to push those signs into the lens of every TV camera they saw."

Each of Courtney's rallies and conferences has been marked by the presence of well-known leaders of the Radical Right.

In 1959, his New Party Rally at Chicago featured a banquet at which Founder Welch of the Birch Society and William Buckley, editor of the *National Review,* a leading magazine of conservative opinion, shared the platform as main speakers. Also taking a leading role at the rally were Birch Society National Council members Tom Anderson and Revilo P. Oliver, and J. Bracken Lee, who is on the editorial advisory committee of the Birch monthly magazine —and Dan Smoot, who apparently came up from Dallas for the occasion.

In 1960, after failing in his race for governor of Louisiana, Courtney called a Solid South Conference at Shreveport whose aim was to explore possibilities for a third party Presidential candidate in the 1960 election. The candidates viewed by Courtney as acceptable at that time included Senators Goldwater and Thurmond, as well as such Birch Society luminaries as Tom Anderson, Dean Clarence Manion, and J. Bracken Lee.

The Goldwater for President rally on the eve of the 1960 GOP convention again featured Welch and Anderson as speakers, along with a surprise appearance by former Senator William E. Jenner of Indiana.

In April, 1961, the Courtneys summoned a Convention of Conservatives at Chicago which again featured Anderson and Lee. As had been the case in 1959, the rally was held in conjunction with a convention of Willis E. Stone's National Committee for Economic Freedom (now called the Liberty Amendment Committee of the U.S.A.). Harry Everingham, who is the executive director of the Chicago-based Far Right group called We, The People!, also was present to give his co-operation, as he did at the 1960 Goldwater for President rally convened by the Courtneys. And Robert Welch sent a telegram of support.

Although Welch has since had some unkind things to say about Kent Courtney and his activities, the New Orleans-based husband-and-wife propaganda team have never flagged in loyalty and praise for Welch and the Birch Society, and it is clear that over and above their Birch affiliation the Courtneys enjoy friendly and co-operative relationships with a number of other big names in the American Radical Right.

Kent Courtney is no fool. As a hopeful politico he knows that any taint by anti-Negro, anti-Catholic, and anti-Jewish groups could be a public kiss of death, and he has made special efforts to avoid such a taint. When he promoted the New Party Rally in Chicago a few years ago, he personally wrote to twenty-five persons known for their activities with hate organizations to tell them they would not be welcome at his meeting. The reception desk had a list of those who were barred and the instructions were firm that they were not to be admitted. When Elizabeth Dilling and Lyrl Van Hyning, both notorious anti-Semites, appeared and were refused admission their loud protests created so big a scene that the receptionist telephoned Courtney for help; she reported they insisted on speaking with him. Courtney refused to see them. The Dillings and Van Hynings are a constant source of embarrassment to the Radical Right.

For the 1964 national elections, the Courtneys' big objective was to weld all Radical Right groups together to roll up a huge Rightist vote. In the absence of a third party, they announced for Senator Goldwater. No matter whom they favor for the Presidency, the Courtneys never forget that the wheels of anyone's propaganda mill turn more easily on money. When they declared themselves for Senator Goldwater for 1964, Phoebe wrote:

"As you know, the work of the *Independent American* is possible because of contributions we receive from our subscribers. Without such continuing help from our friends our activities would grind to a halt within two weeks.

"Therefore, because this is a crucial election year—because this year presents the greatest opportunity that anti-Communist Conservatives have ever had—may we ask that you contribute as much as you possibly can so that all our plans and programs for the coming months can go forward immediately. . . .

"We shall be watching the mails for your response indicating that you approve of our efforts and wish us to go 'full speed ahead' during the decisive year 1964 in this fight against the atheistic Communist conspiracy at home and abroad."

Apparently sufficient funds arrived as a result of the Courtney plea to enable them to set up shop at the Republican Convention in San Francisco. Opening their headquarters as "Independent Americans for Goldwater," in temporary offices at 1175 Mission Street, Kent announced that the premises had been selected "for the convenience of all Conservative voters who wish to work for the nomination of Barry Goldwater running on a Conservative platform, and who want to see Goldwater select an anti-Communist as his Vice-Presidential running mate."

Courtney had several suggestions for the Vice-Presidential slot and listed them without indicating whether he had their prior approval. Included among various solons he named were William E. Jenner, former senator from Indiana, and John G. Tower, senator from Texas.

Careful observation of Courtney's antics immediately preceding the opening of the convention led one to believe his main purpose in San Francisco was to create a movement in opposition to all liberal and moderate tendencies that might otherwise find their way into the Republican platform or the speeches of proposed candidates. Pennsylvania's Governor William W. Scranton, one of the aspirants for nomination, angrily accused Courtney of engaging in a "vicious smear campaign," labeling Courtney a "radical extremist" and charging that Courtney's propaganda "traded on fear and bigotry." The Courtney statement that most offended the governor was the charge that he was "actually an ardent left-winger with a record of actions which prove his softness on Communism."

However out of touch the Courtneys may be with the values

of American democracy as expressed, and debated, by the Republican and Democratic Parties, it is somehow hard to picture the pair involved in fighting a shadowy "atheistic Communist conspiracy at home and abroad"—Phoebe with her swirl of hair and showy furs and Kent with his hail-fellow-well-met salesman demeanor. And yet they say there is such a dark plot in the works, and that they are fighting it, and indeed the contributions keep pouring into New Orleans to help them in the fight.

11

Liberty Amendment Committee

of the U.S.A.

— Willis Stone

The leaders of the Radical Right have their pet hates, pet fears, pet axes to grind. But there is one curious cause in which they are all of one mind: abolition of the income tax.

Along all the strange extremist roads and even in some of the more respectable political neighborhoods of conservatism, the Federal income tax is viewed as Fabian socialism at best—at worst, as a diabolical Marxist scheme to destroy Western civilization. In earlier days, the reactionary Right sought merely to limit the Government in the percentage of income it might collect (the figure usually suggested was 25 percent), and thirty-two state legislatures have adopted measures calling for some sort of ceiling since 1931. But Welch and Hargis, Manion and Smoot and the Courtneys— in short, the loud leadership and most of the followers in today's Radical Right—favor the complete elimination of the income tax itself. They would repeal the Sixteenth Amendment to the Constitution, which had authorized it.

The frenzied advocates of repeal are still far from their goal, but since the 1940's an organized movement has been beating political propaganda drums for the cause. The movement is heavily backed by many of the same individuals and corporations who have lent support to other organizations of the Far Right.

Spearheading it is a sixty-five-year-old industrial engineer named Willis E. Stone. A descendant of Thomas Stone, a signer of the Declaration of Independence, and of the Ralph Waldo Emerson family, Willis Stone is immensely proud of his all-American ancestry. Born in Denver, he served in the Army Tank Corps during World War I, and since 1923 has resided in Los Angeles, where he has been active in American Legion circles. Stone claims to have worked as an engineer on the construction of the Hoover Dam, and has carefully noted that it was not a public power project.

Actually, Stone's ultimate goal is not only the repeal of the income tax. He believes that its repeal would have another effect, his true objective—getting the Federal Government out of various activities which he describes as "business operations." The goal of the so-called "Liberty Amendment," which Stone has been assiduously promoting for fifteen years, is the "de-nationalization" of many Government activities.

Stone claims, without necessarily documenting his assertion, that the United States Government is engaged in some seven hundred business operations for which it has no Constitutional authority—from making fertilizer at the TVA complex to trying to improve Eskimo dwellings. These Government operations, he holds, lose money and consume around $45,000,000,000 in taxes, of which some $38,000,000,000 come from personal income taxes, estate taxes, and gift taxes.

The conclusion, to Stone and his followers and supporters, is obvious: get the Government out of these business activities and sell them to private enterprise, which would, he explains by a complicated process, reduce the national debt by $65,000,000,000. The result would make it possible to eliminate the hated income tax and other direct taxes. A major part of these taxes, says Stone, sustains the Government's "bureaucratic competition against us."

All of which might be just another unreal approach to problems in a democratic society. But the Far Right has latched onto the question and has used it as one anti-social-reform weapon in their arsenal of propaganda. They formalize the issue in their Liberty Amendment, which is brief and to the point:

Section 1. The Government of the United States shall not engage in any business, professional, commercial, financial or industrial enterprise except as specified in the Constitution.

Section 2. The constitution or laws of any state, or the laws of the United States shall not be subject to the terms of any foreign or domestic agreement which would abrogate this amendment.

Section 3. The activities of the United States Government which violate the intent and purposes of this amendment shall, within a period of three years from the date of the ratification of this amendment, be liquidated and the properties and facilities affected shall be sold.

Section 4. Three years after the ratification of this amendment the sixteenth article of amendments to the Constitution of the United States shall stand repealed and thereafter Congress shall not levy taxes on personal incomes, estates, and/or gifts.

The Liberty Amendment was first introduced in Congress in 1952 by the late Representative Ralph Gwinn, long active in reactionary Rightist causes. It was again introduced seven years later by Republican Representative James B. Utt of California, another of the legislative favorites of the Far Right. Those who, like Stone, promote radical surgery on the American body politic in the name of conservatism, have not made much progress since then. But they have been trying.

In 1961, the Congressional Joint Economic Committee published a devastating study of Stone's elaborately "documented" theses and proposals, which Stone, of course, branded as a "fantastic misrepresentation." The congressional study found, among other things, that:

—Elimination of Federal income, estate, and gift taxes would cost the Government $65,000,000,000 a year.

—Federal Government expenditures would have to be limited each year to paying the interest on the national debt and to meeting only a part of other existing obligations. All other obligations, including those for national defense, would have to be eliminated.

—The Federal Government would have to rely on a general sales tax at very high rates—something on the order of 39 percent—which would cut deeply into the revenue sources of the states.

—The Federal Government would have to go much more deeply into debt, resulting in inflation or in very great increases in the borrowing costs for state and local governments.

—The Federal Government would find it much more difficult to meet its responsibilities to the nation and to the free world.

Senator Carl Hayden elaborated on the findings by pointing out that the Social Security Administration and the Veterans Administration, two of the agencies Stone and his supporters would abolish, were involved in serious and solemn obligations to meet human needs. He emphasized that more than five billion dollars were required each year to keep the nation's promises to veterans and their widows and orphans. Senator Hayden did not mention some of the other agencies which the supporters of the Liberty Amendment would abolish:

The Forestry Service, the Federal Housing Authority, the Federal Reserve Banks, the TVA, the Patent Office, the National Labor Relations Board, the National Park Service, the Postal Savings System, the Atomic Energy Commission, the Bureau of Public Roads, the Central Intelligence Agency, the Civil Aeronautics Administration, the Civil Defense Administration, the Soil Conservation Service, the Water Conservation Division, and many other Federal activities.

Nevertheless, proponents of the Liberty Amendment have pressed their cause, pumping out a vast array of literature and propaganda—as many as 4,000,000 printed units in one year, plus film strips, movies, discussion kits, and at least three major speeches a week around the country by Stone himself, plus appearances on radio and TV. Stone has boasted that his organization has had favorable editorial comment totaling millions of lines.

Since 1963, the organizational name under which Stone has operated is the Liberty Amendment Committee of the U.S.A. Before that it was known as the National Committee for Economic Freedom. Stone's original operation was called the American Progress Foundation, which he launched in 1949 to propagandize for his amendment to the Constitution. In about 1956 or so, the American Progress Foundation and the Organization To Repeal Federal Income Taxes, Inc., (ORFIT) began working together. In 1957 they merged. ORFIT was incorporated in the District of Columbia in 1953, with the ex-movie star of silent days, Corinne Griffith, and the late screen actor, Charles Coburn, among the organizers. (Miss Griffith withdrew from ORFIT some time later in a disagreement over policy to campaign for income tax repeal on her own.) But the merger of 1957 was short-lived, at least for Stone, and in 1958 his magazine, *American Progress,* announced that it was thenceforth being published for the National Committee for Economic Freedom, now the Liberty Amendment Committee of the U.S.A. The publication is now called *Freedom Magazine* and is published for the Liberty Amendment organization.

Besides *Freedom Magazine,* Stone also publishes a periodical called *Fact Sheet,* each issue of which documents the story of one of the 700 Government operations which should be turned over to private enterprise as part of the "de-nationalization" program. (Stone originally listed eighty-eight corporations operated by the Government; opposition writers pointed out that twenty-five of them no longer existed and that others never had, plus the fact that there was a substantial number of overlappings, but Stone was undeterred. He later expanded his list to 700.)

Stone's Liberty Amendment Committee reads like a Who's Who of the American Far Right. Composed of some 4,000 persons, the organization boasts committees in 47 of the 50 states, headed by 66 state chairmen and co-chairmen. Of these 66, more than a dozen have been identified with the John Birch Society; five of them are members of the Society's national council, the rest are Endorsers, members, or organizers. Among the state chairmen of Stone's organization are such Birch national council members as Judge M. T. Phelps of Arizona, Robert Love of Kansas, Colonel Laurence Bunker of Massachusetts, and A. G. Heinsohn, Jr., and Tom Anderson of Tennessee. Council member F. Gano Chance was former state chairman for Missouri. Kent Courtney is state chairman for Louisiana. Charles Pavey, M.D., a leading Ohio Bircher, is chairman for the Buckeye State. The Michigan chairman is a former Birch co-ordinator. The former chairman for South Dakota was a volunteer Birch organizer. And so on. There are others perhaps more interesting:

The state chairman in West Virginia, for instance, is Mrs. Jessica Payne, who in 1949 was vice-president of the National Council for American Education. That extremist group was headed by Allen Zoll, a notorious anti-Semite whose American Patriots, Inc., was listed by the U. S. Attorney General's office as subversive.* Once, according to an observer, at a meeting of the Daughters of the American Revolution in Cleveland, Mrs. Payne declared:

"If anyone calls you a Fascist—take a bow. . . . After all, what is a Fascist but a patriotic nationalist . . . and you are looking at one right now."

Milton Lory is Liberty Amendment Committee co-chairman for Iowa. He is a Right Wing Extremist who for many years has been a top leader of the American Coalition of Patriotic Societies, and whose name has appeared on the leadership boards and committees of many Far Right groups, among them the Congress of

* See *A Measure of Freedom* by Arnold Forster (Garden City, N.Y.: Doubleday and Company, 1950) and *The Troublemakers.*

Freedom, Inc., and We, The People! Lory also is associated with Hargis' Christian Crusade, and For America. In 1962, when Bundy's Church League of America opened its headquarters in Wheaton, Illinois, Lory was one of the main speakers at the ceremonies.

The executive committee of Stone's Liberty Amendment organization, composed entirely of Californians, includes some wealthy businessmen, industrialists, and ranchers whose names also appear frequently as supporters of Right Wing causes and organizations. Among them are Walter Knott of Knott's Berry Farm in Buena Park, California, who some years ago decided that it was more important "to save our individual freedom and our free enterprise economy than to build our business larger or to earn a few more dollars." He established a Freedom Center and built a staff to do research, publish materials, and make films for the cause. Mass distribution letters, soliciting support for Stone's organization, often go out on Knott's stationery.

Another leading Rightist on Stone's executive committee is C. C. Moseley, who lives in Beverly Hills and heads the Grand Central Aircraft Company in Glendale. The late Hubbard Russell, a wealthy rancher of Maricopa, also graced the executive committee of the Liberty Amendment group and, like Moseley, was something of a joiner when it came to Rightist crusades.

And then there is Raymond Cyrus Hoiles, a Bible-quoting multimillionaire eccentric who is "agin" just about everything in modern American life, including Community Chests, old age pensions, the United Nations, public roads, public hospitals, our armed forces, police departments, and public schools. He is eighty-five years old, and through a string of newspapers which he owns in ten communities from Ohio to the Pacific Coast, he keeps firing away at these things which he calls "immoralities." Hoiles's personal fortune is estimated at $20,000,000 and he does not want to see any of it going to the "un-Christian and un-Constitutional" modern setup known as public schools. It is his conviction that children who want an education will get it themselves and those who do not want it are better off without it.

This Right Wing Extremist has devoted much of his life to making enemies, even in communities where his papers are published. The *McAllen* (Ohio) *Monitor* is known locally as the "McAllen Monster." Mayor William C. Henderson of Colorado Springs, Colorado, has barred Hoiles's *Gazette-Telegraph* from his own home and once advocated taking "concerted action to remove this cancer from the community."

The publisher is a puritanical moralist who has his newspapers make a point of listing all traffic violators and all those involved in divorces. Once Hoiles himself was arrested for speeding, and his own papers gave front-page coverage to the story of his arrest.

The promise of an end to filing tax returns each April 15 has been so attractive that resolutions favoring the Liberty Amendment have been passed by some state legislatures. Seven states—Wyoming, Texas, Nevada, Louisiana, Georgia, Mississippi, and South Carolina—are on record for the Amendment. Similar resolutions were defeated by only one vote in Colorado, and by a close margin in the Minnesota legislature. In Massachusetts, New York, Michigan, Delaware, Montana, Arkansas, North Dakota, South Dakota, Wisconsin, and Connecticut, the proposed Amendment has made some progress.

The sources of financial support for Stone's Committee are not matters of public record, but there are clues in the identity of the executive committee members and the various state chairmen, as well as in the companies which advertise in *Freedom Magazine*.

Among these, for instance, are the Spindale and Cherokee Mills owned by A. G. Heinsohn, Jr., the Birch council member from Tennessee; Kennametal, Inc., owned by Phillip McKenna, state chairman for Pennsylvania; Coast Federal Savings and Loan Association, headed by Joe Crail, which carries on a lavishly financed program of Rightist propaganda; the Farrel Company, of Connecticut, in which Franklin Farrel, a Birch Society Endorser, is a principal; Moseley's Grand Central Industrial Center; and the Flick-Reedy Corporation of Bensenville, Illinois, in which Frank Flick, Liberty Committee chairman for Illinois, is a principal.

Stone, himself, for all his concentration and dedication to the Liberty Amendment cause, apparently co-operates closely with the Birch Society and in return receives support from the Birchers. He has been listed as a speaker for the Birch-sponsored American Opinion Speakers Bureau. And for all Stone's apparently scholarly research for the cause to which he has dedicated almost two decades, he himself can and does disseminate the same kind of fright and doom and gloom as do other Radical Rightists.

Once, while addressing the extremist Congress of Freedom, Stone declared:

"Every dictionary published in the United States in the last 100 years defines communism as being the use of political force to abolish property and private enterprise. Based upon this historic definition of communism—the United States is, at this moment, rotten with communistic practices."

And Stone may have been the first to denounce the Chief Justice of the United States, Earl Warren, whose proposed impeachment has been a slogan of the Far Right. As far back as 1953, when Governor Warren was named to the high court, Stone told the Civitan Club in Denver:

"He hasn't the remotest idea of how a chief justice or a judge or a Justice of the Peace ought to act."

Stone is, in fact, as extreme an Extremist as one can find on the American Radical Right, and while he has never engaged in any personal bigotry himself, some of the organizations in which he has been involved are somewhat less than pure on the question of anti-Semitism.

The Congress of Freedom, on whose national assembly committee Stone has been listed and before whose conventions he has been a frequent speaker, has been tainted by the presence on its boards and committees of known anti-Semites. So has We, The People! for which Stone formerly acted as West Coast director.

And Stone was on the national advisory committee of Liberty and Property which for five years, from 1955 to 1960, published an anti-Semitic newsletter called "Right." Moreover, in the early 1950's, Stone wrote a regular column for an extremist publication called *The American Reporter* (not to be confused with the highly respected Max Ascoli publication, *The Reporter*) which also carried an often questionable column by former State Senator Jack Tenney. The sharing of space with Tenney in *The American Reporter* did not, apparently, fill Stone with misgivings.

In 1957, moreover, he had kind words for the late Merwin K. Hart, for years one of the nation's more notorious anti-Semites.* Concluding a speech before We, The People! in Chicago, Stone introduced Hart as a man he had "admired and loved."

Such is the judgment of the man who would, by taking from the Federal Government its most vital functions, destroy all of the manifestations of public responsibility in America.

* See *A Measure of Freedom.*

*

The
Extreme
Conservatives

A Preliminary Word

The Right is a band of varying but very similar colors at one end of American's political spectrum. There are no borderlines marking the place where the Radical Right ends and where extreme conservatism begins.

The two factions are difficult to separate at times, particularly when they sit at the same rallies and applaud the same ideas. The difficulty is further complicated by the fact that today's Radical Right sails under false colors, flying the banner of conservatism while in fact advocating the usual Radical Right program. At the same time, the Radical Right accuses all who disagree with it of being pro-Communist, confusing (deliberately or otherwise) communism with all other things it dislikes.

Extreme Conservatives do not advocate impeaching the Chief Justice, but they deplore many of the same Supreme Court decisions as those who do. Most of these Conservatives do not actually urge repeal of the income tax, or American withdrawal from the UN, but they denounce income taxes as confiscatory or socialistic, and attack the world organization with comparable fervor for many of its activities. These Conservatives of the Right do not actually invade supermarkets which sell hams from Poland, but they applaud those who do. The Extreme Conservatives may deplore the extremism of a Robert Welch for calling President Eisenhower a "dedicated, conscious agent of the Communist conspiracy," but they do not reject those who follow Welch. In fact, they are frequently quoted as saying that the Birch Society includes many "good Americans."

Yet if the Extreme Conservatives are not card-carrying Birchers, they often make common cause with them, and the similarities between their views are often more compelling than the differences. Like the Radicals, their conservative allies reject much of America's social, political, and economic history of the last thirty years and would repeal much of that history if they could.

The major differences between these Conservatives and the Radicals is that most of the Conservatives do not, as has been noted, accept the conspiracy theory of American history. The Extreme Conservatives do, however, feel that the liberal domestic policies of the last thirty years have taken the country far down the "road to serfdom" and welfare statism. They attribute this to a blindness, stupidity, bungling, and unsoundness in liberalism, rather than to any subversive plot.

Nevertheless, the similarities of viewpoint between Radicals and the Extreme Conservatives lead to overlaps—not only of ideas, but of people. Supporters and leaders of the Extreme Conservatives often are leaders and supporters of groups on the far fringe also, and often lend their names to causes and slogans of radical origin.

The Extreme Conservatives, in short, are frequent fellow travelers of today's Radical Right. An examination of the Right Wing in America today, therefore, inevitably takes one from the radical elements to their conservative allies and back again, with a way-station stop in the Southern pro-segregation, anti-civil rights, States' rights groups which have flourished for the last ten years in the wake of the Supreme Court's historic decision of May 17, 1954, outlawing segregated public schools.

For the Southern segregationist movement, with its White Citizens Councils and its Coordinating Committee for Fundamental American Freedoms (the latter, early in 1964, spearheaded the Washington lobbying activities against passage of the Civil Rights Bill), exerts an impact on the American body politic which is also essentially Rightist. In pursuit of their stated purpose of preserving segregation, they inveigh against Federal power, charge the existence of plots and conspiracies in the national capital, and propagandize against broad domestic social policies as an invasion of States' rights at best and as dictatorship at worst.

In doing so, these Southern forces of reaction march solidly in step with their Rightist counterparts in other sections of the country, and there have been several efforts in the last ten years to establish formal organizational link-ups between the Rightist forces of the South and those of the North and West. These efforts did not succeed in producing the hoped-for formal coalition of the Extreme Right. But the 1964 struggle against the Civil Rights Bill found the Southern lobby which sought to defeat the bill—the Coordinating Committee for Fundamental American Freedoms—working in harness with the John Birch Society and other Rightist organizations against the proposed legislation.

12

Americans for Constitutional Action
— Admiral (Ret.) Ben Moreell

On August 3, 1958, Admiral Ben Moreell (U.S. Navy, Ret.), president and chairman of the board of Jones and Laughlin Steel Corporation, issued a news release in Pittsburgh announcing the birth of a new political action and educational organization called Americans for Constitutional Action (ACA).

The next day, Senator Karl Mundt of South Dakota took the floor of the Senate with the air of a happy godfather to announce the blessed event, which he called "one of the most memorable dates in the political history of the United States."

The purposes of the new organization were to combat the "shift toward Socialism" in the United States and offset the influence of the liberal Americans for Democratic Action (ADA).

Senator Mundt also quoted "an analysis" of "American political and economic trends" as they were viewed by the founders of ACA. The ACA statement declared that "for the past three decades," there had been "a steady increase in the pressures being exerted . . . on both our major political parties and on all candidates . . . in an effort to push or pressure them toward support of causes which for want of a better term are labeled as 'leftish' in nature. They are the causes which move toward socialism."

Besides the influence of the ADA, the ACA analysis blamed the dangers to the nation on the electoral college system, which it said places too much political power in the hands of voting blocs in "12 vast cities of 8 large states." It also cited the fact that Conservatives are "artificially divided" by the Mason-Dixon line. This, said ACA, has made the Republican Party ineffective in congressional elections in the South. It has also held the South in line for Democratic candidates, even though such nominees are "selected by northern liberals. . . ." As for the ADA, the ACA statement said that group had become the "spearhead" and the "political catalyst" for a combination of labor, big city machine, nationalistic and radical blocs whose influence extended into the Democratic Party national conventions, and into Republican Party nominations for governors, senators, and congressmen in the North and the East.

The original board of trustees announced by ACA when it was formed included Moreell as chairman, the late Henning W. Prentis, chairman of the board of the Armstrong Cork Company, as vice-chairman, former Governor Charles Edison of New Jersey as treasurer, Walter B. Martin, former president of the American Medical Association, and former Representative Ed Gossett of Texas (now out of ACA).

General Bonner Fellers, a hardy perennial in extremely conservative organizations, was listed in 1960 as ACA vice-chairman, and Felix Morley, well-known writer and journalist, had been named as ACA secretary. Other names on the 1960 list of trustees were Howard Buffett (who died in 1964), a former congressman and Birch Society member; Brigadier General Robert W. Johnson of Johnson and Johnson; Allan B. Kline, former president of the American Farm Bureau Federation; Philip McKenna of the Kennametal Company, active in the movement to repeal the income tax and once head of the Gold Standard League; Mrs. R. Templeton Smith, a Pittsburgh civic leader; and Loyd Wright, a former president of the American Bar Association who ran against the liberal Senator Thomas Kuchel in the 1962 California GOP senatorial primary. (Wright was also active in 1963 and 1964 in helping write propaganda against the Civil Rights Bill under the imprint of the Southern-led Coordinating Committee for Fundamental American Freedoms.)

Besides these men, the ACA Board of Trustees has listed other very respectable names: former President Herbert Hoover; Edgar Eisenhower, brother of former President Eisenhower, who is a

Tacoma banker; General Robert E. Wood, who had headed the American First Committee; T. J. Coolidge, former chairman of the board of the United Fruit Company; Bob Cox, a former director of the United States Chamber of Commerce; and the late Ralph Gwinn, a former congressman whose name was a familiar fixture for many years on letterheads of Rightist organizations.

Far from being the newborn and only child of its creators, Americans for Constitutional Action was a younger brother of the Campaign for the 48 States, which came into existence in 1955 to lobby for, among other things, Constitutional amendments to limit income taxes and to revise the electoral college system so as to weaken the voting power of cities. The chairman of the Campaign for the 48 States was Robert B. Snowden of Memphis, Tennessee, who became ACA's first finance chairman, and was later an Endorser of the John Birch Society.

ACA was born in Pittsburgh, baptized in Washington, D. C., and given its first feeding in Memphis, Tennessee, at the headquarters of the Campaign for the 48 States. When Americans for Constitutional Action was being brought into the world, The Campaign was in the process of dying. It had some $25,000 left in its treasury. Early in 1959, this was used to open a bank account for the infant ACA.

The man who heads this increasingly influential organization, Admiral Ben Moreell, set up and directed the famous Seabees during the war. He has an enviable industrial and war record, as well as an arm-long list of honors and citations. Physically, he is a big man, square-jawed and broad-shouldered, who carries his solid poundage on a six-foot frame. His hair is touched with gray and he now wears spectacles, but his full face is still ruddy and his manner vigorous. In his college days at Washington University in St. Louis, where he grew up, he was captain of the track team and a football fullback. Even today, he gives the impression that he could carry the ball through a phalanx of human granite.

This rugged man is a rugged individualist. In a 1963 speech at the Fifth Political Action Conference, sponsored by the Right Wing publication *Human Events* which works closely with ACA, Moreell declared:

"In the idiom of the New Frontier, I am an 'ultra-conservative.' I accept the nomination—provided the title denotes one who tried humbly to follow the trail blazed from tyranny to freedom, through government oppression, by Washington, Jefferson, Madison and the other bold pioneers of our Republic."

He declared that the standard raised by the Founding Fathers, "rooted deeply in religious faith and eternal principles," held that a man "derives, directly from the Creator, his rights to life, to liberty and to the unhampered use of his honestly acquired property," and that "for a man to grow in wisdom and worldly possessions, he must have freedom of choice, a free exchange for ideas as well as for goods." Laudable concepts, indeed, but. . . .

The Admiral believes the American nation is, and has been, "on a suicidal course" because "in recent decades we have been yielding to government our individual responsibility to secure the blessings of liberty for ourselves and our posterity." This, he holds, "will lead ultimately to slavery."

In 1960, addressing the Women's Patriotic Conference on National Defense, Inc., a Rightist and ultranationalist organization, the Admiral declared that it was his "firm conviction that the two greatest intrusions on individual freedom in the history of our Republic" were a 1917 act of Congress which permitted the raising of "a conscript army for use in foreign war," and the Sixteenth Amendment, providing for an income tax. This amendment, he said in another speech, had imposed "on Americans the second plank of the Marx-Engels Communist Manifesto."

"I'm fed up to here," he told the 1963 Human Events conference, "with pseudo-statesmen whose wishbones are where their backbones ought to be, who are past masters of surrender, compromise, appeasement and accommodation. . . ."

He was also "fed up to here," Moreell went on, "with Robin Hood government that promises to rob the rich to pay the poor and, when there are not enough rich left to pay the bills, robs rich and poor alike to pay Robin Hood. . . ."

In an interview, he once said that "any effort to equalize the social and economic status of all individuals by the coercive power of government is a contradiction of nature's laws and can be achieved only by destroying individual freedom. . . ."

Like Robert Welch, Dean Manion, and most Birch thinkers— although not quite as extreme—Moreell sees freedom chiefly in economic terms.

Moreell himself has no affiliation with the John Birch Society. Robert Welch reportedly asked the Admiral to serve on the editorial advisory committee of his *American Opinion* magazine and was turned down. But if Moreell is scrupulous in avoiding any personal connection with Welch and the Birch Society, he is not quite so scrupulous about those who serve with him as leaders of ACA.

He believes that the political and organizational affiliations of his closest associates in the leadership of ACA are none of his business. He has had long relationships with several of these people through his own activities in the American Right Wing movement. Not only was Moreell a member of the national advisory council of The Campaign for the 48 States, predecessor to ACA, but in the 1950's he was also on the National Policy Committee of the right wing For America, which also included Clarence Manion, Dan Smoot, and General Wood.

Moreell's other affiliations include membership on the board of trustees of the Foundation for Economic Education, a conservative organization, and the Intercollegiate Society of Individualists. He is a member of the national strategy committee of the American Security Council, run by former Federal police agents who specialize in servicing business firms and corporations with information about "Communist and other statist movements," and in screening employees from a loyalty file of 1,000,000 names.

The Radical Right and the Extreme Conservatives seem almost to be inextricably intertwined: Moreell was also listed as a sponsor of the American Committee for Aid to Katanga Freedom Fighters, set up a few years ago to oppose "the United Nations' despotic policy" in Katanga. Among the other sponsors were a number of leaders of the John Birch Society—Tom Anderson and Clarence Manion of its national council; Spruille Braden, a former Birch Council member; and such Endorsers of the Birch Society as Frederick G. Reinicke, Archibald B. Roosevelt, and J. Bracken Lee. Other sponsors included such members of the editorial advisory committee of the Birch *American Opinion* magazine as Hans F. Sennholz and former New Jersey Governor Charles Edison, a close friend of Moreell's. Edison is treasurer of ACA. In addition to his Birch ties, he is a sponsor of the Manion Forum and has supported Dr. Schwarz's Crusade.

General Bonner Fellers, ubiquitous in the leadership of Right Wing organizations, is ACA vice-chairman and recording secretary and has been listed as an Endorser of the John Birch Society. Fellers, who serves as national director of the Citizens Foreign Aid Committee (which opposes foreign aid), has also been listed on the advisory committee of Billy Hargis' Christian Crusade and was, with Moreell, a supporter of the old Campaign for the 48 States, the Intercollegiate Society of Individualists, and For America.

In short, these leaders of ACA support, with disturbing impartiality, organizations that are radical and organizations that claim to be conservative, underscoring clearly the ideological blur that exists between the Radical Right and the Extreme Conservatives and the difficulty of making clearcut distinctions between the two.

Certainly ACA's claim to be simply a conservative organization is damaged by the presence, in its leadership, of men who have lent their names and their prestige to Welch's Birch Society and other groups on the extreme political fringes. The same phenomenon shows itself when one considers the sources of financial support which ACA has attracted in the years since it was founded, during which it collected more than $600,000.

The plain fact is that some of ACA's most generous and consistent supporters have ties with the John Birch Society and other groups of the Radical Right. In the five-month period just prior to the 1962 congressional elections, when ACA was in the midst of an all-out drive to elect or re-elect Rightist representatives and senators, the Moreell group collected some $100,000, both in contributions and in loans for its political action drive. Almost 20 percent of that total came from industrialists and others with clear ties to Welch's extremist organization:

—George W. Armstrong, Jr., gave $1,000. He is a member of the editorial advisory committee of *American Opinion*.

—Robert B. Dresser, a Rhode Island lawyer who has long supported Rightist causes, gave $500. He is also on the editorial advisory committee of the Welch magazine and is a Birch Society Endorser.

—Edison, the ACA treasurer and a member of the *American Opinion* advisory committee, made a $1,000 contribution to ACA, plus a $2,500 loan.

—E. Ainsworth Eyre, an Endorser of the Birch Society, gave $1,200 and loaned ACA $2,500.

—William Grede, a Birch national council member, loaned ACA $1,000, and Fred C. Koch, another national council member, contributed $500.

—Dr. Thomas Parker, an Endorser of the Birch group, loaned ACA $2,500.

—J. Howard Pew, the Sunoco oil millionaire and a heavy contributor to Right Wing causes, contributed $3,000, while E. L. Wiegand, a Birch Endorser, loaned $2,500 to the Moreell organization.

—Other ACA contributors and supporters have included Birch national council members Louis Ruthenburg and Paul Talbert, and Birch Endorsers Frank deGanahl, James Doenges, Albert Penn, Robert Snowden, and Mrs. Seth Milliken.

In its 1962 congressional election drive, moreover, ACA endorsed for election the two members of the House of Representatives who openly admitted membership in the Birch Society—Representatives Edgar Hiestand and John Rousselot. Rousselot has since become a top Birch official as national public relations director of the Society. ACA also backed the two other Birch members who were candidates for Congress—H. L. Richardson of California and Jack Seale, the mayor of Birch-scarred Amarillo, Texas.

When these facts were made the subject of statements by liberal congressmen on the floor of the House of Representatives in the spring of 1963, Moreell was quoted as denying "that the ACA is dominated by the John Birch Society." But the Admiral added that membership in the Birch Society by trustees or supporters of ACA was "a matter which does not concern me."

Some of the statements issued by Admiral Moreell have the same doom-and-gloom flavor of broadsides issued by the fright-disseminators of the Radical Right in their frantic efforts to convince the American people that the country is on the verge of disaster. Just before Election Day, 1960, as the Kennedy-Nixon campaign was reaching its climax, Moreell issued such a statement, which was quoted by the late George Sokolsky, the widely read conservative columnist of the Hearst organization.

"The approaching election," Sokolsky quoted Moreell as saying, "is without question the most crucial in the history of our Republic —and the most momentous for the rest of the world."

Sokolsky commented that he had repeatedly heard that kind of prediction ever since he was a little boy and that somehow the Republic had managed to survive despite the candidates who were elected to office.

Sokolsky then quoted another Moreell statement: "I stand with those who believe that the great conflict of our age is between Individualism and Collectivism, to determine whether the individual, as a child of God and endowed by Him with certain inalienable rights, will be permitted to strive for a life in peaceful devotion to his God and in love of his neighbor; or, alternatively, whether his life is to be subordinated to the 'will of the majority,' a majority not guided by eternal and absolute laws of right and wrong, but solely by political and social practices fashionable at the time—a majority whose rule is actually dictated by a minority skilled at political manipulation."

After quoting this, Sokolsky wondered if Admiral Moreell favored a dictatorship, an absolute monarchy, or government by an elite group. Since the alternative to a majority is a minority, the columnist asked, "How does one decide which minority is to be placed in office?"

The answer to this question may be found in the following pages.

By late 1959, ACA had created a going concern to help 1960 congressional candidates who pledged to support the ACA program. Moreell himself took to the road to preach the message of "Constitutional Conservatism." In a September, 1959, talk to four hundred business leaders in Dallas, he warned that "our institutions—political, economic, educational, social and religious—are largely in the hands of the enemy." The enemy, he explained, is not only the avowed Communist but the welfare state and its propagandists.

ACA offices, for a short time in the Human Events building, were established early in 1960 in the Dodge Hotel, not far from the Capitol. The organization set to work to help Rightist congressional candidates seeking forty-five House and Senate seats in the November election. With Kenneth Ingwalson, now an assistant publisher of *Human Events,* as executive director, ACA activated and trained new workers, helped candidates with special problems, devised special newspaper ads, supplied basic speech material, helped raise campaign funds, and prepared a favorable climate for Rightist candidates by a general political propaganda campaign of speeches, films, and pamphlets. Its basic role, as it frankly admitted, was to provide extra support above and beyond what a candidate and his own party organization could supply.

Today, ACA is an effective political action group which already exerts a certain impact on the U. S. Congress and whose influence may well be growing. There are several reasons for ACA's effectiveness and influence. One is the competent and well-organized political help it gives to approved candidates at campaign time. Another is its close relationship with *Human Events* (this weekly publication will be considered in the following chapter) which helps ACA get some of its message to a widespread audience of opinion molders. And finally, there is the *ACA-Index,* which the organization has compiled since its inception and which tells how members of Congress have voted on issues which ACA views as tests of "Constitutional Conservatism." This rating table is one of the major score sheets of its kind and has brought the ACA considerable publicity. (It was General Edwin A. Walker's action in urging troops in his command in Germany to use the *ACA-Index* before casting their military ballots that got him in trouble with the Army and led to his resignation from the service.)

ACA released its first box score as the 1960 elections approached. Fourteen senators and 108 representatives could, ACA reported, be counted on to support "Constitutional Conservatism." On the other hand, the ACA said, 38 senators and 162 representatives—all of them Democrats—had voted 80 percent or more of the time for "welfare state," "large tax," and "high spend" government programs.

ACA's ratings are based on a series of indices, the most important of which is the ACA Consistency Index which measures whether a member of Congress or a senator is a "Constitutional Conservative" or a welfare state fuzzy-head—and to what degree. A pure "Constitutional Conservative" gets a rating of 100 percent if he voted as ACA thinks he should have on every key vote selected by ACA. A senator or representative who voted the opposite way every time would get a rating of zero, and would be viewed as anti-Constitution and as moving the nation toward socialism all the time. The other six indices, which form the basis for the Consistency Index, bear such sloganistic headings as: "For Sound Money and Fiscal Integrity and Against Inflation," "For a Private Competitive Market and Individual Freedom of Choice as Opposed to Government Interference," "For Local Self-Government and the Right to be Let Alone and Against Central Government Intervention in Local Government," "For Private Ownership and Against Government Ownership or Competition," "For Individual Liberty and Against Coercion by Government Regulations," and "For Strengthening National Sovereignty." But it is the Consistency Index that is crucial.

Shortly after the first Index was published in 1960, Ingwalson wrote the *Boston Herald* taking issue with an editorial which, he felt, had revealed a misunderstanding of the Index. The ACA study, he said, merely "shows the degree of consistency with which a Senator voted for principles underpinning the American system and, on the other hand, for those which move us toward socialism—regardless of the subject matter of the proposal before him. (Be it housing, price fixing, labor, etc.)"

The ACA executive director further denied, as the *Boston Herald* had charged, that the *ACA-Index* was "almost completely negative." For, he asked, "how can anything be more positive than to reveal the voting record of Senators and Representatives as being FOR sound money, FOR economy, FOR the private, competitive market system, FOR local self-government, FOR private ownership, FOR individual liberty?"

Alluding to the Democratic national ticket of John F. Kennedy for President and Lyndon B. Johnson for Vice-President, Ingwalson had this to say:

"If you wish, in fact since Mr. Kennedy earned 11% and Mr. Johnson 10% on the ACA Consistency Index (out of a possible 100%), to make this a positive rating, you could say that Mr. Kennedy helped move us 89% of the time toward Socialism, and Mr. Johnson 90% of the time. That's positive. And it's their record."

An ACA rating, as relayed in October of the following year in *Human Events,* found that seven Republican senators and four Southern Democrats had perfect, 100 percent, ACA voting records. Fourteen Republicans and two Democrats had scores of 80 to 92 percent pro-ACA.

The Republicans in the Senate who were rated as "outstanding Conservatives" were Wallace Bennett of Utah, the late Styles Bridges of New Hampshire, John M. Butler of Maryland, Norris Cotton of New Hampshire, Barry Goldwater of Arizona, John Tower of Texas, and John J. Williams of Delaware. The Democrats with perfect scores were Senators Harry Byrd of Virginia, Spessard Holland of Florida, A. Willis Robertson of Virginia, and Strom Thurmond of South Carolina.

In the lower House, the ACA "Human Events" 1961 ratings showed 78 Republicans and nine Democrats with ACA-approved ratings of 100 percent. All nine Democrats were from the South. No Republican voted 100 percent against the ACA line. Of the Democrats, 121 did so, and another 37 Democrats voted 90 percent against the ACA line.

These results have led to charges that the ACA ratings reveal a "heavily partisan bias"—words used by Democratic Senator Gale McGee of Wyoming in a Senate speech on October 4, 1962.

What did ACA expect of a senator, for instance, to justify a high rating? In the two years, 1960-61, Senator McGee declared, it expected him to vote against a majority of the upper house in twenty-seven out of thirty-one roll calls selected by ACA. Included were five votes on foreign aid (ACA wanting to restrict such aid in every case), four votes on extension of the minimum wage (ACA insisting on an opposition vote in each instance), and three votes on area redevelopment and manpower training (ACA requiring an opposition vote each time). There were two votes on the agricultural feed grain program (ACA against it), a vote on a housing bill (with ACA opposed), and a vote on Federal aid to education (again with ACA opposed).

It was the same in the lower House. McGee said ACA required a representative to vote against the majority seventeen out of twenty-two times on votes the ACA selected. There were two votes each on foreign aid, area redevelopment, housing, and pollution control —with ACA opposed to the program in every case. Other votes requiring opposition by a member to win ACA approval were on aid to education, the feed grain program, and extension of the minimum wage.

In 1961, ACA launched a program of Service Awards to congressmen of whose voting records it approved. The awards announced in May, 1961, named 136 members of Congress—22 senators and 114 representatives—as worthy of honor. All were Republicans except 12 who were southern Democrats. In May, 1963, ACA cited 154 members for their efforts to preserve "the integrity of our Constitution." Of the 154, 129 were Republicans.

That the ACA awards were not necessarily viewed as a badge of honor was, perhaps, indicated by the fact that not all of the senators and representatives selected were eager to accept them. In 1961, Republican Senator Thruston Morton of Kentucky and Democratic Senator Frank J. Lausche of Ohio, a special ACA favorite, declined to accept. So did six members of the lower House, all Republicans. In 1963, seven members of Congress declined, one of them Lausche.

By the time the ACA made public its 1963 awards, it had become controversial. On May 20, 1963, Representative Ronald Cameron of California took to the floor to urge his colleagues who had been chosen not to accept the awards. Cameron charged that ACA was "attempting to clothe itself and the John Birch Society with an aura of respectability to which it is not entitled." He said it was "one thing for a Congressman to get a medal for being a conservative, but it is quite another thing to be decorated by a reactionary Right Wing extremist group for its own ulterior motives."

Representative Chet Holifield, another California Democrat, told the House that its own leadership had been rated near zero by ACA. He noted also that several members of the House Committee on Un-American Activities averaged a rating of only 35.5 percent out of ACA's possible 100 percent.

A few days later, several Republican House members rose to the defense of ACA. Representative Bruce Alger of Texas identified himself "rather proudly" with ACA principles, which he listed as a belief in free enterprise, sound money, private ownership of property, local instead of Federal control, and national sovereignty instead of "One Worldism."

Representative Wayne Hays, Democrat of Ohio, went to the heart of the matter. He charged that ACA lists votes of which it disapproves as votes "against the Constitution," and he added angrily he didn't mind a group saying a member voted against what it believed, but "who decides that a vote is against the Constitution?"

Nevertheless, the Right Wing congressional ratings get a wide distribution. In 1963, ACA reported:

"The 1960 ACA-Index was published and sold by Human Events, Inc., for $15 a copy. Over 3,000 copies were sold and used in the 1960 elections. The ACA-Index, because of its role in the 1960 election, achieved national prominence and is now generally recognized as a valuable campaign tool. . . . The 1961 ACA-Index was published and distributed free of charge by ACA. Twelve thousand copies were placed throughout the country.

"Fifteen thousand copies of the 1962 ACA-Index were distributed in the 1962 campaign. This edition was also distributed without charge.

"Permission was granted to candidates to reproduce sections of Index for use as campaign material. In addition, the news media and cooperating groups were permitted to print the ACA scores in their publications."

The *ACA-Index* on congressional patriotism was seized upon by Radical Right organizations which reprinted the findings and used them in political campaigns. ACA reports were, for instance, reprinted in H. L. Hunt's "Life Lines." They were also widely distributed, incidentally, by the United States Chamber of Commerce.

ACA is hard to please. In 1960, when the late President Kennedy and Lyndon B. Johnson were battling Richard Nixon and Henry Cabot Lodge, Admiral Moreell declared that it would be "sad indeed for America" if the platform of either party were enacted into law.

This was understandable, in view of the Admiral's repeated public declarations that only complete elimination of "the existing socialistic virus from our body politic" would save the country. In February, 1960, for instance, he said that we had permitted the citadel of freedom "to be eroded and its foundations weakened to the point where we are in grave danger of losing the entire edifice." The Admiral declared that "we are subjected to compulsory participation in Social Security, mandatory wage rates, compulsory membership in labor organizations, fixed rent controls, restrictions on choice of tenants and purchasers of one's property." To combat this situation, he went on, requires bold action. The nation would have to "refrain from passing more socialistic laws" and would have to undertake the "progressive repeal of the socialistic laws now on our books." Finally, Moreell said the nation would have to "return as many [powers] as possible to the individual states."

There is, in these statements by Moreell—and in ACA declarations generally—a tone and content that is more than faintly reminiscent of the propaganda of the old American Liberty League, formed thirty years ago as the first wave of reaction against the Roosevelt New Deal. The furious activity of the Liberty League as the 1936 Presidential election approached was described by historian Arthur Schlesinger, Jr., (in *The Politics of Upheaval,* the third volume of his overall study on *The Age of Roosevelt*). Of the Liberty League's activity in 1935, Schlesinger wrote:

"It spent twice as much money that year as the Republican Party. Its pamphlets, lavishly printed and widely circulated, depicted the United States on the verge of socialism, bankruptcy and tyranny. Hardly any New Deal policy escaped the League's disapproval. AAA was a 'trend toward Fascist control of agriculture'; the Holding Company Act, 'a blow at invested capital'; The Guffey Act, 'a step toward further aggrandizement of an ever spending government bureaucracy'; relief and social security were 'the end of democracy.' . . . The New Deal was at once infinitely clever and infinitely incompetent."

Schlesinger noted that among the wealthy contributors to activities of the American Liberty League was "Pew of Sun Oil"—the same J. Howard Pew who today supports ACA and other Rightist organizations.

In the 1962 congressional elections, ACA hired eighteen experienced campaign workers and publicity men and sent them into congressional districts to help candidates pledged to work for ACA objectives. When money was needed, ACA laid out the cash to pay for hiring help and printing campaign material. The eighteen men worked as undercover agents, Moreell explained frankly, because if their identities and activities were to become public it "might jeopardize the candidates" themselves. These professional political relations experts were sent into sixteen states to help forty-six Conservatives, eleven of whom were running for the Senate and thirty-five for the House. Not until 1963 did ACA finally disclose the states where these secret agents had been active.

In addition to this aid, ACA also gave "supplemental assistance" to 147 other candidates by assisting them with research, writing news releases, and making its help generally available in campaign efforts.

In announcing the help ACA was furnishing to Rightist candi-

dates in the 1962 election campaigns and the reasons for keeping
their identities secret, Admiral Moreell explained, according to *The
New York Times* of October 22, 1962, that ACA had been linked
unfairly in the press with the John Birch Society. The *Times* article
reported that ACA had endorsed, in all, 19 senatorial and 154
House candidates, including the four known members of the John
Birch Society who were candidates.

The Admiral did not explain why ACA had endorsed the four
avowed Welchites, nor did he seek to refute charges, made a few
weeks earlier by Senator McGee in his Senate speech, about the
Birch ties of ACA vice-chairman Bonner Fellers, ACA treasurer
Charles Edison, and some of ACA's more generous and consistent
supporters.

In addition to the Birchers who received ACA's stamp of approval in 1962, some of the candidates directly supported or
endorsed by ACA were just as far Right as the card-carrying
Birchers themselves. It would be difficult, indeed, to make any
valid ideological distinctions between Birchers such as Rousselot
and Hiestand (who were defeated) and such successful candidates
as Representatives James Utt of California, John R. Pillion of New
York, Bruce Alger of Texas, Donald Bruce of Indiana, August
Johansen of Michigan, and a number of others plainly far, far
Right in their political thinking.

ACA spent some $125,000 on the 1962 congressional campaigns.
When the results were in, ACA claimed that 135 of the 184 candidates who had its active support or endorsement had been elected.
Of these, 128 (74 percent) were elected to the House and comprise
some 27 percent of the lower chamber. Moreover, ACA rejoiced,
85 of the 88 House incumbents with an *ACA-Index* rating of 80
percent or better were re-elected.

ACA announced that it was satisfied by the results of its 1962
push and that it would broaden its activities in the 1964 congressional elections. It declared in a news release that "we are mounting all our resources to broaden this fight and probably will wage
campaigns in the 1964 general elections in states not hitherto
entered. . . ." Its purpose in doing so, ACA said, was "to encourage
others to join many millions of voters who unquestionably crossed
party lines in 1962 to vote for Conservative candidates."

The law requires that the name and address of every person contributing $100 or more to a political action group be reported and
available for public inspection. As ACA's finance chairman, Robert
Snowden in 1959 distributed a brochure to potential contributors

who were asked to limit their contributions to $99.99 and thus avoid being listed. This plan did not work out and contributions were subsequently accepted by ACA up to the maximum allowed by Federal statute.

ACA did not get the half million dollars it asked for to launch its major activities almost six years ago, but it has done very well with much less. In its solicitations for money, ACA has pointed out that a $3,000 contribution can be made without paying a gift tax. The organization had begun life with only a token sum, but when its plans for the 1960 elections were announced in 1959 it received more than $197,000, and in the campaign year itself it received another $126,000—a war chest of $323,000—almost a third of a million dollars. In 1961, an off year, receipts dropped to $61,000.

For the 1962 campaign year and its drive to elect Rightists to Congress ACA collected about $145,000.

ACA top contributors include names well known in the business and professional world, some of whom contribute to other Right Wing causes. In the period since January, 1962, some of the biggest contributors to ACA included Mr. and Mrs. DeWitt Wallace, publishers of the *Reader's Digest*, who gave more than $5,000; Mrs. Seth Milliken, an Endorser of the John Birch Society, who sent along $5,000; General Robert E. Wood, who gave more than $3,000; J. Howard Pew, the Sun Oil Company millionaire, who gave $3,000 (as did three other members of the Pew family for a combined total of $12,000); Donaldson Brown, former vice-chairman of the board of General Motors, and his wife, who combined for $2,000, and Walter Harnischfeger of Milwaukee, a heavy machinery industrialist, who gave $1,200.

Others who have generously supported ACA include Bernard Peyton, the former president and chairman of the board of New York Air Brake Company; T. J. Coolidge, former chairman of the United Fruit Company; Lemuel R. Boulware, a former vice-president of General Electric; John S. Lehmann, chairman of the board of the Petrolite Corporation; John Airey, former president and chairman of the board of the King-Seeley Corporation and a former director of the National Association of Manufacturers; Robert W. Johnson of Johnson and Johnson; Max McGraw, chairman of the executive committee of the McGraw-Edison Company, and many others.

Is this highly financed political party-line organization merely a respectable reactionary group? In his October, 1962, speech pointing to the interlocking relationships between ACA and its close allies—*Human Events* on the one hand, and the John Birch Society and other Radical Right organizations on the other—Senator Gale McGee gave his answer to that question:

". . . in the extensive discussions of the right wing which have taken place since the discovery of Mr. Welch and the John Birch Society, a great deal of effort has gone into attempts to draw a line of delineation between so-called responsible conservatism and the extremists, by which is usually meant Mr. Welch—if not his society. . . . Perhaps the facts which I have set forth regarding Human Events and Americans for Constitutional Action will serve to contribute some light to this discussion. Often regarded as responsible conservatism, these two organizations certainly are located at the point on the spectrum at which the so-called responsibles and the so-called extremists tend to come together. I submit . . . that on the basis of the foregoing report it is a fair conclusion that, in terms of basic philosophy, major objectives and active leadership, the balance of power at ACA and Human Events rests on the extremist side."

And it is to *Human Events*, an influential and growing organ of the American Right, and handmaiden of ACA, that we now turn.

13

Human Events
— James L. Wick

In February, 1944, General Robert E. Wood gave a luncheon in Chicago to which he invited six influential men who had been active with him in the isolationist America First Committee which flourished in the months preceding Pearl Harbor.

Present were Colonel Charles A. Lindbergh; the late Sterling Morton, salt company executive; the late Colonel Robert R. McCormick, publisher of *The Chicago Tribune*; W. H. Regnery, Sr., book publisher; General Thomas Hammond, manufacturer; and Clay Judson, a prominent Chicago attorney.

Present also was the late Frank C. Hanighen, a writer, editor, and author of muckraking books in the 1930's, including *The Secret War*, which dealt with the international oil industry, and *The Merchants of Death,* of which he was co-author and which was an exposé of the munitions industry.

Hanighen had an idea for which he needed backing and the luncheon was arranged by Wood to give him a hearing. The writer wanted to issue a four-page newsletter from Washington, D. C., which would give thumbnail reports on national events to a select list of subscribers who would thus be kept up-to-date on what was going on in the national capital and alerted to protect their personal and business interests. Everyone liked the proposed title for the newsletter—*Human Events*, taken from the Declaration of Independence, which begins, "When in the Course of human events. . . ."

Each of the six guests paid in advance for subscriptions to be sent to a list of 127 persons who thereby became charter subscribers to *Human Events*.

From this modest beginning, with a capital outlay of $500 in subscription money, *Human Events* has grown steadily in size, circulation, and influence. Today it is a sixteen-page, tabloid-size weekly newspaper widely read by politicians, educators, clergymen, and other opinion molders both in Washington, D.C., and around the country. Its circulation is over 100,000 and its annual gross sales are more than $1,000,000. The publication claims—and there is no reason to question it—that its readers include not only business, professional, and political leaders in the United States, but the personnel of foreign embassies as well.

Human Events is, perhaps, one of the most important Rightist publications in the United States, serving as a kind of ideological cement that keeps the American Right in touch with itself and with the activities of the "Liberal Establishment," against which it wages unceasing propaganda warfare. In this adhesive role, *Human Events* is supported by both the Radical Right and the Extreme Conservatives, and in turn it supports both the Radicals and the Extreme Conservatives with an impartiality and lack of discrimination which belies its claim to true conservatism. It is, as Senator Gale McGee said in his October 4, 1962, speech in the Senate, "located at the point on the spectrum at which the so-called responsibles and the so-called extremists" of the American Right "tend to come together. . . ."

That *Human Events* would reflect the interest of today's Radical Right as well as that of its conservative fellow travelers may well have been indicated from the start, not only from the names of those who attended General Wood's 1944 Chicago luncheon, but from the names of those for whom they purchased charter subscriptions to Hanighen's newsletter. General Wood himself was and has been identified with many of the major Far Right causes of the last quarter century. And included among the 127 charter subscribers to *Human Events* were the following Rightists, listed with some of the current Rightist organizations to which their names have been linked:

—Former Governor of New Jersey Charles Edison (Americans

for Constutional Action, John Birch Society, Manion Forum).
—W. J. Grede (Americans for Constitutional Action, Citizens Foreign Aid Committee, John Birch Society, Manion Forum).
—Walter Harnischfeger (Americans for Constitutional Action, Citizens Foreign Aid Committee, Manion Forum, National Economic Council).
—H. L. Hunt (Life Line).
—J. Howard Pew (Citizens Foreign Aid Committee, Americans for Constitutional Action, Foundation for Economic Education, Christian Freedom Foundation, John Birch Society).
—Admiral Ben Moreell (Americans for Constitutional Action).
—A. G. Heinsohn, Jr., (John Birch Society, Manion Forum, National Economic Council).
—E. L. Wiegand (John Birch Society, Manion Forum, Americans for Constitutional Action, National Economic Council).
—Frank deGanahl (John Birch Society).

Although in its appeals for contributions and for lifetime subscriptions (at $150), *Human Events* pictures itself as one of the "ideological publications" which is "non-subsidized," the fact is that in recent years it was the recipient of consistent subventions from an organization called the National Foundation for Education in American Citizenship, which, until a few years ago, enjoyed Federal tax-exempt status. This NFEAC support is a classic example of how tax-exempt money can legally be funneled into support for a commercial venture which is engaged in political propaganda on the American Right Wing.

The NFEAC was established in Indiana in 1940. As with so many groups of its kind, its announced objectives were admirable: "To make better known the American way of life among adults, college, high school, and elementary school children by grants to writers of books, pamphlets and addresses dealing with the American theme. . . ."

The Federal Government and the state of Indiana require that tax-exempt organizations file annual reports on their income and expenditures. Not all such reports of the NFEAC are available, either because the reports were not filed or were filed and lost. Such records as are available indicate that in 1951 and 1952, NFEAC gave $5,800 each year—and in 1953, about $11,000—to *Human Events,* then a struggling Washington newsletter.

In 1957 or 1958, however, the NFEAC began pumping money into *Human Events* operations at the rate of anywhere from $38,000 to $60,000 or more a year. Whether one uses reports filed with the state of Indiana, which indicate contributions of $330,000 by NFEAC to *Human Events*, or Federal reports, which indicate a lesser amount, it is clear that over a period of years, NFEAC poured several hundred thousand dollars into the publication. In the years 1958 to 1962, it appears that *Human Events* received somewhere between 95 percent and 98 percent of the funds disbursed by the Foundation.

In 1962, the Internal Revenue Service revoked the NFEAC's tax-exempt status.

Whether the funds made available to *Human Events* by the NFEAC in the late 1950's and early 1960's had anything to do with the sensational growth of its circulation is not clear, but in 1961 the publication's circulation and sales figures began to skyrocket. In 1954, its circulation was 9,063. By 1961, when the American Radical Right burst forth with mushroomlike effect on the American scene, *Human Events* circulation had climbed to 85,000, and in 1963, it had boomed to about 100,000. Gross sales, which were only $81,000 in 1954, had reached the $1,000,000 mark by 1962.

Human Events has demonstrated that it has a legitimate claim as perhaps the most durable and among the most influential publications on the American Right. Its growth is further indicated by the fact that it started as a four-page newsletter in 1944 and expanded to the point in the early 1960's when a normal issue averaged four or five sections of two or four pages each. Early in 1963, shooting for further circulation, it was converted to a tabloid-size-newspaper format of sixteen well-edited and attractively produced pages, complete with color, and available on newsstands for the first time.

When Frank Hanighen died in January, 1964, at the age of sixty-four, supporters of *Human Events* moved at once to form a Frank Hanighen Memorial Fund, to continue his publication as a living memorial to the man who had started it. The Hanighen Memorial Fund Raising Committee membership is, perhaps, as revealing and indicative of how, on the American Right today, the Extreme Conservative and the wild Radical Rightist make common cause, and how the line of demarcation between them is blurred or even completely invisible.

The Memorial Committee is heavily larded with Birchers. Eleven men whose names have graced the national council of the John Birch Society were listed on the Hanighen Memorial Fund Raising Committee. Perhaps another dozen have been listed as Endorsers of the Birch Society. Two others have served on the editorial advisory committee of Welch's *American Opinion* magazine. And still others were publicly identified as members of the Society, if not among its higher echelons. Of approximately 125 names listed as members of the Hanighen Memorial Fund Raising Committee, about 20 percent were linked, in one way or another, to the John Birch Society.

Human Events and the Birch Society were linked by bonds of affection and mutual respect back in the early days of the Society— in fact, from the start. The ties were so close that for three or four years, bulk subscriptions to *Human Events* and Welch's *American Opinion* magazine were offered by the two organizations at reduced prices.

Welch himself explained that he and the people at *Human Events* believed their publications went well together.

"I think that both Human Events and American Opinion, which complement each other very well, should be put in barbershops . . . just as fast and extensively as we could find the money. Incidentally, Human Events not only feels also that we complement each other well, but for this reason is willing to join us in offering bulk subscriptions to the two periodicals together at a reduced price."

The joint subscription offer was terminated early in 1962. The break did not stem from any sudden realization by *Human Events* that it was linked to the extremism of Welch, the Birch Society, or its spokesmen. Mounting costs, not ideology, had finally put the marriage on the rocks. Welch explained it to the faithful in the Birch Bulletin for January, 1962: Costs had skyrocketed and "neither of us can afford the combination subscription any longer. . . ."

The point is that *Human Events*, which is generally regarded as conservative and which has enjoyed widespread acceptance by respectable and responsible Americans of conservative persuasion, has engaged in flagrant fellow-traveling with the main organization on the Radical Right today.

When early in 1961 a national outcry of protest and indignation over the Birch Society swept the country, following disclosure that Welch had branded President Eisenhower and other American leaders as dupes or agents of communism, *Human Events* was quick to leap to the defense.

In one issue, *Human Events* reported that "many on Capitol Hill appear interested as to why, just now, a profuse press campaign has been let loose on the John Birch Society and its founder, Robert Welch." Citing "observers," *Human Events* said they were asking whether the attack on the Birchers might not be "part of a 'diversionary' movement to take the heat off the Administration?"

Human Events has an odd history of leaping to the defense of Right Wing Extremists—and even those on the anti-Semitic fringe. In 1950, when a subcommittee of the United States House of Representatives on lobbying investigated the activities of Merwin K. Hart's National Economic Council and Joseph P. Kamp's Constitutional Educational League, the June 21 issue of *Human Events* published an attack on the House subcommittee for its investigation of Hart, and of Kamp, whose writings over the years have often been marked by ill-concealed anti-Semitic innuendoes.* Later that year, *Human Events* deplored the jailing of Kamp for contempt of Congress, and early in 1951, it shed bitter tears over the fact that the late Upton Close, an extreme Rightist radio commentator and a virulent anti-Semite,† had lost his broadcasting time.

In 1962, as the elections approached, *Human Events* supported Representative Edgar Hiestand, an avowed member of the Birch Society, who was seeking renomination in the California primaries. Two weeks later, *Human Events* reported that "despite contrary reports in the eastern press, the John Birchers made an impressive showing in the [California] campaign." The Rightist publication rejoiced that "two Birch Society members, Representatives John Rousselot and Edgar Hiestand, were renominated handily on the GOP ticket. Another Bircher, H. L. Richardson, swept the GOP primary for congressman in the newly carved 29th District. Max Rafferty, considered a Birch sympathizer, led the field for the state-wide office of Superintendent of Public Instruction."

A month later, as November loomed, *Human Events* published a special article favorable to Birch candidate Richardson.

When the United States Supreme Court, in June, 1962, handed down its decision barring prayers in public schools, *Human Events* printed a statement by a school-board member from Long Island, New York, who declared: "It looks like Robert Welch of the John Birch Society had the right idea in asking for the impeachment of the Supreme Court." (Welch in fact agitated for the impeachment of the Chief Justice only.)

There is some question in the minds of many as to who is more radical on the subject—Welch, who seeks the impeachment of the Chief Justice, or *Human Events,* which supports a Constitutional amendment that would alter the American form of government established by the Founding Fathers. *Human Events* called on its

---

* See *A Measure of Freedom* and *The Troublemakers.*
† *Ibid.*

readers to urge members of their state legislatures to support amendments which would curb the powers of the Supreme Court as established by the Constitution. One of the proposals would establish a so-called "Court of the Union," composed of the Chief Justices of each of the fifty state supreme courts. The Court of the Union would have the power to overrule decisions of the United States Supreme Court.

Human Events has carried frequent approving mentions of *Nine Men Against America*, a book attacking the Supreme Court by Rosalie Gordon, an official of America's Future, Inc. The Washington publication has, moreover, carried such articles as "Not The Supreme Law of the Land" by Samuel Pettengill, a familiar name in extreme circles for years.

When in 1963 *Human Events* shifted from newsletter format to tabloid size, with newsstand distribution, its pages were thrown open to advertisers. It was no surprise that, as an ideological mouthpiece of the Extreme Conservatives, it was not deluged with orders from major advertisers.

The identity of those who have advertised is worth noting—for example: Grede Foundries, Rock Island Oil and Refining Company, and Spindale and Cherokee Mills, all of which are owned or controlled by members of the John Birch Society's national council. Other ads come from Knott's Berry Farm in California, which is owned by Walter B. Knott, a frequent name on Right Wing sponsorship lists, and Stockham Valves and Fittings in Birmingham, Alabama, a family-owned enterprise whose principals contribute to various Rightist causes both as individuals and through the Stockham Foundation.

Articles by Birchers also appear in *Human Events*. A frequent contributor is Professor Hans Sennholz, an ex-Luftwaffe pilot who heads the Economics Department at Grove City (Pennsylvania) College—an institution heavily endowed by the Pew family. Sennholz is listed as a contributing editor of Welch's *American Opinion* magazine, where his extreme *laissez-faire* economic viewpoints frequently appear. *Human Events* also has reprinted material from *Farm and Ranch* magazine, which until 1963 was published by Tom Anderson, a member of the Birch Society's national council. It also has carried ads for the recording of a speech by Anderson called "Bi-Partisan Treason."

The ties of *Human Events* to other publications and organizations of the American Right extend in all directions. It has given prominent mention in its columns to statements and activities of such groups as the Citizens Foreign Aid Committee, the Manion

Forum, Young Americans for Freedom, the Intercollegiate Society of Individualists—not to mention its close ties to Americans for Constitutional Action. (Former ACA Executive Director Kenneth Ingwalson is now publisher of *Human Events*.)

Human Events absorbed the subscriptions of H. L. Hunt's "Facts Forum News" when Hunt decided to fold up Facts Forum; and a little later, when the Texas oil billionaire launched Life Line Foundation, Life Line officers were for a time located in a rented section of the Human Events building.

In part, the links between *Human Events* and other organizations of the Right stem from Hanighen's own activities as a Rightist. The late editor had been (in 1955-56) on the national advisory council of the Campaign for the 48 States, the now-defunct organization headed by Robert Snowden of Memphis, which had been the predecessor of ACA. Hanighen also was an incorporator of the Intercollegiate Society of Individualists, a Rightist youth group somewhat more intellectual than Young Americans for Freedom. In the mid-1950's Hanighen contributed a column on Washington affairs to *The Freeman,* monthly publication of the conservative Foundation for Economic Education, and various articles to *Christian Economics*, biweekly publication of the Christian Freedom Foundation, once described as "an organization of the far right devoted to rallying ministerial support for 'libertarianism.' "

Contributing editors Frank Chodorov and Edna Lonigan, old-time names on the American Right, have also helped link *Human Events* to other elements of the movement.

Chodorov was founder and president of the Intercollegiate Society of Individualists, served on the national policy committee of For America and on the national advisory council of the Campaign for the 48 States. Miss Lonigan is a researcher and teacher whose articles have appeared at one time or another over the years in most Rightist-oriented publications. Like Chodorov, she was for a time book reviewer for the late Merwin K. Hart's *Economic Council Letter* supplement, "Review of Books." More recently, she has been listed as a member of the national advisory committee of Billy James Hargis' Crusade.

It would be possible to cite endless examples of the Radical Right thinking that pervades *Human Events*, as it wages never-ending propaganda warfare against Federal aid programs of all kinds, foreign and domestic—against urban renewal and public housing, against public schools (as we shall explain later) and so-called "progressive education," against Federal income taxation, against Medicare under social security, against revision of immigration laws based on national origin quotas, against labor unions, against the United Nations, and against "liberalism" in general, whether of the Roosevelt-Truman-Kennedy kind, or of the Eisenhower "modern Republicanism" variety.

Human Events favors the kind of drastic uprooting of established Federal activity endlessly promoted by the inhabitants of the most extreme Right—not only the curtailment of Federal activities but their return to the area of private enterprise operation. Even our schools, say articles in *Human Events*, should be returned to private enterprise competition.

The chief advocate of placing public and private schools in competition with each other is Frank Chodorov, for some years an associate editor of *Human Events*. His writings during the 1950's (when he merged his own publication, *Analysis,* with Hanighen's) urged that the education of American children be put on a free-enterprise, competitive business basis through a plan of Government tax rebates to the parents of children attending private schools in amounts equivalent to the tuition fees.

In the June 16, 1954, issue of *Human Events*, Chodorov, who held to the view that the only thing a government does is confiscate private property, wrote: "All the legitimate functions of the national government could be carried on . . . in a good sized kitchen."

Another 1954 issue of *Human Events*, that of March 10, declared that "we will never have efficiency in the service of delivering mail . . . until the Post Office is turned over to private enterprise."

The flavor of radical thinking can be seen in many articles in *Human Events*, as the following quotations may indicate:

—"Social security and the health of the aged will stay political footballs. They will tend to socialize the minds of the people and condition us mentally and materially for more socialism." (January, 1962)

—"The plain fact is that the welfare state is destroying the character of a large portion of the American people. . . . The only way to relieve suffering and provide for the unfortunate . . . is voluntary Christian charity." (April, 1962)

—"The Roosevelt Administration, wittingly or unwittingly, followed the Soviet line and Harry Dexter White, an important and trusted official in the Administration drafted a note to Japan that produced the war for which Roosevelt had long been looking." (December, 1960)

—"Indeed, a [balance of] payments crisis may afford the occasion to the Kennedy Administration to usher in socialism." (December, 1960)

—"Today the Reds and Pinks are out in the open proclaiming their godless religion and waving a red flag or a mongrel one from the rooftops, and with such effectiveness and in such high places, that American patriots are now on the defensive." (June, 1961)

Human Events is not always on the defensive, however. Its relationships with the Radical Right are further underscored by the twice-a-year Political Action Conferences which it sponsors in Washington—usually in January at the start of a congressional session, and again in July when sessions are supposed to be at the windup stage. The fee is $75, with a cut rate of $45 for students, teachers, clergymen, and members of Rightist youth groups with which *Human Events* co-operates.

These conferences have grown in attendance since January, 1961, when the first one was held, and they have offered a sounding board for Rightist members of Congress. Republican Representatives Edgar Hiestand and John Rousselot (Birchers of California) attended the first conference. Rousselot was again present at the fourth conference in July, 1962, as were Tom Anderson and Colonel Laurence E. Bunker of the Birch Society's national council, James D. Bales of Harding College, Kent and Phoebe Courtney, and Ward Poag, a former co-ordinator for the Birch Society who became field organizer for the Courtneys' CSA.

Also present were Charles Winegarner, nephew of Gerald Smith and a staff member of Smith's rabidly anti-Semitic *The Cross and The Flag*, and Dr. Hugh S. Ramsey, a Bloomington, Indiana, physician who contributes to Smith and supports causes of the Far Right.

Pro-Birch feeling at this fourth conference ran high, and when H. L. Richardson of California, then running for Congress, expressed the belief that he would be the third Bircher to sit in the House, his statement prompted wild applause and shouts of approval from his audience. Present at the Fifth Human Events Conference, in January, 1963, were W. J. Grede and A. G. Heinsohn, Jr., of the Birch Society's national council, as well as council member T. Coleman Andrews (former U. S. Commissioner of Internal Revenue and third party candidate for President in 1956), and former Major General Edwin A. Walker.

The Human Events conferences, however, reveal much more than the mere fact that *Human Events* and the Birchers seem to share the same political paddock from time to time. They serve as a gathering place for Republican Far Rightists and Southern

Democratic Far Rightists. Senators who have appeared frequently are Barry Goldwater of Arizona, John Tower of Texas, and Strom Thurmond of South Carolina. At the third conference, in January, 1962, the Republican Party National Chairman, Representative William Miller of New York, used the Human Events platform for what was described as a "searing" attack on the Kennedy Administration's domestic and foreign policies. He urged his listeners to do everything possible to elect opponents of "socialized welfare programs." Among such measures, Miller listed Federal aid to education and the financing of medical care for the aged through social security.

At the fourth conference in July, 1962, Senator Barry Goldwater, who received a standing ovation at the start and finish of his speech, charged that the New Frontier sought "control over our daily lives and over our business lives," and declared that the division between those who favored a "superstate" and those who opposed it had become clear. He branded Liberals and Radicals, but urged party regularity and support by Republicans of such party Liberals as Senator Jacob Javits of New York—advice which received a very cool reception from his audience. (An even cooler reception greeted Republican Representative Louis Wyman of New Hampshire at the fifth conference when he declared: "If Nelson Rockefeller should be the party's choice, some will be disappointed. If Barry Goldwater is the choice, others will be disappointed. But no matter what the choice is, when it is finally made we must close ranks and unitedly support our nominee." That's when the booing started.)

The Sixth Human Events Political Action Conference, held in July, 1963, had a quality all its own. It was opened with a series of anti-Communist films and cartoons produced by the National Education Program, Dr. Benson's Radical Right propaganda mill at Harding College. But the conference highlight was the participation of 150 members of Young Americans for Freedom, the Rightist youth organization. Many of them acted as moderators and took part in panel discussions. Among these young participants were Lee Edwards, editor of YAF's *New Guard,* son of *Chicago Tribune* reporter Willard Edwards, and later a Goldwater campaign staff man; Robert Bauman, President of YAF, and his wife Carol, a leading YAF activist in the District of Columbia; Fulton Lewis III; and Marilyn Manion, daughter of Dean Clarence Manion. The speakers, Senators Goldwater and Thurmond, received enthusiastic receptions from the fledgling Right-Wingers.

Human Events has actually served as a training school for some of YAF's key leadership. A Human Events journalism school was established in 1957 to train young Conservatives. This was done in co-operation with the Intercollegiate Society of Individualists. The first class at the journalism school included Douglas Caddy, who later became executive director of YAF; David Franke, who became an assistant to William Buckley at the *National Review*; and William Schulz, later an assistant to radio broadcaster Fulton Lewis, Jr.

Part of the *Human Events* staff is shared with the YAF magazine, *New Guard*. *Human Events* Capitol Hill editor Allan H. Ryskind, and former *Human Events* editorial assistant Garry Russell have been listed as contributing editors of *New Guard*.

One of the more distinguished "alumni" of the *Human Events* staff is M. Stanton Evans, a young and able man who went on to become editor of the *Indianapolis News*. A much sought-after speaker at Rightist gatherings, Evans is an author who, in collaboration with fellow-alumni William Schulz and Allan Ryskind, wrote *The Fringe on Top*. According to *Human Events*, the book, which appeared in 1962, exposed the "left-wing extremist advisers surrounding the President"—meaning the late President John F. Kennedy.

When Hanighen died in 1964, his long-time associate, James L. Wick, replaced him at the helm of *Human Events*. Wick had become associated with the publication ten years earlier, when Hanighen's doctors warned that his heart was a question mark; Hanighen then invited Wick to step aboard and become his eventual successor. The succession was smoothly accomplished in January, 1964.

Wick is a veteran editor and author, now in his middle sixties. He had been editor of the Prentice-Hall newsletter called "What's Happening in Washington," and general manager of *The Freeman*. Wick also had worked in two Republican Party Presidential campaigns—the Willkie campaign in 1940, in which he was a national defense specialist for the GOP National Committee, and the 1944 Dewey campaign, in which he served as a research specialist on the New York governor's campaign staff. (Wick later expressed his dissatisfaction with the conduct of those campaigns in a book called *How Not to Run for President*, published in 1952. In it, Wick voiced the now-familiar complaint of the Right Wing—that too much "me-tooism" by Willkie and Dewey had alienated the conservative core of Republican voters.)

In 1959, Wick became president of Human Events, Inc., which remains his present title.

Today, *Human Events* functions as a potent, vital propaganda arm for the forces in our political life which would joyfully repeal much of American history since 1933. It fields a powerful arsenal of propaganda weapons: its own pages, which supply propaganda material to the forces of Reaction; its twice-yearly Political Action Conferences, providing a propaganda sounding board for the Right people and serving as a training school for youth; its weekly tape-recorded interviews with Rightist members of Congress, which are offered as pre-packaged fifteen-minute programs to local radio stations at less than $10 a recording, and which in a recent one-year period featured forty-six Republicans and six Southern Democrats of Rightist persuasion; its reprints of articles, which form the basis for a massive program of political "pamphleteering"; and its publication of the various ACA congressional voting indices.

The titles of some of the *Human Events* reprints, which have been circulated in the millions, are revealing, as are some of the authors:

"Abolish the Income Tax," by T. Coleman Andrews; "Why the Income Tax Must Go: Questions I've Been Asked," by Corinne Griffith; "The Income Tax is Making Us a Dishonest People," by J. Bracken Lee (Mayor of Salt Lake City and a Birch Society Endorser); "The Web of Warren," written by Hanighen himself; "Supreme Court vs. Bill of Rights," by Frank Chodorov; "Corruption Unlimited: Urban Renewal," by James Wick; "One Man's Fight Against 'Fair Housing,' " by Robert Dresser (a Rhode Island lawyer, a Birch Endorser, and a familiar supporter of Rightist causes); and "The Truth About 'Operation Abolition,' " by Representative Rousselot.

Shrill attacks by *Human Events* on all the administrations of recent years, whether Democrat or Republican, reflect the frustration that has pervaded the American Far Right from repeated rejection by the electorate. Since 1952, *Human Events* has sought to bring about a Rightist coalition of Extreme Conservatives and radicals composed of Republicans and Southern Democrats that could be translated into political victory at the polls.

When the late Senator Taft, whom it supported, lost the GOP nomination to General Eisenhower in 1952, *Human Events* began almost at once its harsh criticism of the new Eisenhower Administration. At the same time, searching for a successor to Taft as leader of the American Right, the magazine began to support the establishment of Knowland for President clubs in an effort to push that conservative California senator into the White House. Knowland's views on foreign affairs and his advocacy of right-to-work labor laws conformed sufficiently to the positions taken by *Human Events* itself, and throughout 1957 the editors confidently predicted that the senator would have no trouble winning the governorship of California—a step from the White House in 1960.

Knowland lost the gubernatorial race to Governor Pat Brown, and Vice-President Nixon emerged as the leading GOP hopeful for 1960. *Human Events* coupled support for Mr. Nixon with increasingly open praise for Senator Barry Goldwater.

In the 1960 Presidential campaign, the magazine went all out in its assaults on Senator Kennedy. One flyer, of which more than half a million copies were distributed, bore the title: "Kennedy for President? A Catholic Priest Says 'No.' " The author was Father Juniper B. Carol. The late Senator Estes Kefauver charged that *Human Events*, by publishing it, had engaged in an attack on Senator Kennedy on religious grounds.

Human Events denied the charge, protested that Hanighen himself and two of his four assistant editors at the time were of the Catholic faith. The magazine further charged that the "signal" for the attack on the Father Carol article was a piece that had appeared in *The Worker*, official organ of the Communist Party.

Father Carol himself shed some light on the whole controversy, declaring that the *Human Events* reprint of his article had been edited to omit criticism of Vice-President Nixon. Moreover, the priest disavowed the extensive pre-election distribution of his article.

With the election of Senator Kennedy, *Human Events* swung into a steady stream of criticism directed at the New Frontier, an onslaught epitomized by the assertion that in President Kennedy, the United States had "a smooth talking Chief Executive [who] actually heads a Fabian Socialist Administration." In another article, entitled "Communist Party Calls for Defeat of GOP," published in July, 1963, before the assassination of the President, the same implication was strikingly clear.

On another occasion, *Human Events* reprinted an editorial from the *Chattanooga News-Free Press* which declared that "maybe somewhere along the line, the American people will become sufficiently disgusted with Kennedy failures and subterfuge and dictatorship that they will sweep Washington clean of its destructive influence."

Bircher Hans Sennholz, in articles condemning the "bankruptcy" of the New Frontier in labor-management relations, wrote in *Human Events* that "All New Deal labor laws must be repealed."

Human Events launched an extensive promotion of the anti-

Kennedy book by journalist Victor Lasky entitled *JFK: The Man and the Myth*, which was described as "the book that will defeat Kennedy" in his bid for re-election. Even after the assassination, in December, 1963, January, 1964, and February, 1964, the promotion continued. The ads for the Lasky book on several occasions consumed the entire back page of the Washington weekly tabloid.

Meanwhile, as the 1964 election year approached, *Human Events* went all out to help Senator Goldwater win the Republican nomination for President. Rarely did an issue appear without favorable mention and glowing headlines for the Arizona senator. Hardly a page of any issue did not carry his name. Headlines like "Growing Goldwater Boom," "Goldwater Band Wagon Rolls," "Goldwater Forges Ahead," "Goldwater Boom Expands," "The Polls Smile on Goldwater," and "Everybody 'Wants' Goldwater" suggest the breathless enthusiasm and the intensity of the *Human Events* commitment to the Arizona Conservative.

When the senator, in January, 1964, officially announced that he would seek the nomination, *Human Events* published one of its special supplements to aid the campaign. (Earlier special supplements, published since 1962, devote an entire issue of *Human Events* to one subject: "The Case Against Socialized Medicine," "The Truth About A.D.A.," "The Labor Monopoly," "A Conservative's Guide to Political Action," and "The Case Against Urban Renewal.")

Obviously designed for campaigning purposes, the back page of the Goldwater supplement unabashedly bore the headline "How To Use the Goldwater Portrait Edition To Win Votes. . . . Get This Portrait Edition to Friends, Neighbors, Clergymen, Teachers and Commentators." It suggested that the faithful place the edition on newsstands by forming "newsstand distribution committees," that they "saturate" their neighborhoods, that they reach precinct chairmen and block captains and cover "talk-stimulating centers."

The Goldwater Edition of *Human Events* consisted in large part of a digest of a book published in the spring of 1964 called *Barry Goldwater, Portrait of an Arizonan*, written by Edwin McDowell, an editorial writer for the *Arizona Republic*. The prepublication digest by *Human Events* was dressed up with the usual and appropriate pictures. The candidate embracing his attractive wife. The candidate and his family. As a boy, as a young man, as an aviator, in uniform as a general in the Air Force Reserve, as a hobbyist in photography, as a successful department store executive, as a Westerner with roots in the pioneering tradition. Appropriate pictures with senatorial colleagues of conservative outlook, a smiling portrait

of the late Senator Taft, and a statement by the publisher of a
Negro newspaper who was quoted as saying that the senator had
"done a great deal for Negro integration in Arizona."

Meanwhile, *Human Events* was not neglecting the other side of
the coin. As it assiduously promoted Senator Goldwater's candidacy
for the GOP nomination, it sought also to dent the favorable image
and popularity achieved by President Johnson in his first half year
in office.

As early as December 21, 1963—a bare month after Mr. Johnson was catapulted into the White House by the tragic assassination
—*Human Events* carried a front-page article by conservative columnist Holmes Alexander under the headline "LBJ's First Mistake?" The February 1 issue reprinted a *Chicago Tribune* editorial
under the headline "President Johnson: Blessed Are the Poor;
They'll Elect Me."

The issue of February 15, 1964, carried a column by *Chicago
Tribune* reporter Walter Trohan headlined "The New Status Symbol: 'Skinny Dippin'' With LBJ," which purported to inform the
public of reports that the President was inviting favored guests to
swim in the raw in the White House pool.

On February 22, the regular *Human Events* feature "This Week
in Washington" bore such subheadings as "Secret Diplomacy,"
"Press Cools Toward LBJ," and "LBJ Loves ADA," while another
item spoke of "LBJ's penchant for picking controversial people to
carry out Administration policy. . . ."

On March 7, an article warned that the Administration was
"Out To Buy the Farm Vote." A week later, the top headline on
the front page asserted that "Fear and Weakness Mark U.S. Foreign Policy." Inside, the reader was told that labor leader Walter
Reuther (a favorite whipping boy of *Human Events,* as he is of
the whole American Right) was "Closer to LBJ Than He Was
to JFK."

The April 11 issue carried an ACA ad announcing the avail-
ability of the "Lyndon B. Johnson Special Supplement to the ACA-
Index" which—said the ad—was "considered by experts as one of
the most devastating political documents available to conservatives"
because "It exposes LBJ for what he is." (The same issue carried
a two-page spread defending F. Gano Chance, a member of the
John Birch Society National Council from Centralia, Missouri, who
had been the target of a critical series of articles by the *St. Louis
Post-Dispatch.*)

A front-page cartoon in the April 18 issue was drawn to make
President Johnson resemble the late President Franklin Roosevelt

and bore the caption "Mah Friends. . . ." A front-page article by conservative intellectual leader Russell Kirk declared, in comment on the Johnson anti-poverty program, that "there are worse things than poverty."

And so it went, as the 1964 political pot boiled and the *Human Events* two-pronged propaganda campaign—for Goldwater and against Johnson—mounted in intensity. It was a campaign spearheading a major political push by the American Right—by both the Extreme Conservatives, who saw their opportunity to overturn the thirty-year dominance of the Liberal Establishment, and of the Radical Right, who envisioned the very last chance to "save America" from a Communist take-over. And both camps had as their herald a Washington weekly which often had difficulty in seeing the difference between them.

For what, in sum and substance, is *Human Events?*

It is a Rightist organ which reflects the thinking of the Extreme Conservatives and often that of the Radical Right. As such, it is an example of the ideologoical blur that exists between them— the blur that, often as not, makes it difficult if not impossible to determine where one ends and the other begins.

As has been shown, the magazine was spawned twenty years ago by the Right Wing, and through the years it has remained true to the doctrines of those who gave it birth and whose support has nurtured and nourished it. As it grew out of adolescence, it showed an easy virtue about its political bedfellows, embracing both the Birchers and the white knights of extreme conservatism like Senators Knowland and Goldwater. It carried on with the Birchers and the Goldwaterites, as though the two were the same—and so, for all its size and growth, it has emerged as a Rightist political weapon of uncertain allegiance and loyalty.

But if *Human Events* would clothe itself in the mantle of conservatism, it ought better answer the question of what it seeks to conserve. Certainly anyone reading its pages can readily conclude that it would conserve little of the last thirty years in American political, economic, and social life, in which, so it would seem, it sees small good.

It does not, as has been pointed out, call for the impeachment of Chief Justice Warren, but would alter the Constitution of the Founding Fathers to curb the Supreme Court's jurisdiction. If it does not call for repeal of the income tax, it does publish articles by those who do. If it does not cry treason and betrayal by Washington in the cold war, it does accuse American leaders of softness and accommodation in dealing with Moscow. If it does not charge that Red agents have made domestic policy in Washington for thirty years, it does charge that the United States has embraced un-American socialism.

Human Events is, in short, an influential fellow traveler of the Radical Right—neither responsibly conservative in avoiding extremism, nor quite as far over on the political spectrum as are the Birch Society and the other extremists. It does not dwell with them, but it conducts a continuing dalliance.

14

Intercollegiate Society of Individualists

The Old Guard continues as a force in political life because it has always thought to provide heirs.

Human Events, for example, had been founded by America's Old Guard in 1944. It since has helped to spawn a whole new generation of tadpole Rightists whose mission it is to carry forward into the future the Right Wing revolt against the recent past. This new generation calls itself—as in the title of the magazine of Young Americans for Freedom—the New Guard, but its cry is the cry of the Old Guard from which it has taken its instruction.

The story of the fledgling Rightists really begins with the story of an ailing man now in his seventies.

Frank Chodorov was a firebrand Leftist who swung to the other side of the political spectrum. Born and raised in New York City, he was a youthful street-corner orator when a student at Columbia University. Before World War II exploded, he became disillusioned and swung to the Right and to isolationism. He wrote for *Scribner's Commentator,* the intellectual organ of the America First movement. As the bombs began to fall on Pearl Harbor, the America

First Committee fell apart, and by 1946, after the victory of the Allied forces, Chodorov began expressing his views in a monthly newsletter he called *Analysis*. He had swung so far that he became a board member of the Americans for Justice for Tyler Kent Committee, along with a half-dozen Extremists of the Right who had banded together in support of Kent. (Young Kent had been convicted of passing secret information from the American Embassy in London to the Nazis and had been sentenced to prison.)

Chodorov believed that in his lifetime he had witnessed "the transmutation of the American character from individualist to collectivist," and that the process had actually begun when Jack London, Upton Sinclair, and other writers and intellectuals met on September 12, 1905, in New York's lower Manhattan and formed the Intercollegiate Socialist Society "to awaken an interest in Socialism among the educated men and women of the country." Out of this Society there emerged, in 1921, the League for Industrial Democracy. Through some of its active people—Norman Thomas, Walter Lippmann, Walter Reuther, John Dewey, and Clarence Darrow, to mention only a few—the League for Industrial Democracy attained a status of intellectual and academic respectibility.

In Frank Chodorov's view—expressed in *Human Events* in a now significant 1950 article entitled "For Our Children's Children"—these intellectuals and their disciples had wrought a profound transformation in American thinking in the course of half a century, a transformation which was unthinkable in 1905 when he said the movement really started.

The heart of the matter, he felt, was the planting of "collectivist seed . . . in the soft and fertile student mind forty-odd years ago."

"We are not born with ideas," Chodorov wrote in his *Human Events* article, "we learn them. If Socialism has come to America because it was implanted in the minds of past generations, there is no reason for assuming that the contrary idea cannot be taught to a new generation."

Chodorov's article was the germ of today's Intercollegiate Society of Individualists, which indoctrinates college students in basic concepts of old-fashioned rugged individualism as if they were something fresh and new.

A businessman read the article and sent Chodorov a check for $1,000 to get "freedom" clubs, or something of that sort, started on American campuses. In a visit to the Foundation for Economic Education (FEE), a conservative propaganda organization supported chiefly by big corporations, Chodorov mentioned the $1,000 check. The Foundation's executive secretary suggested that if

Chodorov gave him the names of students who would read "libertarian" literature, the Foundation would send them material. Chodorov discussed the idea with other Rightists, notably Frank Hanighen of *Human Events,* and in 1952 the Intercollegiate Society of Individualists was born.

For the ISI, Chodorov wrote a manifesto called "A Fifty Year Project"—ISI's long-range goal for transforming America's thinking.

"We are dealing with ideas," Chodorov wrote. "Ideas are acquired by reading and listening. Hence, the job consists of distributing individualistic literature on the campus and supplementing the literature with lectures. . . . There is plenty of good individualist literature seeking readership, and more will be produced if a market is opened up."

The market was opened up. In its first year (it operated as a mailing-list outfit from the offices of *Human Events*) ISI sent out 8,000 pieces of literature, most of it contributed by the business-supported Foundation for Economic Education. Two years later, the literature total was up to 160,000.

The Old Guard was now on its way to producing heirs who would cast their shadow over the decades ahead. The young Rightists have already been heard from—in the Goldwater youth movement, at the Human Events Conferences in Washington, and in hundreds of Conservative clubs on America's college campuses. These young Rightists fly two flags—one, that of the ISI, and the other of Young Americans for Freedom.

ISI is primarily an educational group which seeks to recruit American college youth to the Rightist cause. YAF is a political action group for those who have been recruited.

When ISI was first formed, its announced aims were to "weld together" existing Rightist groups on the campuses, to form new groups where none existed, and to give encouragement and tangible assistance to students and organizations in the colleges opposed to the "socialist indoctrination" they were supposedly receiving.

To run ISI, Frank Chodorov hired thirty-year-old E. Victor Milione, who was then working for Americans for the Competitive Enterprise System, an organization that arranged tours of industrial plants for high school students. Chodorov had a few thousand dollars and he offered Milione $75 a week and expenses, and said that the job would last as long as the money did.

There are no worries about money now. ISI reports, filed with Internal Revenue Service as a tax-exempt organization, show that in 1958, Milione's salary was $10,000. By 1962, it was $14,500. When he started, he had a part-time secretary. In 1958, he had two full-time aides. A few years later, he had nine. And so on.

ISI's gross income has also risen through the years. By 1958, its receipts—entirely from contributions—were almost $100,000. By 1961, they were $181,600, and by 1962 they had crossed the $200,000 mark.

A substantial proportion of ISI's receipts comes from foundations established by large corporations and by leaders of business and industry, many of whom are consistent and frequent contributors to Right Wing causes. The rest comes from companies and individuals.

In one year, for instance, the William Volker Fund of Burlingame, California, gave ISI more than $48,000. The Lilly Endowment of Indianapolis, Indiana, supplied $25,000, the Marquette Charitable Organization gave $19,000, and various other foundations contributed smaller amounts for a total of more than $130,000— almost 75 percent of ISI's income for the year. In the same year, the Gulf Oil Corporation contributed $5,000, U.S. Steel $1,000, and the Pennsylvania Manufacturers Association $1,000.

Another year, Harry Bradley of the Allen-Bradley Company (which has supported Fred Schwarz's Christian Anti-Communism Crusade) gave $5,000, while Lemuel Boulware, the former vice-president of General Electric, contributed $5,800. J. Howard Pew of Sun Oil gave $2,000.

ISI's first president in the early days was William F. Buckley, Jr., the intellectual *enfant terrible* of the Right Wing youth movement, who will be discussed in a later chapter. But, as Buckley recalled ten years later in an article in his own Rightist magazine, *National Review*, he was only "a figurehead" at ISI, as Chodorov soon let him know. Buckley wrote that soon after he was named, Chodorov wrote him: "I am removing you as president. Making myself pres. Easier to raise money if a Jew is president. You can be the V.P. Love, Frank."

Because the organization was distributing only Foundation for Economic Education propaganda, those concerned concluded that ISI would better operate out of FEE's headquarters. The infant, swaddled in diapers of folded *Human Events,* was moved to Irvington-on-Hudson, New York, where it remained until 1958, when it moved into its own offices on Philadelphia's Independence Square.

By 1956, ISI boasted a student membership of 3,400 and was

shipping FEE propaganda to more than 400 universities and colleges in 45 states. FEE assumed the costs. Today the mailing list is around 18,000, and 60,000 students have received Rightist literature through ISI auspices since the organization was founded.

How much of the rapid expansion was due to a carefully nurtured desire of students to meet corporation executives for good job opportunities will probably never be known. ISI leaders themselves call the students' attention to employment possibilities when they join the organization. Chodorov wrote in *Human Events* in September, 1956, that there would be an "employment bureau which will put employers in touch with graduates who have shown enthusiasm for free enterprise."

ISI, as such, has no campus chapters. Members belong as individuals. But since it was started, Right Wing campus organizations and self-styled "conservative clubs" have mushroomed in various colleges and universities. The number is not yet very large—last year there were about seventy such ISI-affiliated campus organizations. ISI requires that they be solely educational groups and that they refrain from political activism. They are to be interested in principles and philosophy—in ideology, not action. (Young Americans for Freedom makes the real noise on the political scene for the young Turks of the Far Right.) The membership in ISI-affiliated campus clubs ranges from as few as a dozen students to as many as a hundred or more, each of them operating without any central direction, but with the assistance of ISI, and with a zealous and fanatical dedication to the Rightist cause as their main unifying force.

These clubs use a wide variety of names: the most common is the Conservative Club—as at the University of Wisconsin and at Michigan State. At the University of Pennsylvania it is the Eleutherian Society, at Queens College the Robert A. Taft Club, at DePauw the George Washington Club, at Purdue the Society for Individual Insight, and the Cornell Conservative Club, whose publication flies an elegant banner—"The Gentlemen of the Right."

These Right Wing students are verbal and articulate, and their publications are scholarly and well-written. The best, perhaps, is the *New Individualist Review*, published at the University of Chicago, an intellectual center for the Rightist youth movement, having had on the faculty such conservative thinkers as economist Milton Friedman and the late Professor Richard M. Weaver.

ISI has its own publications as well. One of these is *The Individualist*, launched in October, 1961, and issued six times a year, usually in two sections—the first containing essays and book reviews by noted scholars or by students themselves, the second usually containing a longer article by a professor or a noted Rightist business leader. A second publication, *The Campus Report,* is published four times a year ("finances permitting," says an ISI brochure) as an eight-page newspaper roundup of club activities, guest lectures, and book notices. A third, called *Under 30,* is published twice a year and is a digest of what ISI considers the best in campus writing of a Rightist slant.

By any standard, the writing and the intellectual quality of *The Individualist* and *Under 30* are of a high order, and it is clear that many of those students who march under the banner of ISI are the youthful elite of the American Right.

ISI's effort to expand and train this elite centers on the distribution of booklets and short essays, mainly because such booklets are the cheapest way of communicating with the 18,000 young Americans who are on ISI's mailing list. There is no effort whatsoever made to deal with current political issues as such; the approach is academic.

The titles tell the story. For the academic year 1963-64 they include "The Private and the Public Sector: Which Is Which and Why," by Professor William H. Peterson of the N.Y.U. Economics Department; "Resistance or Death? The Perils of Surrender Propaganda," by Dr. Stefan Possony, director of international political studies at Stanford's Hoover Institution on War, Revolution and Peace; "Modern Art as an Expression of Our Times," by Professor Thomas Molnar of Brooklyn College; "The Communist Mind," by Dr. Gerhart Niemeyer; and "Standardization Without Standards," by Professor Russell Kirk, author of *The Conservative Mind.*

Young Stanton Evans contributed "The American Revolution: A Study in Conservatism," in which the ISI luminary argued that the American Revolution was a "conservative revolution."

ISI also sponsors a vast panoply of lectures through its speakers bureau, which makes available to campus ISI-affiliated organizations some prominent Right Wing members of the academic world. These speakers are also available for campus seminars, and they also lecture on political theory, economics and history at ISI-sponsored summer schools, which were inaugurated in 1960, and which are well attended.

An example of the subjects considered at these gatherings is "A Conservative Approach to American Foreign Policy," at the Columbia Club in Indianapolis during 1961. Speakers included Dr. Gerhart Niemeyer, University of Notre Dame political science professor, and Frank S. Meyer, senior editor of the *National Review.* At a Princeton seminar in 1962, the topic was "The Responsible Right." Speakers were Senator John Tower of Texas, M. Stanton Evans, and Dr. Wiliam Peterson, the N.Y.U. economist.

Besides the hundreds of thousands of short and inexpensive booklets, ISI also distributes thousands of books whose cost is borne by the wealthy tax-exempt foundations, the corporations, and the business leaders who are bankrolling the ISI effort to generate a Right Wing intellectual Reformation.

As its scope of activities broadened, so too did ISI's organizational apparatus. Victor Milione became its president. Under him were a publications director, a national field director, and three regional directors—one for the East, one for the Midwest, and one for the West, the latter two based in Indianapolis and in Menlo Park, California. A southern office was also planned.

The other officers of ISI include Chodorov, as honorary chairman of the board, and John G. Pew, Jr., a member of the Pew Sunoco family who is a vice-president of the Sun Shipbuilding and Dry Dock Company in Chester, Pennsylvania, as ISI chairman. Charles H. Hoeflich, president of the Union Bank and Trust Company in Souderton, Pennsylvania, is ISI secretary-treasurer.

ISI lists among its advisors such Birch Society supporters as Clarence Manion, J. Bracken Lee, Roger Milliken, E. Merrill Root, and former Congressman Wint Smith. Another advisor is Samuel Pettengill, a well-known name in Extreme Right Wing circles.

ISI trustees also include Birchers—retired Brigadier General Bonner Fellers, the hardy perennial on lists of extreme conservative causes, and Professor Hans Sennholz, who writes for *Human Events*, lectures for both ISI and the Birch American Opinion Speakers Bureau, and who contributes quite regularly to the Birchers' *American Opinion* magazine. Other trustees include Admiral Moreell, the ACA chieftain; Stanton Evans; James A. McConnell of Corn Products Company; Peter O'Donnell, Jr., of Dallas, financier and young leader of the pro-Goldwater movement in Texas; and a liberal sprinkling of nonliberal professors.

ISI spokesmen either ignore or blandly fluff off the presence of Birchers in their senior leadership. They attribute the presence of the Radical Right in their midst to "coincidence" and to "overlapping interests."

The phenomenon is, however, less coincidental than the young ideologues of the American Right would like the public to believe.

For if the ISI is indifferent to the Birchers, the Birch Society is not indifferent to the ISI, which was among a list of sixteen organizations which Founder Welch, in May, 1961, urged his membership to help in every way possible.

The picture is, however, unclear when one attempts to evaluate the attitude and the relationship of the ISI to the Birchers. ISI seeks the counsel of Birch supporters as advisers and trustees, and it numbers among its contributors those whose names and energies also nourish the Birch Society. Yet the ISI members also revere the thinking of Russell Kirk, the conservative scholar who—among all the spokesmen of the Right—has gone farthest in attacking what he termed "the fantastics" of the Extreme Right. And an ISI forum at Princeton in 1962 heard Senator John Tower of Texas attack the leadership of Founder Welch. Tower said the Society's leadership was "terribly misguided" and had used "bad judgment minimizing the serious threats and maximizing the less serious ones." He declared: "I demand that conservatives reject Mr. Welch's leadership."

The young eggheads of ISI are in fact quite as ambivalent and as soft on radical rightism as are their seniors on *Human Events,* in ACA and elsewhere on that front which claims to be nonextremist. One of them, a bright young man from Fordham named John Hilberg, wrote a piece for the first issue of *The Individualist* in October, 1961, which was called "The Necessity of Right Wing Extremism."

In it, Hilberg said: "If the continuity of Anglo-Saxon political institutions—whose dominating characteristic is a compulsion for the moderate—is to be safeguarded from submersion of the Left, a racial [sic] Right-Wing movement must manifest itself."

Referring to Senator Goldwater's now-famous book, Hilberg declared that "a candidate today who would run on a platform such as Conscience of a Conservative has no one to his starboard side. If, however," Hilberg continued, "there was such a group, it would draw the majority of the invective that always attaches itself to the extremist," while in its absence, the conservative candidate "must alone defend his traditionally indefensible position."

Followers of the "Conservative school," Hilberg concluded, "can hardly expect to gain a major electoral victory unless they can emulate their opponents in projecting themselves as some compromise solution to a fantastic aberration of the far Right. It is, therefore, in the interests of all Conservatives to support the illusions of Rightist extremism circulating around such groups as the John Birch Society. . . ."

Because ISI members are concerned with theory, with ideology, and with trying to define their own political philosophy, neither they nor ISI carry on propaganda on the day-to-day issues that concern the rest of the Right Wing. It is, therefore, difficult if not impossible to gauge where they stand on the political spectrum by any public positions. Many of them, perhaps most, are Right Wing Republicans at the minimum; many of them probably find their political home even farther to the Right than that.

For instance, one segment of the ISI membership worships at the shrine of authoress Ayn Rand and her bizarre philosophy of "Objectivism"—a viewpoint which elevates self-interest to the cardinal principle of life, and which is specifically anti-religious. Its high priestess, Miss Rand, is said to wear a brooch in the shape of a dollar sign. Those among the Rightist youth who follow her superindividualistic philosophy seem to find that her ethics and the completely *laissez-faire* economics of, say, Ludwig von Mises go hand-in-hand.

Most of the young eggheads of the Right, however, appear to root their philosophy in concepts of natural and moral law and oppose "relativism," which they scorn as the root of liberal philosophy and thinking. In short, these young Rightists believe that there is such a thing as absolute good and absolute truth—and being of tender years, they believe they have the key to these absolutes and the answers that flow therefrom.

One thing is certain. Their revolt is against the dominant ideas and reforms of the last thirty years. They oppose the use by the people of the instrument of government to improve the economic and social well-being of individuals. This they reject, in the sloganistic language of their elders, as the welfare state. They vehemently oppose Keynesian economics because they oppose any interference with the free market and they stand, in their words, for "economic freedom." They see the last thirty years as years of "discretionary government action" in contrast to "constitutionalism," which they favor.

They view liberalism as Old Hat and Liberals as the Old Guard. And if they claim to fight "statism" while defending Senator McCarthy's exercise of the state's power against individuals (as well as loyalty oaths for students receiving government educational aid and the House Committee on Un-American Activities), they can always write learned essays and treatises to prove that such exercises of the power of the state are right and good, while other government actions on the economic and social front are bad.

Are they, then, really conservative? They are aware that they may not be, and that many do not view them as Conservatives, but as Extremists. They are too smart not to know the chinks in their own ideological armor. M. Stanton Evans, the articulate voice of these young tads, tried to cover this obvious problem in his book *Revolt on the Campus*. He admitted that their critics charge that they want to "change everything—to dismantle 'social gains'; in addition to favoring individualist goals, they want to use radical means. If they were truly 'conservative,' say their detractors, they would be content to accept the status quo—to rest with the 'gains' legislated by the New Deal and its Democratic and Republican successors."

Evans acknowledged that the factual foundations of these criticisms of today's youthful Right are "sound." "The young conservative of today," he conceded, "*is* (1) determined upon change; (2) devoted to the cause of freedom; and (3) sometimes prone to use 'radical' means."

"But," he asked, "do these things indicate that he is not conservative?" The answer, he said, lay in what one means by conservative. He saw it, and presumably so did his eager and self-consciously serious young contemporaries, first and foremost as a set of principles, "a way of looking at man and his universe." Circumstances, said Evans may change, "but principles do not."

"In general," he said, sneaking across a truism, "the conservative will resist change during periods in which the values he cherishes predominate." Since his values by and large have been those of Western civilization, the Conservative usually is "quiescent" and has been content to preserve the existing order. And as certain changes occur, he weighs the situation. He accepts changes of degree, and is unwilling to use "radical" methods to overturn those changes, once established. "But," Evans wrote, "there comes a point where changes in degree fuse into a change in *kind*: where the essential tradition is not amended, or modified, but violated; when the changes enacted are . . . revolutionary acts conspiring to deny those principles. . . .

"It is just such a condition," Evans continued, "which today prevails in America, indeed throughout the West, and it is just such a condition which confronts the young man or woman who . . . decides that he or she is a conservative."

In short, Evans says, quoting another author, these young people believe that "a revolutionary force" has shattered "the unity and balance of civilization" and they feel compelled, by the altered circumstances as they see it, to become ideologues. "Confronted with an established revolution, the conservatives must seek to *change* the status quo; he has no other means of affirming his tradition. And in seeking that alteration, he must invoke certain of the techniques which are effective in producing change."

And this, perhaps, may be used to justify the John Birch Society's policy of employing the techniques of secrecy in order to disturb the status quo.

In any case, the young Turks of the Right see that they are confronted by a revolution wrought by "Liberals" who have overturned all that they believe in. They admit they seek change—far-reaching change. They wish to tear down an era, and go back to a bygone age. They fly the banner of conservatism, but they are as extreme as many of their Rightist elders.

And they know what they want. They are conscious of the fact that they seek nothing less than an economic revolution, an overturn of established policies and perhaps of established American reforms themselves. Evans has admitted as much.

Despite the promise of Chodorov five years ago of an employment bureau to bring the youngsters in touch with business leaders interested in hiring students showing an enthusiasm for free enterprise, it would be a mistake to view the youth movement as a pack of ambitious self-seeking, would-be junior executives. While many of them are, in fact, graduating into the ranks of American industry, business, and the professions, they are not abandoning their rebellious ardor in doing so. Many of them are graduating significantly, into the Right Wing movement itself, continuing to work for the Cause even after their diplomas are safely nailed to the wall.

The significance of ISI lies in the fact that in a decade it has indoctrinated hundreds of young men and women and has already spawned the cadres of what the American Right seeks—an ideological movement that will wreak a counterrevolution on the political and economic front and eventually restore the America of 1928— or perhaps 1828.

There is no reason to think that Chodorov was kidding when he spoke of ISI as a "Fifty Year Project" to accomplish for the Right what he felt the League for Industrial Democracy had accomplished on the other side between 1905 and the middle of this century. For the plain fact is that in only ten years, ISI has already shown signs of achieving what Chodorov once predicted when he wrote that "in a few years students will supply their own crop of writers and lecturers." ISI-indoctrinated men and women are scattered around the country—making their voices heard in teaching, in writing, and on the political front. With very few exceptions, they are barely thirty and will be on the scene for years to come.

There is Bill Buckley, and there is Stanton Evans, who went on from Yale to the staff of *Human Events* and who is now editor of the *Indianapolis News*. Evans is thirty.

There is Garry Wills, Ph.D., Assistant Professor of Classics at Johns Hopkins, a contributor to Buckley's *National Review* and formerly a staff writer for the *Richmond* (Virginia) *News Leader* whose editor, James Kilpatrick, is a leading figure in the Southern States' rights and pro-segregation movement. Wills is twenty-nine. He succeeded Richard Whalen, also twenty-nine, another young Rightist of promise, on the Richmond paper. Whalen, who also contributes to the *National Review*, went on to become an editorial writer for the *Wall Street Journal*.

There is Edwin McDowell—another twenty-nine-year-old—an editorial writer for the *Arizona Republic,* a good friend of Senator Goldwater and author of *Barry Goldwater: Portrait of an Arizonan.*

Some are active as leaders of YAF, and others help publish YAF's magazine, the *New Guard*. Still others are on the staff of *Human Events*. Others have worked for Right Wing members of Congress, and some for congressional committees. Some work for conservative molders of opinion in the broadcasting field.

Wherever they are, wherever they go, they write, they speak, they instruct. They turn out a good round dozen or more of well-written, well-edited collegiate publications. As far back as 1960, they were in the forefront of the movement for Senator Goldwater and more and more of them are active in today's political scene.

They may not be the wave of the future, but these youngsters of extreme conservatism are already a detectable ripple. Their energy, their dedication, and their talent for the written and the spoken word appear to overshadow anything that the more liberal youth on or off the campus can offer. The young Liberals of today do not appear to have produced leaders of stature and energy to do battle with them. These young Rightists spawned in the last decade undoubtedly will make a substantial impact on American life.

It is not especially relevant that today, or even tomorrow, the Rightist youth movement remains a minority. Counterrevolutions are wrought by dedicated, energetic—and even fanatic—minorities, who know what they want, and who have the energy, the will, and dedication to strive and work for it.

15

Young Americans for Freedom

It is always a bit of a jump from the pure and tranquil world of the thinkers and the writers to the moist, sweaty world of the doers and activists. The intellectuals of the ISI who engage in learned discussion and controversy over the theories of Edmund Burke, Ludwig von Mises, Ayn Rand, or Russell Kirk must, and do, face a plain fact: that beyond their ivied halls and tree-shaded campuses, there is a real world, and that the hated Liberal Establishment is entrenched there.

As they see it, the Liberal Establishment has sought to brainwash them during their college days with dangerous doctrines of welfare-ism and Keynesianism, and though they have survived four years of propaganda by Liberals in the classroom, they are now graduating into a world in which the Liberal Establishment runs everything—the Government, the press, the magazines, the radio and television networks. Worse still, it controls the Democratic Party in the North and segments of the hallowed Republican Party seduced by the Modern Republicanism of Eisenhower, Dewey, Lodge, and Rockefeller. All this they believe.

Their feelings of persecution are palpable. But they persevere as they graduate from their academic ivory towers into the smoky world of political action, Rightist style. Many have already had several years of experience as cheer leaders for the Right Wing political heroes of the moment.

In the last few years, their idol among American political figures has been Senator Barry Goldwater of Arizona, and a tremendous proportion of the youthful energy and zealous enthusiasm of the Young American Right has been poured into the movement for "Goldwater in '64." This love of America's Right Wing youth for the handsome and personable senator is reciprocal; he has been one of their most ardent champions and sources of encouragement. Senator Goldwater has spoken at scores of college campuses in recent years and has urged the students to form their battalions and to become part of what he and they believe to be the wave of the future in American politics.

It was, in fact, the warm attraction between the youngsters and the senator that inspired an important new organization on the Right—a bouncy, energetic, chesty, and somewhat ruthless outfit called Young Americans for Freedom. In its four years on the American scene, it has had a certain discernible impact on campus life and on American politics itself.

YAF (*Yaff*, as it's called) is guided by men and women who, for the most part, have been out of college for quite a few years— but the membership consists of students in high schools, colleges, and universities, and young people up to the age of thirty-nine who are presumably the Young Marrieds of the American Right.

The membership of YAF is said to include somewhere between 20,000 and 30,000 young men and women on more than three hundred campuses as well as in cities, suburbs, and towns all across the United States. (That is the same general membership figure claimed by YAF leaders as far back as 1961, after YAF had been in operation about a year. Thus, it would seem that the wave of the future is hardly a tidal wave.)

The YAFers are an active lot, and have campaigned extensively in local and national elections for Rightist candidates of all kinds, from moderate to extreme. Since YAF was formed in September, 1960, members have taken part in innumerable political campaigns, have distributed countless pieces of printed propaganda, and have sponsored a perpetual calendar of Rightist rallies.

They have also formed front organizations for specific activities, and have campaigned long and loud against the influence of the National Student Association, a well-established and thoroughly respected organization that is the largest of all American student groups. NSA, representing campus organizations that embrace more than a million students, is a favorite target of YAF, which charges NSA with the unpardonable crime of liberalism and with being unrepresentative of the majority of American students today.

In 1963, YAF launched a drive to establish itself on almost every American college campus. Senator Strom Thurmond of South Carolina, Dixiecrat candidate for President in 1948, revealed the drive in a December, 1963, letter soliciting funds for YAF. The senator, a favorite of the Radical Right, wrote:

"Recently the National Board of Directors in a 2-day meeting in Washington, D. C., set a goal of starting YAF chapters on 1,000 college and university campuses by November 1964.

"The prospect of patriotic anti-Communist youth groups on 1,000 college campuses is truly an inspiring and heartwarming thought. I am convinced that if we are to be successful in defeating atheistic Communism it will have to be done by the young people. A YAF chapter will prepare a young man or woman for the struggle ahead with Liberalism, Socialism and Communism."

All recipients of the Senator's letter (which he put on United States Senate stationery even though it included a solicitation for funds) were assured that "the vital work that these young people are doing is without doubt the most encouraging sign on the American political scene today." Included was an announcement of a Human Events Political Action Conference to be held in 1964. One theme: "How to elect the next President."

YAF came into existence as the result of a bill introduced in the United States Congress during 1959 to repeal the requirement for a loyalty oath from students receiving Federal aid under the 1958 National Defense Education Act.

Two young Rightists in Washington—Douglas Caddy and David Franke—opposed the bill. Caddy and Franke started recruiting their associates for a student committee favoring retention of the loyalty oath requirement. (Both of the founders were members of ISI. Caddy, a Georgetown University student, was also chairman of the District of Columbia College Young Republicans, while Franke, a student at George Washington University, was editor of ISI's *The Individualist* and of *The Campus Republican,* official organ of the College Young Republicans.)

In January, 1960, the two announced formation of the National Student Committee for the Loyalty Oath, with some thirty colleges represented by members on its governing board. The ruckus the student group generated helped, their admirers claimed, to stop the movement in Congress to repeal the pledge. Right Wing congressmen and senators were lavish in their praise for the committee.

Stanton Evans wrote in his book, *Revolt on the Campus,* that the loyalty oath brouhaha gave young Conservatives a taste of political action and a "sweet sensation of victory." He said it had "established a network of contacts" and that the students involved had been bound closer together in something resembling a "movement" with a common language and common goals. "They had," he wrote, "taken their first real step from philosophical speculation to political action."

In the spring of 1960, with the Republican nomination for President pretty well assured for Richard M. Nixon, a meeting of the Midwest Federation of College Young Republican Clubs was held in Des Moines. It was a Donnybrook between liberal and conservative young Republicans. The moderates narrowly succeeded in electing their man as chairman, but the Rightists pushed through a surprise resolution supporting Senator Goldwater for the GOP Vice-Presidential nomination.

The victory on the resolution surprised even the young Rightists among the young Midwestern Republicans. A Northwestern University student named Robert Croll saw the possibilities in a drive to marshal support among students and young people for Goldwater on the GOP ticket. He got in touch with Caddy and Franke and with two other young activists and the five of them formed an executive committee of a new organization called Youth for Goldwater for Vice-President. They announced their new enterprise in May, 1960.

By early July, the Youth for Goldwater group claimed local units in thirty-two states and the District of Columbia, and chapters on sixty-four college and university campuses. By convention time, the group was proclaiming that "American youth" was "swinging to the right" and that conservatism was growing stronger "and must inevitably triumph."

Newsmen and political reporters at the GOP convention in Chicago noted that the drive for Goldwater as Nixon's running mate was largely a youth movement. But it was not entirely so. On the eve of the convention, a mammoth Goldwater rally was held in the Morrison Hotel. The moving spirits behind that rally were Kent and Phoebe Courtney, the New Orleans publishers of the *Independent American.* A Goldwater for President committee, which wanted no part of Nixon, trotted out mass petitions bearing a claimed 50,000 signatures supporting the senator for the *top* spot on the GOP ticket. Of the 1,000 persons at this noisy affair staged under the Courtneys' extremist auspices, a generous proportion were youngsters. The featured speaker was former Senator William E. Jenner of Indiana, a Rightist luminary of the McCarthy era.

The conglomeration of pro-Goldwater activists at Chicago succeeded in generating sufficient enthusiasm for the senator's name to be placed before the convention for the number one spot, and this was the occasion for a gigantic demonstration. The Courtneys later claimed they had arranged for the hundreds of placards and had seen to it they were nailed to sticks in time for a wild demonstration, complete with a band of marching Indians. Youth for Goldwater officers later complained that the convention leadership had interfered with the demonstration, not allowing enough Goldwaterites to enter the convention arena and interfering with chances for proper exposure on TV. But whatever the auspices and whatever the obstacles, the demonstration for Goldwater that erupted at the convention helped to catapult the senator into a position of greater prominence on the American political scene.

After the convention, the executive committee of Youth for Goldwater stayed on, joined by half a dozen other young Rightists. They wanted in some way to keep the momentum they had generated for young conservatism. They issued a call for a national conference of young Conservatives in the early fall of 1960. Caddy was named to head up an interim committee to plan the conference.

William Dunphy, a philosophy teacher at Fordham University, wrote in *Commonweal* of April 14, 1961, that Senator Goldwater himself met with the Youth for Goldwater leaders right after the convention to thank them for their role in the demonstrations, and that the senator suggested that these youth leaders form a national organization for young Conservatives.

Then, on the weekend of September 9-11, 1960, about a hundred young men and women from forty-four colleges met at the large family home of William Buckley, Jr., in Sharon, Connecticut. When the meetings had ended, Buckley—the first of the postwar young Rightists—baptized Young Americans for Freedom. A manifesto was issued, which has come to be known as The Sharon Statement. It is a four-hundred-word document which states the basic views of the Young American Right and which revises the concepts of the Declaration of Independence and the United States Constitution in more than minor ways. The Sharon Statement reads as follows:

IN THIS TIME of moral and political crisis, it is the responsibility of the youth of America to affirm certain eternal truths.

WE as young conservatives, believe:

That foremost among the transcendent values is the individual's use of his God-given free will, whence derives his right to be free from the restrictions of arbitrary force;

That liberty is indivisible, and that political freedom cannot long exist without economic freedom;

That the purposes of government are to protect these freedoms through the preservation of internal order, the provision of national defense, and the administration of justice;

That when government ventures beyond these rightful functions, it accumulates power which tends to diminish order and liberty;

That the Constitution of the United States is the best arrangement yet devised for empowering government to fulfill its proper role, while restraining it from the concentration and abuse of power;

That the genius of the Constitution—the division of powers —is summed up in the clause which reserves primacy to the several states, or to the people, in those spheres not specifically delegated to the Federal Government;

That the market economy, allocating resources by the free play of supply and demand, is the single economic system compatible with the requirements of personal freedom and constitutional government, and that it is at the same time the most productive supplier of human needs;

That when government interferes with the work of the market economy, it tends to reduce the moral and physical strength of the nation; that when it takes from one man to bestow on another, it diminishes the incentive of the first, the integrity of the second, and the moral autonomy of both;

That we will be free only so long as the national sovereignty of the United States is secure; that history shows periods of freedom are rare, and can exist only when free citizens concertedly defend their rights against all enemies;

That the forces of international Communism are, at present, the greatest single threat to these liberties;

That the United States should stress victory over, rather than coexistence with, this menace; and

That American foreign policy must be judged by this criterion: does it serve the just interests of the United States?

The Sharon Rightists held to a narrow view of government, and while wrapping themselves in the United States Constitution—itself a fine idea—revealed their concept of American government as restricted to preserving internal order, setting up and operating a system of courts, providing for the national defense, and protecting the right of everyone to make a dollar without any special restraints. They conveniently overlooked the fact that in Article I, Section 8, the Founding Fathers gave vast powers to Congress: the right to lay and collect taxes; to pay the debts and provide for the common defense and general welfare of the United States; to borrow money on the credit of the United States; to regulate interstate and foreign commerce; to coin money and regulate the value thereof; to promote the progress of science and the useful arts; to call out the militia to execute the laws of the union; and to make all laws necessary and proper for carrying out those powers.

The Founding Fathers, in short, gave the Congress of the United States, the Executive, and the Judiciary, far-reaching powers. And they did not mention the market economy nor did they conceive the powers of the Federal Government to be limited by the law of supply and demand.

The document they drew was for the centuries to come. The Sharon Statement is a series of slogans that seeks to wed the Objectivist self-interest concepts of Ayn Rand and the *laissez-faire* principles of economists like von Mises to the Constitution of the United States—while at the same time grafting on the foreign policy of Senator Goldwater. It clearly showed those who founded YAF as longing for a government stripped of any real power over the market place and the economic affairs of men and corporations.

It might be pointed out that the "individual freedom" to which these Young Americans are so loudly devoted is almost invariably economic.

Those who joined Buckley in helping to found the infant YAF organization were not all especially young. There was, of course, Stanton Evans, who is generally credited with drafting The Sharon Statement. There was also Marvin Liebman, a former Communist who has emerged in recent years as public relations consultant for a whole panoply of Right Wing organizations, fronts, and promotions—some of them children of the Buckley brain. Liebman served as public relations man for Fred Schwarz when the Christian Anti-Communism Crusade came to New York in 1962 for the rally that started the Aussie on the downhill road.

YAF's national advisory board of forty-one congressmen and five United States senators represents varying shades of the political Right. Noncongressional members included former Leftists who had swung over to the Right, such as Dr. Bella V. Dodd, once a well-known Communist leader, and John Dos Passos, the novelist who in the long ago was a contributor to the *New Masses,* a Communist publication. In addition, there was Igor Cassini, who was later convicted of failing to register as a representative of the Dominican Republic. There were such old reliables of the Extreme Right as General Robert E. Wood and Charles Edison, and several editors of the *National Review,* and of course a dozen or so leaders of the John Birch Society.

YAF has a national chairman, an executive director, a financial secretary, eight regional chairmen, and a nineteen-member board of directors. There is no provision in the organization's bylaws which makes the board accountable to the membership. The bylaws, in effect, give seven persons power to make decisions binding on the entire membership. An even smaller "policy committee quorum" consisting of three persons can make binding decisions "when the board of directors is not in session."

Like ISI, Young Americans for Freedom, assures prospective recruits that it will help them find jobs when they graduate. A YAF brochure says:

> YAF Young Conservative Employment Service. Every YAF member has available the services of the national headquarters as the clearing house for part-time or full-time jobs on Capitol Hill and elsewhere. It is hoped that this will soon be expanded to include business and industry employment for young Conservatives.

YAF leaders, in fact, have found opportunities to serve the Rightist cause, both in Government and out. Douglas Caddy, the first national director, has worked for *Human Events,* has edited the McGraw-Edison Public Affairs Newsletter (where he succeeded Edwin McDowell, biographer of Senator Goldwater), and has since worked for the United States Chamber of Commerce. Another ex-YAF leader, William Cotter, Jr., has worked for the National Association of Manufacturers. Other YAFers have worked for Buckley's *National Review* and for Admiral Moreell's ACA.

Scott Stanley, Jr., one of the earliest YAF officials, went on to become managing editor of *American Opinion.*

The new youth organization was not yet dry behind the ears

when its political mentors decided to stage a political rally in New York City—a big bite for a baby with no experience and less money. But the older mentors of YAF understood the publicity value of youthful political rallies and apparently underwrote the cost of the project.

Manhattan Center was rented in March, 1961, to give awards to deserving individuals "for contributions to American Conservatism and the youth of the nation." The recipients were James Abstine (chairman of the Indiana College Young Republicans), William Buckley, Jr., novelist Taylor Caldwell, Professor Russell Kirk, industrialist Herbert Kohler, publisher Eugene Pulliam, columnist George Sokolsky, former AEC chairman Lewis Strauss, the House Committee on Un-American Activities, the McGraw-Edison Company, and the Republic of China. The Center was packed and the audience was told that 6,000 persons had been turned away for lack of room. The high point of the evening was a speech by Senator Barry Goldwater. *The New York Times* described what happened when Goldwater arrived:

> Senator Goldwater's appearance . . . set off a tumultuous ovation from the 3,200 persons crowded inside the Center. . . . The crowd came to its feet as he walked out. Hundreds of yellow, pink and blue balloons stamped with his name filled the air, their colors picked out by roving spotlights. "We want Barry! We want Barry!" the audience shouted and the rhythm was picked up by a marching band in front of the stage. Huge placards with the Senator's picture waved over their heads. . . .

Senator Goldwater told the assembled young Rightists that the American people were being caught up in a wave of conservatism. He asserted that this fact could easily become "the political phenomenon of our time." That quotation has since been emblazoned on countless pieces of YAF literature as if, somehow, the constant repetition of the hope might somehow make it reality.

The publicity didn't hurt, however. Nor had the press notices of constant YAF-sponsored showings of the "documentary" film, *Operation Abolition*—a controversial and not scrupulously accurate story of demonstrations in San Francisco during the 1960 hearings conducted there by the House Committee on Un-American Activities. The narrator for the film was Fulton (Buddy) Lewis III, a YAF leader, son of the radio commentator. A showing of the film by the YAF Greenwich Village unit in New York provoked picketing by young Leftists and was good for more newspaper publicity.

Nor do the young Turks of the New Right shun the tactics

and techniques of the Old Left itself. A classic example of the use of time-honored Far Left tactics by the YAFers took place weeks after the 1961 Manhattan Center rally. A meeting to examine the Peace Corps proposal advanced by the Kennedy Administration had been called by the respected National Student Asociation at the American University in Washington. Some three hundred delegates were present, including some fifty delegates sympathetic to YAF views, some actually representing YAF, some representing the Young Republicans and other sympathetic student groups. It appears that the whole Rightist intrusion was part of a well-conceived and thoroughly planned strategy by YAF and its allies. They operated under the banner of a front group set up specifically for the conference itself and later dropped. The name of the front was the Students for an Effective Peace Corps, and its hard core was composed of YAF leaders.

At a late hour, toward midnight, the hard core laid down its own political position for the next day's plenary session: The Peace Corps should not be based on altruism but on cold war realism. Peace Corps members should have to pass top security screening and sign loyalty oaths. U.S. citizens working abroad should enjoy the legal protection of extraterritorial rights. The following day a diluted resolution supporting the Peace Corps was adopted.

Once the conference was over, the front group was disbanded and little or nothing has been heard from YAF since on the subject. But the publicity achieved did little harm and added to the illusion of YAF strength. And the NSA was harassed.

There was still another assault by YAF and other young Rightists against the National Student Association at the now-famous fourteenth annual NSA congress at Madison, Wisconsin, in August, 1961. Weeks before the conference date, YAF leaders charged that an "elite" was running NSA for its own "far left" purposes. YAF threatened a region-by-region coalition to push Rightist resolutions through the annual congress, as well as a walkout by member colleges if these Rightist resolutions were voted down. At the same time, YAF headquarters warned that "bus-loads" of young Right-Wingers would descend on the Madison conference to prove that they were in fact the "wave of the future."

When the Madison gathering opened, the YAF hard core had established and was operating behind a front set up for the purpose—the Committee for a Responsible National Students Organization (shades of an effective Peace Corps). The barrage of propaganda ground out from the YAF command post in a luxury motel near Madison bore the organizational front name, with a New York address that was identical with YAF's national headquarters address at the time—the offices of Marvin Liebman's public relations firm.

The YAF floor tactics were noisy and inflammatory. YAF activists were described as jumping up, seizing the microphone, and making fiery speeches. Moderate students who attended, as well as some other conservative delegates, said later that the YAFers had alienated the congress and had pushed it toward the Left. Other students criticized YAF tactics as "noisy," or "disruptive," or "underhanded." Adult observers, *The New York Times* later reported, suggested that the YAF tactics resembled the Left Wing student tactics of the 1930's. In any event, most of the one thousand students who attended the 1961 NSA congress at Madison came away repelled, rather than attracted, by YAF.

It was perhaps significant that at Madison YAF relied largely on senior spokesmen—Bill Buckley himself, Fulton (Buddy) Lewis III, and Representative John Rousselot. Rousselot implored the students to join him as members of the John Birch Society—not inappropriate advice.

By May, 1963, M. Stanton Evans, writing in the *National Review Bulletin,* told of a new approach by YAF in its war against NSA. Most of the anti-NSA group had concluded that reform from within NSA could go only so far and had little chance for success. He said that the anti-NSA group was turning increasingly to a different approach—that of challenging NSA "at the source of its apparent authority, the campus itself." And Evans claimed that the new approach was having great results.

An example—perhaps an extreme one—of how YAF operated against NSA on individual campuses was reported in a May 15, 1962, *New York Times* article which told of strange events at the University of Oklahoma in Norman. There, early in 1962, a referendum was scheduled on the question of withdrawing the school from NSA affiliation.

Two weeks before the referendum, two YAF officials, Scott Stanley, Jr., and Bill Cotter, checked into a motel in Oklahoma City, twenty miles from the campus. Only once, according to the news dispatch to *The New York Times,* did the pair have a meeting with the president of the Student Senate. Six students saw the YAF officials casually, and perhaps twenty knew they were even in the vicinity.

Stanley (who was to become managing editor of Robert Welch's magazine) and Cotter had other work. They were also in Oklahoma for an intensive speaking tour of civic clubs and parent groups in Tulsa, Oklahoma City, and other communities. In these talks they repeatedly implied that the National Student Association was unrepresentative of majority student opinion and was actually a Leftist front. Many parents then communicated with their children and with the university administration to protect their children from NSA's presence on the campus.

YAF strategy was successful. The referendum vote was the largest cast in the history of the university. NSA lost three to one; the vote was to dissociate the school from the National Student Association.

YAF subsequently issued a press release in which it boasted of the influence it had exerted to win this extraordinary vote. It said that two of its national officers had "directed the attack" against the National Student Association: "In barely two weeks of operation in Oklahoma, we succeeded in motivating parent groups from three of the largest cities in Oklahoma to go to the University administration to protest the school's affiliations with the radical group. The students' response to the exposé of the ultra-Leftism of the NSA reaffirms our belief that the students of today are predominantly Conservative."

In a 1963 report about the National Student Association, YAF boasted of its successes against NSA and said that since 1961, some thirty-three schools, including some of the largest in the nation, withdrew from NSA. It added that fourteen other colleges turned down suggested affiliation with NSA.

On the reverse side of the coin, in 1962, the Reverend John Caine, director of student activities at the Roman Catholic Niagara University, announced that the YAF chapter there had been banned. The school's objections were based on tenets of The Sharon Statement which, said the clergyman-teacher, were contrary to sound Catholic principles and to the American way of life.

Protests by the YAF chapter chairman and well-known Rightists were fruitless.

In 1962, when YAF held its first national convention at New York's Commodore Hotel, it elected a new national chairman. He was Robert E. Bauman, now twenty-six, a graduate of Georgetown University's School of Foreign Service and a member of its Law School's Class of 1964. Bauman was re-elected in 1963. He and his wife, the former Carol Dawson, are activists on the Right Wing youth front. Carol became executive secretary of Youth for

Goldwater near the end of 1963. She also served as managing editor of the *New Guard,* and has worked for Admiral Moreell's ACA, and for Representative Donald Bruce of Indiana.

Bob Bauman, a Marylander, had grown up breathing the air of Washington politics. His knowledge of Capitol Hill began when he was a congressional page; he had served as an aide to the minority leader of the House, Representative Charles Halleck of Indiana, and knew many congressmen personally.

With its new headquarters a few blocks from Capitol Hill, YAF works with congressional leaders and a number of Right Wing organizations, including the Human Events Political Action Conferences and the ACA.

Under Bauman's administration, YAF branched out in the services it provides both to individual members and to YAF chapters. A YAF Speakers Bureau was set up to provide Rightist speakers for college and community chapters, and presumably to local civic groups. A Film Library has been established—it sells and rents Rightist films, including a special YAF movie called *A Generation Awakes,* which features William Buckley and Senator Goldwater. In the field of radio, YAF co-operates with the Manion Forum and distributes a weekly radio tape suitable for YAF sponsorship on local radio or campus radio stations. The free service features most of the Extreme Rightist personalities heard on the Manion Forum. The fact that the former Dean is a member of the Birch Society's national council doesn't seem to bother Bauman or the national office of YAF one bit.

In the field of political action, YAF provides all chapters with information on how to raise funds, organize, recruit, get publicity, hold rallies. Each member of YAF, in addition to the *New Guard* magazine, also receives *YAF Washington Report,* a monthly newsletter which includes the ACA vote ratings of individual members of Congress.

YAF members have been bombarded with ads and offers for all sorts of Goldwater-for-President novelties—sweat shirts, bumper stickers, books, recordings, folk songs to "bug Liberals" (by "The Goldwaters"), Gold Water cologne and after-shave lotion, buttons, crayons, and premium quality soap marked "AuH$_2$O '64."

YAF also set up a "Hot Line Service" and informed potential supporters, members, and contributors that it was prepared to co-ordinate nation-wide political action on a crash basis, including picketing, demonstrations, letter-writing, and petition campaigns. The "Hot Line" is YAF's method, so its promotional literature says, "of activating chapters on a 24-hour basis."

Picketing and counterpicketing have become standard YAF operating technique. In 1962, for instance, some 4,000 non-YAF students from colleges throughout the country converged on Washington, D. C., by train, bus, or in jammed automobiles. Most of them traveled long distances to participate in a series of peace demonstrations before the White House, in front of foreign embassies, around the Washington Monument, and in other selected places. At almost every demonstration about two hundred young persons from the Washington, D. C., area who said they were members of YAF promptly showed up with placards reading "End The Cold War With The Sword"; "They're Not Red, They're Yellow," and "A Test A Day Keeps The Commies Away."

When President Kennedy drove to the National Gallery of Art in January, 1963, to view the unveiling of the "Mona Lisa," eighty YAFers, with placards already painted, started "a spontaneous demonstration" against "UN atrocities" in the Congo. When, in October, 1963, Adlai Stevenson was spat upon, shoved about, and struck on the head with a picket sign at a Dallas UN Day celebration, some of the anti-UN demonstrators identified themselves as members of YAF.

Four years after its founding, with thousands of members spread throughout the country, YAF is proud of its achievements. In pleas for money to continue its expansion of activities, it reminds potential contributors that on the night of March 7, 1962, it staged "the most significant gathering of Conservatives in recent U. S. history as 18,500 people jammed Madison Square Garden in New York City."

This meeting was staged with rally tactics commonly used at nominating conventions. Students in blazers were everywhere. Usherettes with YAF ribbons emblazoned on their dresses escorted excited students to their seats; on every seat was placed the latest issue of YAF's magazine and an announcement of a special introductory offer to *National Review*. There were 340 policemen in uniform and in plain-clothes. Officers on horseback, six abreast, patrolled the street corners. At a side exit were an ambulance and more policemen.

The performance began with stirring band music. Fourteen American flags suspended from the ceiling rippled and confetti fluttered from the balconies. Students in the upper balconies from time to time launched paper gliders which floated down upon the older people who packed the floor.

In the tradition of Madison Square Garden rallies over the

years, whether Left or Right, the four-hour rally featured a long parade of speakers, introductions, responses, awards, and musical selections, ending around midnight after the climactic speech by Senator Goldwater.

Before their idol mounted the rostrum, however, the audience saw a battery of crimson-colored award folders presented to bell-wethers of the American Right, both individual and corporate. One such award went to the Deering Milliken company, and was accepted by Roger Milliken, a top official of the company, who also happens to be an Endorser of the John Birch Society. Other awards went to Senator Strom Thurmond; Professor Ludwig von Mises; actor John Wayne (who could not attend); former Governor Charles Edison of New Jersey, who supports many Rightist causes, including the Birch Society; the late Professor Richard Weaver; author John Dos Passos; YAF public relations man Marvin Liebman; and Stanton Evans.

The Kennedy Administration was repeatedly booed and hissed. Bill Buckley's brother-in-law, Brent Bozell, an editor of *National Review*, brought down the house and summed up the spirit of the Rightists when he told the audience that to save the "Christian West," orders should go out from Washington for sweeping new policies:

> To the Joint Chiefs of Staff: Make the necessary preparations for a landing in Havana.
> To our commander in Berlin: Tear Down the Wall.
> To our Chief of Mission in the Congo: Change sides.
> To the Chief of CIA: You are under instructions to encourage liberation movements in every nation of the world under Communist domination, including the Soviet Union itself.

The high point came when Goldwater was introduced as the Conservatives' choice for President. A huge banner reading "For the Future of Freedom—Goldwater in '64" was unfolded as the band burst into the "Battle Hymn of the Republic." The audience sang " 'Glory, Hallelujah' " over and over. The senator stood patiently through a five-minute ovation. Spotlights played on him. Confetti fluttered everywhere. Balloons cascaded from the upper reaches of the Garden as the audience chanted "Goldwater for President." And the band played on.

The senator told the audience that "Conservatism . . . has come of age at a time of great national need" and voiced doubts that the Liberals understood the struggle against communism. He predicted "the twilight of Radical Liberalism as it has been practiced in this country." He declared that "Conservatism is young, virile, alive" and that it was "the wave of the future come to life after 30 years of apathy."

Seats at the rally had been scaled from $1 to $25, with eighteen Patron's Boxes at $250 each. YAF reported gross receipts of $80,000—an amount equal to its entire budget in 1960-61.

Was this indeed the first swelling of the wave of the future?

There is, within YAF, within ISI, and within the whole Rightist Movement, a deep-seated philosophical cleavage between the Rugged Individualists and the so-called Traditionalists, both of whom claim the mantle of true conservatism. The main cry of the Rugged Individualists is against statism—against use of the instrument of government to improve living standards, social conditions, and the domestic "general welfare." Fearing statism, they nevertheless support the exercise of state power to investigate the ideas of individuals, and to promote prayers in public schools. And in the name of freedom and limited government they would adopt radical measures to turn America backward to the political, economic, and social conditions that existed in the McKinley era.

The Traditionalists emphasize the need for order and authority as the essentials for the virtuous society. They stress law, Constitutionalism, value and virtue, and the lessons and experiences of the past.

For the present, the two schools of Rightist thought are united in an alliance by the urgency, as they see it, of overturning the Liberal Establishment.

This uneasy alliance, held together by a common target and a common goal, exists within the extreme conservative youth movement as it does among older veterans of the Right. It enables YAF to welcome the support of men who also support the Birch Society and other Radical Rightist causes. It enables YAF to give awards and to honor those who nourish the growth of Right extremism. The only criterion of the movement is: Is it anti-Liberal?

In practical terms, YAF today includes two basic groups: the first from the College Young Republicans, essentially youthful Eastern politicians on the make, and active because they hope eventually to enhance their careers inside the Republican Party. The second group, a coalition of young Rightists in revolt against liberalism, are essentially ideological fundamentalists who are more interested in the future of what they call conservatism than in the future of the Republican Party. These fundamentalists are strongly under the influence of Bill Buckley, and they are willing to support such moves as the formation of Conservative parties. They are ideologues, not politicans, and veer farther toward the Radical Right than do the young politicians.

Like their intellectual allies in the Intercollegiate Society of Individualists, the young men and women of YAF are a generation of political creatures whose experience is limited and whose grasp of events and issues is narrow. They have never seen the bread lines of Depression, or the chow lines of shooting war. They are unequipped for the "long, twilight struggle, year in and year out" of which the late President Kennedy spoke so eloquently.

The one, basic, all-important fact about the Rightist youth movement in America today, minority though it is, is that it is here. And the people in it are going to be around for a long time to come. Whether right or wrong, green or case-hardened, they will in all likelihood be the Rightist makers and shakers, wheelers and dealers of tomorrow. Among them are tomorrow's Rightist candidates, politicoes, writers, commentators, authors, businessmen. And they are not likely to moderate their political views as they grow older.

And so the Young American Rightists beat the drums in 1964 for Senator Goldwater, and like their elders they leap to their feet with roars of approval when one of their young tribunes shouts for the invasion of Cuba, or for the tearing down of the Berlin Wall, and the liberation of captive peoples.

The zest for the oversimplified solution to the complex problem is as much a disease of the Young American Right as it is of the Old American Right. Both feed and grow on the fears and frustrations of the twilight struggle. The Moderates of our nation, with long responsibility for governing, can offer only a call for patience, for fortitude, and for resolution. And this has no attraction for those who, seeking militant action, march today under the banner of YAF.

16

The National Review
— *William F. Buckley, Jr.*

When it comes to deploring the extreme and dangerous condition of the United States and of all Western civilization, you have to get up pretty early in the morning to outdo William F. Buckley, Jr., the aging Boy Wonder of the American Right and a leading light of unabashed Reaction.

Now thirty-nine and barely a year away from the magic age when he will lose his franchise as a young Turk, the one-time *enfant terrible* of Yale University has emerged in the last decade or so as a major figure on the American Right—one of its most articulate writers and voices, and undoubtedly its most polysyllabic.

Buckley is the editor of *National Review,* a well-written and important "journal of fact and opinion" which appears fortnightly to wage ideological warfare against the Liberal Establishment and which has provided an outlet for an assortment of middle-aged ex-Leftists and rising young hopefuls of the Right Wing. Started in 1955, beset by the usual financial, circulation and advertising problems which plague journals of opinion, the *National Review* has nevertheless survived, and has grown to impressive proportions for a magazine of its kind.

Buckley, in addition, writes a syndicated newspaper column that is carried once a week in thirty-eight newspapers, with an estimated circulation of 7,000,000. He appears frequently as a debater, a lecturer, or a TV guest panelist, as do a number of those whose names are associated with *National Review*. These speaking engagements and appearances on the mass media by Buckley and his colleagues have run as high as several a week throughout the year.

Buckley and his entourage at *National Review* have, in short, become a noticeable influence in the field of American public opinion generally, and almost "must" reading for the American Right in particular. In a sense, the *National Review* is to the contemporary Extreme Right Wing what the *New Masses* was to the Extreme Left Wing three or four decades ago. It is the intellectual outlet for Rightist thinkers. In the semantics of this book, Buckley and his publication are Extreme Conservatives.

As an individual, Buckley himself performs an important role in the activities of the American Right. He is a link between the senior and junior members of the Extreme Right Wing, binding the Old Guard with the young warriors. He also serves as a kind of catalyst for the promulgation of new ideas and new activities, the most noteworthy of which is Young Americans for Freedom. As described earlier, YAF was founded at Great Elm, the Buckley family estate at Sharon, Connecticut. In the four years since, Buckley has served as its mentor and greying eminence.

Not only does Buckley link Rightist generations; he also serves as a kind of ideological bridge between leading Radical Rightists and the Extreme Conservatives. Buckley has been quoted as calling himself a "Radical Conservative," and the self-chosen label is apt—for in fact, Buckley is one of the leading fellow travelers of the American Radical Right. On a number of subjects, his own political thinking and the *National Review*'s line fall just short of Radical Right.

Buckley is too smart to accept the Radical Right mythology that the Communists are already in operational control of the country. Nor does he think the United States has been sold out by Presidents who have been part of the Bolshevik conspiracy. What Buckley believes ails the United States in its domestic and foreign policy is liberalism and its seeming blunders. What Buckley calls liberalism, Founder Welch of the Birch Society calls communism, and the only essential difference is that Welch thinks the United States has been degraded by traitors, while Buckley thinks it's been degraded by blunderers. It's a difference—but whether it's a difference of anything more than degree is another question.

There are other differences: Welch thinks the menace to the United States is from the internal Red conspiracy. Buckley correctly realizes the danger to the United States is posed by Moscow and Peking. Like Welch, however, he thinks that thirty years of internal liberalism has undermined the nation's capacity to meet the threat from abroad.

The major outlet for Buckley's views is, of course, *National Review*, which modestly describes itself as "a magazine of discourse and criticism edited for the well informed citizen and written by some of the most accomplished essayists, poets, analysts and critics of our time."

Surveys of *National Review*'s readership show that it is read by an affluent (annual income of over $15,000) and influential segment of the population. The magazine, although far from homespun, is pretty much a family affair. Buckley is editor, sister Priscilla is managing editor. Sister Aloise writes political articles. Another sister handled all the correspondence. Brother-in-law L. Brent Bozell is on the editorial board and second in command.

When the magazine was launched, the directors, besides Buckley himself, included Clarence Manion, who has since become a member of the John Birch Society national council and proprietor of his own Manion Forum; Godfrey Schmidt, a Rightist attorney; Morrie Ryskind, a playwright; Edwin S. Webster, Jr., whose name had previously been identified with numerous Right Wing causes, and General Albert Wedemeyer, also a supporter of myriad ultraconservative organizations. A memorandum announcing the new magazine said it hoped "to change the nation's intellectual and political climate—which, at present, is preponderantly leftist."

The back cover of the first issue, dated November 19, 1955, carried messages of greeting from well-known names: Admiral Ben Moreell, J. Bracken Lee, Bonner Fellers, Spruille Braden, Charles Edison, J. Howard Pew, and many others. In a statement, Buckley declared that the new periodical "stands athwart history, yelling 'Stop!' at a time when no one is inclined to do so, or to have much patience with those who urge it."

National Review was financed by $290,000 capital raised from 125 investors. Buckley said he invested $10,000 himself. He said the magazine expected a loss of $210,000 in its first year, $100,-000 in its second, that it hoped to break even in its third year, and earn $100,000 in the fourth. The actual results were far different. According to newspaper reports, the *National Review's* balance sheet on June 30, 1958, showed assets of about $270,000 and debts of almost $1,500,000. The loss in 1956 was more than $252,000, in 1957 more than $292,000 and in 1958 more than $388,000.

Exactly how these tremendous losses were met is not known, but the Buckley family is wealthy, and when Buckley's father, an oil industrialist, died in 1958, his son wrote in the *National Review* that it was "to his encouragement, moral and material, that the magazine owed its birth and early life." Young Buckley added that the magazine had become his father's "principal enthusiasm."

In 1957, in an apparent effort to offset the magazine's losses, National Weekly, Inc., the parent corporation, purchased a radio station in Omaha for $822,500. In 1962, a second station, an FM outlet, was acquired, also in Omaha. The radio operations have helped, but the deficit continues, although substantially reduced with constant circulation growth of the magazine.

By 1961, *National Review* circulation had reached about 36,000; by the end of 1963, it had reached about 66,000, with a press run of 96,000. (Some 30,000 copies of each issue were not accounted for.) There were still financial problems, and in the spring of 1964, an urgent appeal was sent out, suggesting the horrifying possibility that the *National Review* might fold. A few months later, however, Buckley announced to his public that the magazine would be around for at least another year.

Although he asserts that *National Review* policy is set by an editorial board, the magazine is widely regarded as being in the grand tradition of the one-man publication that mirrors the personality of the man who dominates it. Buckley founded the *National Review* to express his own arch and unequivocal views, and the magazine is as much William Buckley, Jr., as the John Birch Society is Robert Welch.

Despite the fact that the *National Review* is the best-written and best-edited Rightist publication in the country, a contributor who knows Buckley and the magazine well described it as one of the "most unprofessional" of all the journals of opinion and "hopelessly Amateur Night." He said "staff absenteeism compares favorably with that of the U.S. House of Representatives."

The writer, Noel Parmentel, Jr., also noted that despite Buckley's own skill as a writer, he was less than big league in his taste for the journalese of others, especially members of his family. He noted that the *National Review* sometimes seemed to be the spiritual successor to *Grelmschatka,* a private Buckley family newspaper. (It was so dubbed from an amalgam of the names of the Buckley family homes in Sharon, Connecticut, and Camden, South Carolina—Great Elm and Kamschatka, both sprawling plantation-like manses in the best tradition of American nineteenth-century wealth.)

William Frank Buckley, Jr., was to these manors born on November 24, 1925. His father, William F. Buckley, Sr., was a lawyer and independent oil man whose holdings in seven countries around the world were estimated at $110,000,000 when he died in 1958. The senior Buckley had been born in Texas, the son of a second-generation Irish-American who had successfully engaged in merchandising, politics, and sheep-raising in Duval County, and had served several terms as county sheriff. Although his paternal grandfather had been a Protestant in Ireland, William F. Buckley, Sr., was raised as a Roman Catholic in the faith of his mother.

William F. Buckley, Jr., one of ten children, was also raised as a Catholic. In addition to the financial and religious legacy he received from his strong-willed father, William, Jr., also inherited a rigid political and economic ideology that stemmed from his father's career as a self-made, ruggedly individualistic oil operator who handed down to his son a devout belief in free enterprise and in the survival of the fittest.

Bill Buckley, Jr., was reared in England, in France, and in the United States, was educated at St. Thomas More School and St. Johns in England, and was privately tutored before entering Millbrook School in Millbrook, New York, where he finished his secondary education in 1943 and was generally on the honor roll. His prep school interests were music, the school newspaper, and the yearbook. It is perhaps worth noting that the kind of upbringing and the kind of education Buckley received rarely, if ever, brought him in contact with youngsters of different social and economic backgrounds. His family referred to him as the "Young Mahster," and his father later recalled that they had thought him "slightly deficient in a sense of humor, and unbearably arrogant and dictatorial."

The elder Buckley recalled, as "illustrations of the character and imperiousness" of his son, that when he was six years old the youngster had written to the King of England demanding that England pay her war debt. At ten, two days after his arrival at a school in England, he called at the office of the president of the institution, a distinguished scholar, and told him there were a number of things about the school he did not like, which so flabbergasted the educator that he could not speak. By the time he had recovered, the elder Buckley recalled, William, Jr., had explained the deficiencies of the old and established institution of learning.

And there were other episodes which Buckley, Sr., included in his reminiscences about his son: the correspondence maintained by young Billy with members of Congress and his youthful pre-occupation with global affairs; his appearance, uninvited, at a faculty meeting at the Millbrook School to complain that a teacher had deprived him of the right to express his political views in class (followed by a discourse before the stunned teachers on the virtues of American isolationism, the dignity of the Catholic Church, and the political ignorance of the school staff); his arrival, while in the Army, at a military base in Texas which was followed, in forty-eight hours, by a letter to the commanding general de-ploring the waste of manpower and the inadequacy of the staff, plus a plan redesigning the entire system at the base—a letter that was intercepted before it reached the commanding officer.

When young Buckley was fifteen, his father—who wrote fre-quent advisory memoranda to his brood of ten—told Billy that while his parents liked his strong convictions and his readiness to express them, he should "learn to be more moderate in the ex-pression" of his views and to express them in a way that would give as little offense as possible to his friends.

Young Buckley took part in horse shows, but was not other-wise especially inclined toward athletics; today he skis and is a passionate yachtsman, owner of a forty-two-foot cutter which he sails out of Stamford, Connecticut, where he lives in a twenty-room house on Wallack's Point.

In the year following his graduation from Millbrook, Buckley studied at the University of Mexico, a country from which his father had been expelled in 1921 for backing the unsuccessful side in a revolution—a deportation later rescinded with an invita-tion to return to the country whose oil development he had aided. Young William entered the United States Army during World War II as a private and was discharged in 1946 with the rank of second lieutenant. He then entered Yale University, where he concentrated on history, political science, and economics, distin-guished himself as a debater, served as chairman of the *Yale Daily News,* and achieved membership in the Torch Honor Society, the Fence Club, and Skull and Bones.

Buckley graduated in 1950. A year later his first book, *God and*

Man at Yale, was published by Regnery, the Rightist publishers, and it brought him nation-wide attention, as it was widely reviewed and heatedly discussed.

The book was a severe indictment of Buckley's alma mater, the content of its curriculum, and the political and economic views of many of its faculty members. In the foreword, Buckley declared that before entering Yale, he had been taught that "an active faith in God and rigid adherence to Christian principles were the most powerful influences toward the good life." He said he also believed, although he had scanty knowledge of economics, that free enterprise and limited government "had served the country well and would probably continue to do so in the future."

He "therefore looked eagerly to Yale University for allies against secularism and collectivism." While he was still an undergraduate, he said, he had advanced the viewpoint that the faculty was morally and constitutionally responsible to the trustees, who were in turn responsible to the alumni at large. "I contended," Buckley wrote, "that the trustees of Yale, along with the vast majority of the alumni, are committed to the desirability of fostering both a belief in God, and a recognition of the merits of our economic system"—and he added he believed it was the responsibility of the trustees to guide the teaching at Yale toward those ends.

He wrote that he proposed to "expose what I regard as an extraordinarily irresponsible educational attitude that, under the protective label 'academic freedom,' has produced one of the most extraordinary incongruities of our time: the institution that derives its moral and financial support from Christian individualists and then addresses itself to the task of persuading the sons of these supporters to be atheistic socialists."

The October 15, 1951, *Yale Daily News,* in a front-page article on Buckley's book, summed it up this way:

". . . he says, the alumni of Yale believe in Christianity and capitalism. He does not feel that all her professors do.

"He would fire those who do not."

Buckley wrote in the foreword of his book that he had little real hope that the situation would be remedied but added:

"I consider this battle of educational theory important and worth time and thought even in the context of a world-situation that seems to render totally irrelevant any fight except the power struggle against Communism. I myself believe that the duel between Christianity and atheism is the most important in the world. I further believe that the struggle between individualism and collectivism is the same struggle reproduced on another level."

Some Yale graduates disagreed with Buckley's elaborately documented effort to prove that Old Eli was irreligious and collectivist. One of them, McGeorge Bundy—later to become an advisor to Presidents Kennedy and Johnson—wrote in the November, 1951, *Atlantic Monthly:*

"As a believer in God, a Republican, and a Yale graduate, I find that the book is dishonest in its use of facts, false in its theory, and a discredit to its author."

Yale, founded in 1701, managed to survive Buckley's onslaught and his notion that education should consist of indoctrination in religious orthodoxy and *laissez-faire* economics. *God and Man at Yale,* nevertheless, launched Buckley into the public arena as an acid and articulate voice of the Right. The book was diligently promoted by the habitués of the Right, all the way from the Near to the Far, including some on the anti-Semitic extremist fringe. This was not, of course, Buckley's fault; he is no anti-Semite and will have no truck with anti-Jewish bigotry.

Buckley became a sought-after Rightist personality, and during 1951, he wrote frequently for *Human Events,* where Frank Hanighen and Frank Chodorov were in charge. In 1952, Buckley served a brief time on the staff of the *American Mercury* just before that once-great magazine descended into a long period of frequent and undisguised anti-Semitism. He resigned to free-lance, and soon afterward, Chodorov named him as president of the newly formed Intercollegiate Society of Individualists.

The fairest fruit of this two- or three-year period was a second book, which Buckley co-authored with his Yale chum, Brent Bozell. Bozell was an ex-One-Worlder type who fell under Buckley's influence while at New Haven, in short order became a Rightist, a Roman Catholic, and somewhat later the husband of Buckley's sister, Patricia. Today, Bozell, a co-founder of the *National Review,* is a personality in his own right on the starboard fringe. The new book was *McCarthy and His Enemies,* and was a defense of the late Wisconsin senator and the activities he perpetrated in the early 1950's which will be known to the ages as McCarthyism. Bozell and Buckley made concessions all over the place in a show of disarming fairness, admitting that the senator had at times tended to exaggerate in his charges, sometimes was a little short on facts to back up his allegations. But, they said, he had rendered a national service, regardless of these occasional departures from truth, because he had generated a greater concern for internal security in the Government—particularly in the State Department.

Critics were quick to point out that the book, which appeared in 1954, completely ignored some of McCarthyism's major aberrations—his reckless attacks on the Voice of America and the United States Information Agency, the bizarre behavior of McCarthy aides Roy Cohn and David Schine, and the Fort Monmouth "investigation." But the most startling disclosure of the book was that Buckley and Bozell—two staunch young opponents of statism and the power of government over the economic affairs of men—were stern advocates of statism when it came to security probes.

Reasonable regulations for internal security are necessary. But Buckley and Bozell went so far as to urge that in the case of government employees, the whole concept of presuming a man innocent until proven guilty should be chucked in the internal security program.

Exactly why statism is dangerous in the market place but not in cases of individual justice is one of the contradictions which Buckley has not been able satisfactorily to explain.

He stands as an unrepentant defender of McCarthy, and of what the term McCarthyism has come to mean as a dark and sordid period of recent American history. That probably doesn't bother Buckley, who is not inclined to have doubts. He knows fervently what he thinks, and the verdict of American public opinion leaves him cold.

Commenting on the stand taken by Buckley and Bozell—that despite questionable methods, McCarthy had rendered a public service—William S. White, not at all the harshest reviewer of *McCarthy and His Enemies*, wrote in *The New York Times*: "What is urged is not only that the end justifies the means, but that a moral end justifies immoral means."

In this period, like any young and dedicated radical, whether Left or Right, Buckley became a bit of a "joiner"—lending his name to several of the major Radical Right causes of the mid-1950's peopled by some of the more prominent names on the extreme fringe of American political life. He popped up in 1954 on the advisory committee of the U.S. Day Committee—an outfit inspired (by, among others, the late Merwin K. Hart) to counteract the annual United Nations Day celebrated around the country. A little later he was listed on the national council of the Campaign for the 48 States—one of the major Radical Right efforts of the 1950's, as was For America, which in 1955 listed Buckley on its national policy committee.

In October, 1959, about two years before he delivered an all-out repudiation of Founder Robert Welch (but not the John Birch Society), the Sage of Stamford journeyed to Chicago to attend a two-day conference staged by Kent and Phoebe Courtney. The parley, at which Buckley was a speaker, included Welch himself, and Birch Society national council member Revilo P. Oliver, the University of Illinois classics professor who was then listed on the masthead of the *National Review* and has since emerged as one of the most extreme voices of the extremist Birch Society. Other Birch supporters present at Chicago included Tom Anderson, J. Bracken Lee, Medford Evans, and Bryton Barron, an ex-State Department official who has since broken with the Birchers as being too totalitarian. And there were such other luminaries of the Radical Right as Dan Smoot and Willis Stone.

Since Bill Buckley calls himself a "Radical Conservative," some may wonder whether he went to Chicago as an innocent Conservative who thought he was attending a conservative gathering, or whether he was, in fact, a Radical attending a meeting of political soul mates. The *National Review,* in its issue of November 7, 1959, described the Welch-Buckley-Oliver-Smoot-Courtneys meeting as "a spirited conference of conservatives" and in listing the names of those present, declared that it added up to "a lot of right-wing firepower."

Since Buckley is a leading advocate of individual responsibility for individual action, one can only conclude that he knew what he was doing—that he made a conscious decision to break bread and share the speaker's platform with this noisy collection of Extremists. And since he himself is ever ready to chastize those of Leftist political persuasion who have strayed beyond the portside pale in bygone years, it can be assumed that he will not assert that he is the target of "guilt by association." In any event, Buckley associated in 1959 with quite an assortment of Radical Rightists. He was thirty-four, out of college eight years, and was no longer politically unsophisticated.

Buckley's willingness to let his name be used in common cause with such individuals continues. As late as 1962, when the Committee for the Monroe Doctrine was formed during the Cuban crisis, with Captain Eddie Rickenbacker as chairman, Buckley and sister Priscilla were listed as members, along with a wide assortment of Extreme Conservatives and Radicals of the Right, including about a dozen names prominently linked with the John Birch Society. These included five present or former members of the Birch national council, nine or ten Endorsers of the Society, and one or two others identified with Robert Welch's magazine.

Coming as it did some ten months after Buckley's now-famous and quite devastating denunciation of Welch as harmful to the cause of anti-communism, it could only be concluded that while Buckley would not associate with Welch, he would make common cause with those who did, however closely. (It has already been noted that Young Americans for Freedom, of which Buckley has been a mentor since it was formed in 1960, shows a broad tolerance for those whose names have been linked with the Birch Society and other extreme causes.)

Perhaps Buckley's easy attitude about marching under Rightist banners with Birchers can be explained by the main thrust of his widely read editorial, "The Question of Robert Welch," which appeared in the February 13, 1962, issue of the *National Review*. The editorial repudiated Welch but declared that the Birch Society included "some of the most morally energetic self-sacrificing and dedicated anti-Communists in America."

Addressing itself to those Birch members, the editorial called on them to reject, "out of a love of truth and country, his [Welch's] false counsels." Buckley said that for Rightists there were "bounds to the dictum" that "anyone on my right is my ally." On moral grounds, he asked, "can one endorse the efforts of a man who, in one's judgment, goes about bearing false witness?" This was all the more true, said Buckley, because Welch insisted that there be no disagreement on the part of his followers with the central Welch thesis—that the Government of the United States is, and has been, under the operational control of the Communist Party for a number of years. Yet by the time the Committee for the Monroe Doctrine was formed in October, 1962, those identified with the Birch Society who joined the Committee had not, with perhaps a few exceptions, disassociated themselves from the Society nor had they succeeded in ousting Founder Welch. But Buckley's name was linked with theirs. Anyone on his near right was apparently his ally.

The Buckley editorial, cutting up Welch while kissing Birchers on both cheeks, shook the American Right, caused anguished comment by the Founder, and was widely interpreted as a conservative manifesto reading the Radicals out of the whole American Rightist movement. In truth, it was a lot less than that; Buckley had taken a hard line on Welch and a soft line on Birchers.

When the smoke cleared, Welch—like Yale—had survived the wrath of Buckley's typewriter. Since February, 1962, Buckley and the *National Review* have resumed saying nice things about the Birchers and some of their activities.

It has already been noted that in 1959, after Welch had formed the Society, but before he and it became notorious, Buckley took common counsel with Welch and some of the leading Radical Rightists at the Courtney meeting in Chicago. Late in 1960 and early in 1961, Welch, the Birch Society and some of Welch's extreme and outrageous viewpoints came to light in the nation's press —headlined was the charge that President Eisenhower was a "dedicated, conscious agent of the Communist conspiracy."

In March and April, 1961, came the national outpouring of indignation over the Birch Society and Welch which we have described in previous pages. Newspapers, magazines, broadcasters, national political figures, and clergymen, it will be recalled, denounced the extremism which had been exposed. In an article headlined "The Uproar," which bore Buckley's by-line and which appeared in the April 22, 1961, *National Review,* Buckley interrogated himself on the subject.

Q. Would you say that the structure of the John Birch Society is totalitarian or fascistic? A. No, I consider it reasonable that a man who founds an ad hoc organization of this character should have as much dominance over its affairs as he considers to be in the best interests of the organization's objective. If members of the John Birch Society do not like the way it is run, they can resign from it. . . . Q. What is the future of the John Birch Society? A. I hope it thrives, provided, of course, it resists such false assumptions as that a man's subjective motives can automatically be deduced from the objective consequences of his acts.

A week later, when news came of the suspension of Major General Edwin Walker for seeking, allegedly improperly, to indoctrinate his troops with Rightist propaganda, the *National Review* leaped to the defense of Walker.

In June, 1961, as the wave of anger about the Birch Society continued, the *National Review* testily complained of the denunciations: "Why, it's enough to make one join the John Birch Society."

By 1962, alarm that the national outcry against the Birch Society might harm the whole Rightist movement in general must have hit home with Buckley. *Ergo,* his editorial of February 13, 1962:

"Mr. Welch, for all his good intentions, threatens to divert militant conservative action to irrelevance and ineffectuality. There are, as we say, great things that need doing, the winning of a national election, the re-education of the governing class. John Birch chapters can do much to forward these aims, but only as they dissipate the fog of confusion that issues from Mr. Welch's smoking typewriter. Mr. Welch has revived in many men the spirit of patriotism, and that same spirit calls now for rejecting, out of a love of truth and country, his false counsels."

By 1963, however, when it was clear that the rejection had not taken place, the inevitable zag by the *National Review* followed the zig. As the so-called "card party" movement—plugged, promoted, and manned by Birchers across the nation—sought to stop the retail sale of goods manufactured behind the Iron Curtain, the *National Review* had some nice things to say:

"President Kennedy says it doesn't do any good, but he just doesn't read the papers. This happy new enterprise of scattering little cards among Communist merchandise in local stores has paid huge dividends. . . ."

Two months later, in March, 1963, Buckley again took the soft line on Birchism:

"I tend to fear not that the pendulum is going too far in the direction of Mr. Robert Welch, but too far in the direction of total nonchalance about the fact that a) conspiracies do exist, and b) that they do accomplish great purposes."

By November, 1963, Buckley found himself called upon to go even further in his "anti-anti-Birch" position. In a piece called "Goldwater and the John Birch Society," he wrote: "I had occasion last March, before . . . Senator Goldwater had become an odds-on favorite to receive the Republican nomination, to comment on the tendency among opponents of the American Right to fasten on the John Birch Society as a means of sandbagging conservative candidates. With the rise of Senator Goldwater, the tendency is assuming the form of a national political obsession."

Buckley wrote that Senator Goldwater had never been a member of the Society and that he had repudiated Welch's "spectacular theses." He added that on several occasions the senator had called on Welch to resign his leadership "as the result of his manifest disqualifications as a political analyst."

Buckley said that ". . . certainly it does not follow that Senator Goldwater has any obligation, in morals or in intellect, to repudiate all those who have associated themselves with Mr. Welch to make common cause against Communism and socialism."

Referring to a reported statement by Senator Goldwater that "all the members of the John Birch Society I have met are good people," Buckley said that "a society is not to be judged by the excesses of individual members of it, any more than it must be judged by the excesses of its leaders." (Buckley did not tell his readers how a society *should* be judged, if not by its leaders and its members.)

Buckley concluded with the declaration that he stood by his statement of a year previous: ". . . that I have nothing against, in fact I have a considerable admiration for, the majority of those members of the John Birch Society, whom I have met or corresponded with—and I judge them as individuals, not as members of the Society. But irrespective of whether one agrees with the general goals of the Society's members, as I emphatically do, genocidal assaults upon the membership of the Society and on candidates who refuse to condemn all members of the Society are unreasonable and undiscriminating."

Buckley has not applied the same nice yardstick to individuals in Leftist or even liberal groups such as ADA; they are all usually lumped together.

The softness of Buckley and the *National Review* on Birchers and Bircher-conducted "card parties" is not the only evidence that the Rebellious Rightist of Stamford and his magazine are sometimes closer than a hair's breadth to the Radical Right. Does the Birch Society call for the impeachment of the Chief Justice of the United States? Not realistic, says Brent Bozell in the September 9, 1961, *National Review*. But he adds:

"There is nothing in the world to prevent the House or Senate or both jointly from passing a resolution of *censure* against the Supreme Court, or against especially offending justices—or, if that is deemed appropriate, against Warren singly. Here is something the John Birch Society could get its teeth into. . . . But let us abandon impeachment. Another way of putting all of this is that Earl Warren has sinned too grandly for that. He has defiled our jurisprudence and made war against the public order. He has not stolen chickens."

Does the Birch Society demand "Get the U.S. out of the U.N. and the U.N. out of the U.S.?" Here's what the *National Review* has to say:

Put most simply, and not quite exactly, we believe that many of the *technical* functions served by the complex of agencies composing what one calls for short, 'the UN,' are desirable or necessary; but that most of the UN's *political* functions are not merely useless, but fraudulent, mischievous and often gravely injurious to major goals—international peace and order—that the UN Charter proclaims. As a technical organization we are, if not unqualifiedly *for* the UN, at any rate prepared to accept it. As a political organization, we are against it, and strongly so. We therefore conclude that the UN ought to be, to the maximum extent possible, *depoliticalized*. If this proved to be impossible, then—since the political aspect has in the past year dropped to an intolerable badness— the UN as a whole ought to be liquidated.

That was in January, 1962, when the Congo was a hot item, and Katanga was very much in the news. *National Review*'s position on Katanga: "We hope they [Tshombe's Katanga] lick the daylights out of the forces of the so-called United Nations."

By the end of 1962, here's what the *National Review* was saying on the UN:

"Our people, in the delegation and secretariat staff alike, really believe all that abstract nonsense saturating the UN air—Humanity, Peace, Universal Rights, Disarmament, World Law, Conscience of Mankind, Last Best Hope. . . . For the Communists, the UN can be a useful forum and political weapon. For us, until we are willing to open our eyes, it can only continue to be a political trap."

Robert Welch denounces democracy as an instrument for demagoguery and a "perennial fraud." Does Buckley? In an April, 1961, lecture at Brooks School, North Andover, Massachusetts, Buckley told his youthful audience that "the commitment by the intellectuals to democracy is inordinate." Buckley added that he did not believe completely in democracy but that he did favor self-rule.

These were ideas Buckley had spelled out in detail in his 1959 book, *Up from Liberalism*, in which he declared that "democracy is mere procedure" and added: "The democracy of universal suffrage is not a bad form of government; it is simply not necessarily nor inevitably a good form of government. Democracy must be justified by its works, not by doctrinaire affirmations of an intrinsic goodness that no mere method can legitimately lay claim to."

Nor does Buckley believe in universal suffrage. In an article that appeared in the January, 1961, issue of *Esquire*, writer Dan Wakefield quoted Buckley as saying that the idea that everyone is qualified to vote was "one of the great self-delusions of democracy."

"I don't have any theory worked out on who should vote," Wakefield quoted Buckley as saying, "but let's say, as a hypothesis, that fifty per cent of the people are qualified to vote—or seventy-five per cent. I don't know how you determine it, but it's certainly worth a study by the Ford Foundation."

Buckley, Wakefield wrote, didn't think purely intellectual qualifications should by any means be the determining factor in who should vote. "I would rather be governed by the first 2,000 people in the telephone directory," Buckley was quoted as saying, "than by the Harvard University faculty." Buckley added that "under certain circumstances, dictatorship is best." Buckley was interested in human freedom and the kind of government that maximizes it. "I think I would have more freedom under Franco, for instance, than I would have had under the Spanish Republic!"

At least as much, certainly. But what of those not on the Right?

The plain fact is that Buckley attaches far more importance to property rights and the freedom of the market place than he does to political rights. He spelled it out in *Up from Liberalism*:

"Let the individual keep his dollar—however few he is able to save—and he can indulge his taste (and never mind who had a role in shaping it) in houses, in doctors, in education, in groceries, in entertainment, in culture, in religion; give him the right of free speech or the right to go to the polling booth, and at best he contributes to a collective determination, contributes as a rule an exiguous voice. Give me the right to spend my dollars as I see fit—to devote them, as I see fit, to travel, to food, to learning, to taking pleasure, to polemicizing, and, if I must make the choice, I will surrender you my political franchise in trade, confident that by the transaction, assuming the terms of the contracts are that no political decision affecting my sovereignty over my dollar can be made, I shall have augmented my dominance over my own affairs."

What is the course of action for Conservatives in the modern age?

"It is," Buckley wrote, "to maintain and wherever possible enhance the freedom of the individual to acquire property and dispose of that property in ways that he decides on. To deal with unemployment by eliminating monopoly unionism, featherbedding, and inflexibilities in the labor market, and be prepared, where residual unemployment persists, to cope with it locally, placing political and humanitarian responsibility on the lowest feasible political unit. . . .

"Is that a program? Call it a No-Program, if you will, but adopt it for your very own. I will not cede more power to the state. I will not willingly cede more power to anyone, not to the state, not to General Motors, not to the CIO. I will hoard my power like a miser, resisting every effort to drain it away from me. I will then use *my* power as *I* see fit. I mean to live my life an obedient man, but obedient to God, subservient to the wisdom of my ancestors; never to the authority of political truths arrived at yesterday at the voting booths. That is a program of sorts, is it not?

"It is certainly program enough to keep Conservatives busy, and Liberals at bay. . . ."

Given that position, it is not hard to understand why, in February, 1964, Buckley wrote that he did not believe everyone should vote and that he did not even believe everyone should have the right to vote.

"I believe in potholing, rather than broadening, the highway to the voting booth."

Buckley conceded that such statements imposed on him a responsibility to state an acceptable alternative. His, he wrote, was this: ". . . Everyone should have the right to vote whose record or accomplishments suggest he attaches an importance to the vote beyond his own immediate self-interests." Like "my dollars," for instance?

Buckley did not, of course, get around to stating how the right to vote should actually be determined—but that is fairly typical. For all his brilliance, Buckley is short on answers to specific questions, short on answers to specific problems that beset ordinary folk. But then, he is no ordinary man. Everyone agrees on that— including Bill Buckley.

In short, on most of the subjects about which the American Right agitates itself, the *National Review* seems always to have one foot poised in the air over the radical camp, while the other appears to remain in the conservative camp. The *National Review* stops short of the radical wilds, yet advocates positions frequently beyond those usually taken by Conservatives.

There is a unanimity as to Buckley's attractiveness, erudition, charm, intelligence, and wit. When he writes, and especially when he speaks or debates publicly, one gets the impression that he is far more eager to use a scintillating phrase than to analyze his subjects soberly and objectively. He delights in public debate and readily meets with adversaries such as Norman Thomas, Arthur Schlesinger, Jr., and James A. Wechsler.

On the platform he is a six-foot, trim, debonair, blue-eyed, and blond-haired Ivy League type whose fading is still almost imperceptible. His manner of delivery has been described as that of a sharp professor rather than that of a politician. He stalks back and forth; sometimes, in moments of concentration, he rises to his toes and touches his face reflectively, or, hands on hips, paces restlessly as he drives home his point in a deep, positive voice. He has a gift for withering ridicule and the flashing phrase, whether spontaneous or well planned and kept in reserve for the proper moment. He loves a shocker—and startles an audience into applause with phrases like "a vindictive vulgarity of a Harry Truman," or "the directionalist vapidity of the unsilenceable Mrs. Roosevelt." Buckley gives the impression that he is not only presenting ideas but is putting on a good show.

A writer in the *New York Herald Tribune* once described him in action:

"The supercilious manner in which Buckley displayed his vast erudition, the flashes of wit and velvety insults that were sprinkled throughout his remarks, reminded me of Noel Coward acting in one of his own plays. Buckley even looked a little like Coward when he delivered a line like 'I wish you wouldn't sound so fatigued when confronted by historical fact.' "

Though he may slash an opponent with a rapierlike phrase, when debate is ended, Buckley is a sociable fellow. If his propaganda strength were not so useful to the Radical Right, he would be very amusing and harmless. In a debate with playwright Gore Vidal, Buckley called his opponent a "philosophical degenerate," but when the debate ended, amiably suggested that they go out for a drink. He's got epithets in every pocket, and one opponent in debate said:

"Buckley has the facility of creating an atmosphere which leads you to believe you are engaging in a reasonable discourse, only to make some outrageous point at the end. You become mellow and amiable, then suddenly discover he is practically calling you a traitor."

A magazine writer noted:

"Before an audience his voice went much deeper, striking bass notes that sounded grim warnings in their very tone. . . . But in private conversation his voice does not plumb those dark lower registers, and during our talk he gave more the impression of the genial and scholarly tutor explaining his subject than the prophet-with-a-mission he often sounds like in public."

Buckley is a devout Roman Catholic. But when Pope John XXIII issued *Mater et Magistra,* an encyclical urging aid for underdeveloped areas, declaring that the advantages of socialization and state welfare programs should be accepted—provided that "the sphere of freedom of the personal initiative of individual citizens" was not reduced—Buckley sharply disagreed with the Pope. He called the encyclical "a venture in triviality." In a *National Review* editorial on July 29, 1961, he said that the encyclical took insufficient notice of the "most obtrusive social phenomenon of the moment . . . the continuing demonic successes of the Communists. . . ."

Catholics and non-Catholics alike were shocked. The Jesuit weekly, *America,* severely condemned Buckley. *America's* editor said that to imply that "Catholic Conservative circles" accepted the Church as Mother but not as Teacher was "slanderous." "It takes an appalling amount of self-assurance for a Catholic writer to brush off an encyclical," said the publication. "The *National Review* owes its Catholic readers and journalistic allies an apology."

Buckley snapped back that the Jesuit weekly's comments were "impudent"; that the *National Review's* editorial was the position of its editorial board, made up of Catholics, Protestants, and Jews.

Buckley seemed to be indifferent to the fact that he was out of step with Vatican policy which favored international co-operation and recognition of racial equality and rights for minorities. American liberal Catholics—and most who are not Liberals— accept the Vatican's teaching and want no part of the reactionary concepts which Buckley advocates.

The main target of Buckley and his magazine is still liberalism. "The salient economic assumptions of Liberalism are socialist," he wrote in *Up from Liberalism.* This, he added, is because "the Liberal sees no moral problem whatever in divesting the people of that portion of their property necessary to finance the projects certified by the ideology as beneficial to the Whole." And the *National Review* inveighs endlessly against this liberal dastardliness, with rarely a word of approval for most of the works of the Roosevelt, Truman, Eisenhower, Kennedy, or Johnson administrations.

Here are some sample quotes:

—On Roosevelt: ". . . the biggest President the U.S. ever had. He spent the most dollars, told the most lies, broke the most promises, fooled the most people. . . ."

—On President Eisenhower: ". . . what a miserable President he was! . . . it is painful to use such language about so good a man. . . . As it happened, Eisenhower, when he was not the laughing stock of the trouble-makers, was the explicit object of their contempt. . . . At home, radiant with good will, he failed. Under Eisenhower, the forces that gnaw at the strength of our country grew stronger—the bureaucratic parasites, the labor union monopolists, the centralizers."

—On President Kennedy: "Our President emerges as the ultimate man in the grey flannel suit: the great accommodator, the weather vane on the perfect ball-bearings—soul-free, immune from any of the frictions of reality."

". . . there aren't enough psychiatrists in the world to cure this crazy administration."

"The White House is not occupied by a man of unalterable principle, but by a man who will balk at nothing—no, not even at right reason—in his desire for the continuing consent of the governed."

"The editors of *National Review* judged John Fitzgerald Kennedy to be a consummate technician of mass politics. His programs and policies—often chosen, by the evidence, in opportunistic furtherance of technical manipulations—we judged to be, for the most part, dangerous to the nation's well-being and security, and to the survival of our perilously threatened Western civilization. Neither his death nor the fearful manner of it provides any reason to change these judgments."

After the dark days of the Cuban missile crisis in the fall of 1962, the *National Review* wrote:

"It is too shocking to feel that a man holding the office of President of the United States could be so infinitely cynical and irresponsible as to risk the fate of his country and the world for a handful of votes. But the timing is hard to explain on any other account."

Neither Buckley nor the *National Review* favors Federal legislation on civil rights. As far back as 1957, when the first civil rights bill was being considered by Congress, the *National Review* published an editorial entitled, "Why the South Must Prevail." It said in part:

"The central question that emerges . . . is whether the white community in the South is entitled to take such measures as are necessary to prevail politically and culturally, in areas in which it does not predominate numerically.

"The sobering answer is YES—the white community is entitled because, for the time being, it is the advanced race."

The editorial added that "it is more important for any community, anywhere in the world, to affirm and live by civilized standards than to bow to the demands of the numerical majority."

When the late President Kennedy submitted the Civil Rights Bill of 1963 to Congress, Buckley wrote in his syndicated column that the individual states should be left to govern their own affairs, and that States' rights should not be abandoned.

What really bothers Buckley most, it would seem, was something which he discussed in *Up from Liberalism*: how the Negro would use the vote if he got it. Buckley wrote that "the problem of the South is not how to get the vote for the Negro, but how to train the Negro—and a great many whites—to cast a thoughtful vote." In a footnote, he worried that if all Negroes in the South were enfranchised, there were two fields in which they could be expected to vote as a bloc—education and economics. In education, he said, the Negroes would vote to abolish segregated schools, and this, he said, could cause violent social dislocations. Thus, he argued, the white men deny the vote to the marginal Negro who could tip the balance. But, he said, even if the whites do not fear violence, the white man is still well motivated if his intention is to safeguard intellectual and moral standards which he is convinced would be diluted under integration. On economics, Buckley said that if Negroes, who generally comprise the lowest economic class, were to be given "plenipotentiary political power," they would likely use it to levy heavier taxes against the white propertied classes. "I believe," Buckley wrote, "it is a man's right to use his political influence to protect his property; but one should be plain about what one is up to, as not all Southerners are."

He said he felt the South should apply voting qualification tests impartially to Negroes and whites in order to show good faith, and expressed the hope that "the Southern crisis, growing in tension, may set in motion the first radical reversal of the long drive to universalize the suffrage." He explained that the drive for 100 percent suffrage might end up by reducing the total vote to say, 25 percent, among whom he felt should certainly be some Negroes. Such a restriction on the vote, he said, "should allay the Southerners' fear that their society will end."

Second to the power of the state, Buckley and the *National Review* fear the power of "monopoly unions." Yet they would use the power of the state to change the situation. From a 1961 *National Review* article:

"The best available counterpoise to overweening union power would be, in our judgment, the enactment and enforcement of antimonopoly laws against the labor unions, and the establishment of a bill of rights for the individual worker which would permit him, according to his own lights, to join, or not join, a labor union."

The *National Review* also favors right-to-work laws: "The Right-to-Work law is a protection against laborism—the blind concen-

tration of dictatorial power in the hands of a few irresponsible
and self-perpetuating union bosses."

Such laws are no doubt *good* statism. Laws to protect Negroes
are *bad* statism.

In explaining his opposition to the Supreme Court decision rul-
ing segregated public schools unconstitutional, Buckley once declared that there were reasons, quite aside from segregation, that
led him to side with the Southern position. "I'm in favor of any
movement," he was quoted as saying, "which brings private schools
into being. I'm afraid of the quality of mass education."

Just as he is sure liberalism is the destructive force in domestic
affairs, so Buckley also believes that it is driving Western civilization toward suicide in world and foreign affairs.

In mid-1964, James Burnham, an editor of the *National Review*,
published his latest book, *Suicide of the West*, in which he argued
that liberalism is not equipped to meet the challenges confronting
Western civilization today, the most important of which is survival.
In his syndicated column hailing the book, Buckley declared that
the West cannot survive unless the present trend is reversed. What
has been happening, he wrote, is that the West has been engaged
in "a prolonged act of suicide."

It is noteworthy that neither Buckley nor, for that matter, Burnham, offers any program for salvation. Nor does the *National Review*.
That, of course, is their privilege. Commenting on the most press-
ing problems of domestic peace, tranquility, and justice—and of
survival in a dangerous world—they criticize broadside all that
those who have borne the burden of responsibility of government
have sought to do for thirty years. It's all wrong, we are told,
almost without exception, whether at home or abroad. *This* won't
work; *that* endangers freedom; *the other* weakens us in the cold
war. Four Presidents and all their assembled advisory brainpower,
not to mention their counterparts in other free countries who have
made Western policy—all of these are not quite as brilliant as the
Boy Wonder of Old Eli, and his assortment of Rightist eggheads,
former Leftists, young Tories, and Buckley kinfolk. But then, as
his family noted many years ago, the "Young Mahster" has always
been "unbearably arrogant."

17

A Final Word

We have made an effort to describe the nature, the scope, and the
thrust of the Extreme American Right Wing—the Radical Right
and its supporters in the ranks of the Conservatives. We have concentrated on the activities of those who cry wolf at phantom
Communist plots involving Presidents and cabinet members. We
have discussed those who find socialism in an era of corporate
prosperity. We have described those who fear statism, belied by
their own freedom to speak, to write, to publish, to earn, and to
spend. This book has tried to show that these alarmists—whether
among the Radicals or not—tear at the fine fabric of this democratic Republic by their fevered fancies and false counsels of fear,
hatred, confusion, and suspicion.

Although these pages have concentrated on the main organizations of the Radical Right and its conservative allies whose impact
is felt today, and which cast a shadow on tomorrow, it must be
borne in mind that there are other such organizations which have
not been mentioned in detail. Some are important, others are not;
some have a national impact, others are strictly local in character.

A few are secretive, a few loud and wild. Neither time nor space permits them to be probed at length or in depth in these pages.*

It is impossible to estimate with any degree of precision the number of Americans who have enlisted in the Right Wing cause, whether of the radical variety or not. But there is throughout this country, in all likelihood, a far greater reservoir of potential membership and support for the Extreme Rightist movement than is generally believed.

A public opinion poll several years ago posed the question: Should the United States withdraw from the United Nations? It was probably as good a yardstick as any other to measure Radical-Rightist sentiment. About 5 percent of those responding answered affirmatively. That is roughly 5,000,000 adult Americans, and some 3,000,000 of the 60,000,000 voters in the 1960 Presidential election.

It is a fairly certain fact that the leaders of the Right Wing—Radicals and their conservative allies—have not yet mobilized anything but a fraction of that potential reservoir of support. And it is reasonable to expect that these leaders may, in the next few years, mobilize and activate new thousands, if not millions, of confused and frightened citizens not now marching in the Rightist ranks.

This is all the more likely because the fears and frustrations of the "long, twilight struggle" seem likely to continue for years. Those who seek the quick and the easy answer to the complex and delicate problem of the cold war will continue to be drawn to the Extreme Right, whose siren song appears to offer such an answer. At home, the tensions of the racial crisis will test the tolerance, the good will, and the steadfastness of the most stable Americans—let alone the citizen who is mercurial, short-tempered, prejudiced, or worse. The latter may easily be drawn to the slogans and banners of the Radical Right.

Meanwhile, the Radicals—Welch, Hargis, Smoot, McIntire, and the Courtneys—who proclaim that the nation is in the grip of a Communist political apparatus, whittle at the very concepts of the Republic they say they would save. They pollute the atmosphere of reasonable discourse and decent respect for the opinions of men, without which republican government cannot function. They charge those who oppose them with treason and subversion at worst, with being dupes of the Communists at best (even William Buckley, Jr., is not spared the odious charge when he attacks Robert Welch).

And what of Buckley and the not-so-Radical Right—the conservative allies who do not accuse their opponents of communism

* Some of these Right Wing groups are discussed in the Appendix.

or warn of massive internal conspiracies, but who blink at the Radical's game out of either softness or blindness?

Should not those who say they are conservative, without abandoning their principles, some day abandon once and for all the Radicals with whom they too readily fraternize? What is needed on the Right Wing is a house-cleaning that would separate the conservative wheat from the radical chaff, so that an Admiral Moreell or a William F. Buckley, Jr., would no longer with such ease agree to lend his name to an organization or group that abounded with leaders or members of the John Birch Society, or to make common cause with those who, like Captain Eddie Rickenbacker, willingly appear in Billy Hargis' carnival of fright.

Those who claim to be true Conservatives must, in short, come to the day when they regard the Birchers, the Crusaders, the McIntires, the Smoots, and the Courtneys as millstones of which they must be free. These Conservatives, if such they really are, will have to reject once and for all the fevered political activities of the Radicals. And Bill Buckley will, if he can, have to condemn Birch member as well as Birch leader, instead of damning the leader while praising the led.

Whether the non-Radical Right can accomplish such a cleansing is its problem. But it is also the nation's problem, because the nation *needs* a truly conservative force on the political scene. It cannot afford confusion on the Right, and if the confusion persists, the public will in the end reject the Conservative along with the Radical.

Our democracy needs a conservative faction. Without it, we will be the poorer, but we will survive.

So, too, will a military-foreign policy that deals with the perilous Communist threat, avoiding both surrender and war. So will the Supreme Court. So will the income tax. So will social security. So will TVA. So will the war on poverty. And so will the cause of civil rights, that seeks the liberty and justice our Constitution promises to all.

The nation has always heard the harsh and dissident voices of extremism, sometimes loud and sometimes muted—and it has survived them all. It has survived because the American decision-making process takes place at, or near, the vital center—sometimes a little to the left, sometimes a little to the right. For that is where the voices of reason and moderation are heard.

Appendix

Other Right Wing Organizations

In the main body of this book, we have surveyed and analyzed the major organizations of the Radical Right and the extreme Conservatives in America—those committees and crusades which have exerted a large and disturbing influence on a certain body of American political opinion, which have achieved sizeable membership and backing, or which have captured the interest of the American people.

There are other organizations and influences which are not quite so large or quite so well known. There should be some mention of these, though they are of lesser importance in the overall Rightist picture. We could mention, for instance, the American Coalition of Patriotic Societies, with headquarters in Washington, D. C., which is a co-ordinating organization for over one hundred "patriotic" groups. The American Coalition was formed thirty-five years ago "to promote patriotism and a better understanding of the American form of government," but today marches in the ranks of the Radical Right—opposing the income tax, foreign aid, the United Nations, for instance—and occasionally co-operating with extremist and racist groups.

We could mention the extremely conservative Circuit Riders, Inc., with headquarters in Cincinnati, which was formed in 1951 to combat "all efforts to propagate socialism and Communism and all other anti-American teachings in the Methodist Church." Its leaders include Myers G. Lowman, its executive secretary, and John Satterfield of Yazoo City, Mississippi, a past president of the American Bar Association who in 1964 was a major figure in efforts to defeat the Civil Rights Bill. The Circuit Riders conducts research into alleged socialist and Communist influences, not only in the Methodist Church, but among clergymen of other faiths and denominations as well. In recent years, it has published "exposés" of alleged Leftist affiliations and activities of Episcopalian, Presbyterian, Baptist, and Unitarian ministers, as well as Jewish clergymen. Its material is widely distributed and used by other Right Wing organizations, such as the Christian Crusade, the 20th Century Reformation Hour, American Council of Christian Churches, and the Church League of America.

On the extreme fringe of the Radical Right is an organization called Liberty Lobby, which is headquartered in Washington, D. C., and whose leadership and staff include anti-Semites or individuals who have maintained ties with the anti-Semitic and racist underworld. Curtis B. Dall, as chairman of Liberty Lobby, has made anti-Semitic statements in testimony before a congressional committee. Willis Carto, a staff member, has been associated with non-bigoted Rightists and with peddlers of racial and religious hatred.

In May, 1964, Liberty Lobby joined with two other groups with whom it works closely—Americans for National Security, and Government Educational Foundation—in staging a three-day so-called "Project America." Among the speakers on Liberty Lobby's phase of the program were such men as Kenneth Goff, an ex-associate of Gerald Smith and for some years leader of his own hate group, Soldiers of the Cross; Ned Touchstone, an extreme segregationist who edits *The Councilor* in Shreveport, Louisiana; and Westbrook Pegler.

Among other extremely conservative organizations, which fellow-travel with the Radical Right, are Christian Freedom Foundation, the Foundation for Economic Education, the American Economic Foundation, America's Future, Inc., Citizen's Foreign Aid Committee, and the American Security Council.

The first three—the CFF, FEE, and AEF—preach essentially the same *laissez-faire* message, sometimes co-operate with each other, and spend between $1,000,000 and $1,500,000 of tax-exempt money every year warning Americans against government regulation of business activities and the danger of any social reform legislation. All three organizations are heavily supported by wealthy industrialists of very Rightist views, by corporations and by foundations. They pump a veritable Niagara of "educational" material into the information channels of American life in a large-scale effort to influence the economic and social thinking of the opinion molders and the younger generation of the country.

The American Economic Foundation, headed by Fred Clark, is headquartered in New York and its main targets are the American elementary and secondary school teachers and their students. An extremely conservative movement, AEF conducts teacher institutes at more than one hundred colleges, and programs utilizing its films and other materials have been established in more than seven thousand high schools. AEF also has published an "Economic Fallacy Series," pamphlets designed for the general public, and "Economic Facts of Life," designed for editorial use by publications throughout the nation. AEF also supervises projects to aid corporations in their public relations and employee relations programs. It takes in and spends in the neighborhood of $500,000 a year.

Christian Freedom Foundation, also based in New York, seeks to rally the support of Protestant clergymen for rugged individualism and has for years been supported almost entirely by J. Howard Pew of the Sun Oil Company and members of his family. They have contributed well over a million dollars to its operations in the last five or six years.

CFF is directed by Howard Kershner, an extreme Conservative who edits its biweekly tabloid newspaper *Christian Economics,* which is sent free to 200,000 Protestant ministers and laymen. CFF also distributes a syndicated column called "It's Up To You," which goes to 225 daily newspapers and, in abbreviated form, to 450 weekly newspapers—all free of charge. Finally, CFF produces a radio program—"Howard Kershner's Commentary on the News" —which is available to radio stations on a sustaining basis.

In CFF propaganda, social security is described as "the older generation stealing from the younger," the income tax is branded as "Communist doctrine," labor unions are described as "stemming from Socialism," and foreign aid is pilloried as subsidization of "Socialistic schemes and experiments." The United Nations is described as "being used to promote Marxist philosophy throughout the world" and as "the most powerful engine now in existence for destroying a free society and ushering in authoritarian government."

The extent of Pew support for CFF can be seen from the following figures:

In 1958, when the organization grossed $470,000, Pew contributed $420,000. In 1959, when CFF took in more than $200,000, Pew gave $115,000 and Mrs. Mabel Pew Myrin gave $50,000. In 1960, CFF received $242,000, and Pew gave $180,000, the J. Howard Pew Freedom Trust $10,000, and Mrs. Myrin about $19,000. In 1962, CFF took in more than $30,000, and Pew gave $230,000.

The Foundation for Economic Education, with headquarters in Irvington-on-Hudson, New York, was formed in 1946 for the broad general purposes of promoting and supporting research in the field of economics and related branches of social science, and distributing the results of such research. Today, as an extremely conservative organization, it appears mostly to concentrate on issuing a huge volume of material aimed at overcoming "state interventionism"—which it defines as socialism, Communism, Fabianism, Nazism, the welfare state, and the planned economy.

Director of this half-million-dollar-a-year political propaganda mill is Leonard Read, a former Chamber of Commerce functionary, who founded FEE in 1946 with the aid of ten major contributors, each of whom put up $10,000 to launch the project. In its first four years, FEE received almost $1,200,000 from some of the top corporations in the Who's Who of American industry—companies like General Motors, Chrysler, U. S. Gypsum, E. I. duPont de Nemours, Gulf Oil, Consolidated Edison, Marshall Field, Montgomery Ward, Sun Oil, U. S. Steel, B. F. Goodrich, and the Armour Company. Among the more generous individual contributors was J. Howard Pew, who remains a FEE trustee.

Today, the burden of its support appears to be spread among some 12,000 contributors who provide the organization with the wherewithal to carry on its widespread propaganda. FEE publishes *The Freeman*, a monthly magazine which claims a circulation of some 55,000 and which is mailed free to students, teachers, clergymen and business executives. It is well-written in a clear, straightforward style that is geared to a lay audience, as is all FEE literature. FEE also sponsors lectures and seminars, and provides material for high school debates on the merits of free enterprise. It has produced a vast array of books, pamphlets, leaflets, and other materials, which are offered to several thousand high school principals and school superintendents. FEE also sponsors a college-business exchange program to indoctrinate college professors through fellowships provided by some fifty corporations.

FEE's purpose was best summed up by Read in a recent Dallas speech when he declared that FEE was dedicated to "reversing

our [America's] present unholy trend toward all-out Statism. . . ."
FEE's role in providing literature for ISI, when that Rightist youth
group was first formed, has already been mentioned.

Another extremely conservative organization closely identified
with American industrial and business corporations is the Chicago-
based American Security Council, which was originally formed
around 1956 to help companies screen personnel for Communist
affiliations or sympathies. Many of the professionals hired by ASC
are former government agents. In recent years, ASC has broadened
the scope of its operations to serve as a clearing house for information about Communist and other Leftist and statist movements,
and its information is available only to "member companies, government agencies, carefully selected writers, scholars and other
qualified persons."

ASC publishes a newsletter for its subscribers and a biweekly
Washington report on developments affecting national security, and
maintains a film library and speakers bureau.

It is financed by dues paid by member companies on the basis
of number of employees and operates on a budget of over a quarter
of a million dollars a year, provided by some three thousand companies and individuals. Executives and top officials of major corporations comprise the membership of various committees set up
by ASC. Some of these individuals have been identified with Rightist causes. In the spring of 1964, General Robert E. Wood sent
out a letter soliciting support for ASC.

America's Future, Inc., is another quarter-of-a-million-dollar-a-
year operation among the Extreme Conservatives. Based in New
Rochelle, New York, it is an offshoot of the ultraconservative Committee for Constitutional Government, which was active fifteen
years ago, but in recent years America's Future, Inc., has had an
identity and a separate operation all its own. It describes its role
as "helping our citizens understand and fight for the fundamentals
of private ownership, willing exchange, open competition and limited government." In recent years, it sponsored the late John T.
Flynn in a weekly radio program of news commentary called "Behind the Headlines"; produced another radio program called "Americans Speak Up"; and distributed reprints of the texts of both
programs. It also published book reviews, book digests, and other
materials.

In 1959, America's Future, Inc., created a Textbook Evaluation
Committee to make comprehensive and corrective studies of textbooks in use at the high school level—studies which it has carried
out in a number of communities. Members of the committee have

included educators such as E. Merrill Root and Charles C. Tansill, both identified with the John Birch Society's magazine *American Opinion,* and Felix Morley, formerly of *Human Events.* The president of America's Future is Rudolf Scott, and trustees have included leaders of business and industry identified as supporters of other Right Wing causes. One of them, for instance, is Walter Harnischfeger, the Milwaukee industrialist.

Another extremely conservative organization on the scene, in which the same Harnischfeger plays a leading role, is the Citizens Foreign Aid Committee. Despite its name, it opposes foreign aid and its national chairman is General Bonner Fellers. Clarence Manion of the Manion Forum and Birch Society national council has been listed as the Committee's legal counsel, and many members of its national committee are also members of the Birch council or Birch Society Endorsers.

Still another extremely conservative organization with a special interest is the National Right-To-Work Committee, with headquarters in Washington, D. C. It was formed almost ten years ago by Edwin S. Dillard, a North Carolina industrialist, and former Representative Fred Hartley of New Jersey, co-sponsor of the Taft-Hartley Law. The committee conducts a nation-wide campaign against compulsory unionism and its main activity has been to press for passage, by the various state legislatures, of laws prohibiting compulsory union membership as a condition of employment. At first, the Committee carried on its work through newspaper advertisements, publications, and personal contacts, but in recent years it has produced a wide variety of pamphlets, manuals, books, and reprints. It publishes a monthly newsletter, and distributes color slides, filmstrips, and motion pictures for TV and for showing before civic groups. A radio program called "The Blessings of Liberty" is supplied to radio stations free of charge, and the Committee maintains a Speakers' Corps.

The Committee's spokesmen find ready platforms in organizations of the Radical Right. One member of the Committee's board, Frederick C. Fowler, has appeared on several occasions at meetings of Billy James Hargis' Christian Crusade. Glenn Green, who became a Committee vice-president several years ago, was identified as an active member of the John Birch Society and formerly was associated with the National Education Program of Harding College, where he produced the film *Communism on the Map.* The Committee's first chairman, Mr. Dillard, has been listed as a Birch Endorser, and such Birch Society national council members as Robert Love and Fred Koch of Wichita, Kansas, have been active.

Love was a main speaker at the 1961 National Seminar of the Committee, held in Chicago. Committee spokesmen have also participated at meetings staged by Kent and Phoebe Courtney, have written for *Human Events*, and have appeared on Manion Forum broadcasts.

The National Right To Work Committee has a gross income of more than $400,000 a year, provided by some 15,000 members.

The Cardinal Mindszenty Foundation, with headquarters in St. Louis, is an anti-Communist study organization but of the extremely conservative variety. The Foundation claims some five thousand active local study groups in all fifty states, and publishes a monthly periodical called *The Mindszenty Report*. The operating leadership is in the hands of Mrs. Phyllis Schlafly, its research director, who has been described by Founder Welch of the John Birch Society as "a very loyal member." Mrs. Schlafly is the wife of J. Fred Schlafly, an Alton, Illinois, attorney who has spoken at numerous Rightist forums, including the Schwarz schools of anti-Communism of which Schlafly has been a "faculty" member. Executive director of the Foundation is Miss Eleanor Schlafly.

Sources of Finance of the
American Right Wing

No one really knows how much money is being poured into the American Right Wing every year to support the massive reactionary Rightist propaganda campaign which seeks to influence and to change American political opinion.

Nevertheless, as is pointed out in the opening pages of this book, it is a fair and conservative estimate that the minimum cost of the overall Rightist propaganda assault on the American mind is in the neighborhood of $14,000,000 a year. This encompasses the known expenses of the American Right, ranging from the extremely conservative organization to the Radical Right. It does not include the far-out organizations tainted with racism and anti-Semitism; they raise more than a million dollars for their own special purposes.

A substantial portion of the $14,000,000 that is poured into extremely conservative and Radical Right propaganda comes this way: from some 70 or more foundations (almost all tax-exempt), 113 business firms and corporations, 25 public utilities, and some 250 individuals who can be identified as having contributed at least $500 each in recent years.

It is unwise, with the imprecise information that can be collected, to venture a breakdown of the money supplied to the American Right Wing by each of the three groupings—the foundations, corporations, or the individuals—or by any particular foundation, corporation, or individual. It should also be borne in mind that a considerable proportion of the money comes from small contributors—most of whom do not contribute anything near $500 each.

Foundations

Included among the seventy-odd foundations are some of the most public-spirited agencies in the United States—agencies whose money nourishes civic, educational, religious, health, and charitable work of the most worthy kind. Their annual outlays for such worth-while causes are, in many cases, of staggering proportions, often millions of dollars. The contributions such giant foundations make to Right Wing causes may perhaps be only a drop in the bucket to them, but surely are of considerable importance to the annual budget of the ordinary Rightist organization. Contributions, for instance, of $1,000, $5,000 or even $25,000 may be a negligible part of a giant foundation's annual giving; they are substantial items to a Rightist group.

Clearly then, with rare exceptions, most of the foundations which contribute to the Right Wing organizations were not set up for the express purpose of financing such causes. Worse still, these gifts to Rightist groups are usually included with grants to schools, to colleges, to churches, and to other recipients whose work is entirely free of any political connotation.

On the other hand, some of the foundations are the creations of individuals or families whose names are to be found among the leaders and sponsors of Rightist organizations. Still other foundations are the creatures of companies whose principals personally support Rightist causes and who often influence their companies to support such Right Wing groups.

Examples are not hard to find. The Chance Foundation in Centralia, Missouri, is the creation of F. Gano Chance, a member of the Birch council and board chairman of the Chance Company. The Grede Foundation, Inc., in Milwaukee, Wisconsin, is the creation of William J. Grede, also a member of the Birch Society national council. The Ada Hearne Foundation in Sevierville, Tennessee, is the outlet for contributions by A. G. Heinsohn, Jr., still another Birch council member, and a principal in Spindale and Cherokee Mills. And the Harnischfeger Foundation of Milwaukee is the creation of the Harnischfeger Corporation and of Walter Harnischfeger, who has for a number of years given support to Right Wing organizations.

These very foundations support worth-while civic work, but their contributions also go to Right Wing organizations. The Chance Foundation, for example, in recent years, sent generous gifts to the Hargis Christian Crusade, the Schwarz Christian Anti-Communism Crusade. McIntire's American Council of Christian Churches, as well as to the Intercollegiate Society of Individualists, Harding College, and America's Future, Inc.

Some foundations appear sometimes to allocate a *major* portion of their annual giving to Rightist causes. During 1959, for instance, Heinsohn's very modest Ada Hearne Foundation made total contributions of a little over $20,000. Almost $15,000 of that total went to the American Economic Foundation and the Christian Freedom Foundation (see page 267), $1,000 each went to Harding College, the Intercollegiate Society of Individualists, and to the National Foundation for Education in American Citizenship—the latter a major source of funds in recent years for *Human Events.* Against this, some $200 went to the Knoxville Symphony Society, $100 to Smith College, $500 to a Baptist school, and another $1,500 went to two churches.

The O'Donnell Foundation of Dallas, heavily financed by Peter O'Donnell, Jr., a leading supporter of Senator Goldwater for President, has also channeled a fair proportion of its annual outlays to Rightist purposes. In fiscal 1962, for instance, when O'Donnell Foundation grants totaled $65,000, $20,000 went to the Intercollegiate Society of Individualists, which had received a total of $10,000 in two earlier years.

Sometimes, the stated purposes for which a foundation is created make its objectives quite clear. For instance, when J. Howard Pew created the J. Howard Pew Freedom Trust in 1957, the statement of purposes in the trust agreement declared:

"Socialism, Welfare-state-ism, Marxism, Fascism and any other like forms of government intervention are but devices by which government seizes the ownership or control of the tools of production."

It added that the trust would seek to "acquaint the American people with the evils of bureaucracy and the vital need to maintain and preserve a limited form of government." It also would point out the "dangerous consequences that result from an exchange of our priceless American heritage of freedom and self-determination, for the false promises of Socialism and a planned economy" and "expose the insidious influences which have infiltrated many of our channels of publicity." Finally, the foundation planned to acquaint the American people with the values of a free market, the dangers of inflation, and the need for a stable monetary standard.

When the Trust applied for tax exemption in 1958, a year after it was formed, it declared that it sought to make grants to "religious, charitable, and scientific, literary or educational organizations . . . to be used for the teaching on the meaning of individual liberty and freedom." During the calendar year 1962, $24,000 of the $59,000 spent by the J. Howard Pew Freedom Trust went to the Christian Freedom Foundation ($20,000), the Foundation for Economic Education ($2,000) and the American Economic Foundation ($2,000) (see pages 266–268).

With the caveat that any example of foundation support for the American Right Wing is not necessarily typical of its giving, and that any foundation named may also support the most worthwhile causes, it is possible to cite some revealing examples of foundation support for Rightist causes, some of which have been mentioned elsewhere in this book:

ITEM: The large contributions by the Alfred P. Sloan Foundation of New York to Dr. Benson's establishment on the campus of Harding College in Searcy, Arkansas, helped launch Benson's National Education Program of today. Other foundation money has helped keep it going—for instance, $38,000 from the Donner Foundation of Philadelphia in 1959 and 1960.

ITEM: In the fiscal year 1961–62, the William Volker Fund of Burlingame, California (now being liquidated), donated $48,066.50 to the Intercollegiate Society of Individualists. The Lilly Endowment supplied $25,000, the Marquette Charitable Organization $19,000, the Relm Foundation $5,000, Curran Foundation $3,000, the Ingersoll Foundation $4,050, and the Ada Hearne and Deering Milliken Foundations $2,500 each. There were numerous other, and smaller, foundation grants to ISI. Of a total income from contributions of $181,616.00 for the fiscal year, the Intercollegiate Society of Individualists received $129,404.85 in foundation funds.

ITEM: In the five-year period, 1956 to 1961, the William Volker Fund contributed almost $270,000 to the Council for Basic Education, Washington, D.C. The Council has received frequent favorable mention in the Right Wing publication *Human Events*, which has reprinted articles from the Council Bulletin attacking "progressive" education and the "unethical practice" of teachers joining "professional" organizations. The Council also opposes Federal aid to education. (In 1958, the first phase of a "basic curriculum study" by the Council was financed by a $34,000 grant from the Relm Foundation, Ann Arbor, Michigan.) In the same five-year period, 1956 to 1961, the Volker Fund also contributed more than $320,000 to the Foundation for Voluntary Welfare, of which $192,887 was contributed in fiscal 1960, when Medicare was a major issue on the national scene. The Volker Fund also has served as a source of support for research and writing in the social sciences by economists and scholars of Rightist viewpoint, like Ludwig von Mises, and it heavily underwrote the distribution of "basic books" to college libraries over a period of years.

ITEM: During 1958–62, $125,000 was contributed to Dr. Fred Schwarz's Christian Anti-Communism Crusade via the Glenmede Trust Company of Philadelphia, which serves as trustee for Pew Foundation funds.

ITEM: More than $30,000 of Pew Foundation money was contributed between 1958 and 1962 to the Christian Freedom Foundation. (The overwhelming bulk of the Christian Freedom Foundation's annual budget is supplied by individual contributions from Mr. J. Howard Pew and Mrs. Mabel Pew Myrin, whose donations to the CFF between 1958 and 1962 were well over $1,000,000.) The CFF is not, itself, a foundation in the sense that it provides grants and other contributions. It is, rather, a recipient of funds which it expends on its own activities.

ITEM: Between 1955 and 1961, the Donner Foundation, Philadelphia, Pennsylvania, contributed $95,000 to the American Economic Foundation. Between 1958 and 1961, the Donner Foundation gave $57,500 to the American Enterprise Association, now called the American Enterprise Institute for Public Policy Research. In 1956 and 1957, the Donner group contributed a total of $50,000 to Americans for the Competitive Enterprise System. Harding College, Searcy, Arkansas, received a total of $38,000 in 1959 and 1960.

ITEM: The Relm Foundation of Ann Arbor, Michigan, whose resources are somewhat smaller than those of many other foundations, has nevertheless consistently supported a number of Right Wing groups. Between 1957 and 1960, the Relm Foundation gave $38,800 to the American Economic Foundation, $8,500 to the American Enterprise Association, almost $25,000 to the Council for Basic Education, $29,500 to the Foundation for Economic Education.

ITEM: As noted in this book, the National Foundation for Education in American Citizenship, Inc., Indianapolis, Indiana, has for some years been a consistent supporter of the Right Wing newsletter, *Human Events,* and these contributions appear to be the largest single item of annual expenditure by the Foundation. For the years 1957 to 1962 inclusive, the National Foundation for Education in American Citizenship gave a reported $330,000 to *Human Events.* In recent years, more than 90 percent of contributions made by the Foundation went to *Human Events.*

The foregoing few instances of how foundation funds are channeled into organizations and propaganda arms of the American Right Wing are obviously only examples.

Corporations

A total of 113 industrial, mercantile, and banking firms, and twenty-five electric and gas companies have been identified as having contributed in the last few years to organizations of the American Right Wing. This represents the minimum number of firms which have channeled significant amounts of funds into Right Wing causes.

Broadly speaking, oil, steel, and heavy machinery producers, and manufacturers of motors and motor controls, tend to predominate among corporate and business firms which support the American Right. So do chemical and textile companies. The names of electric light, gas, and power companies in various sections of the country appear as contributors with noticeable frequency.

Some individual organizations of the American Right Wing have been, over the years, substantially dependent on business and corporate contributions for their continued existence.

Dr. Fred Schwarz's Christian Anti-Communism Crusade, for instance, has benefited heavily from support furnished by the Allen-Bradley Corporation of Milwaukee, and Technicolor, Inc., a holding company whose subsidiaries include the Technicolor Corporation of America and Eversharp, Inc. The enthusiast here is Patrick Frawley, Jr.

Harding College and the National Education Program located on its campus have received corporate contributions that total hundreds of thousands of dollars over the years. The Republic

DANGER ON THE RIGHT

and United States Steel corporations, as well as Gulf and Humble Oil companies, were among the major corporate contributors to the Searcy operations.

The Intercollegiate Society of Individualists has also benefited from corporate gifts, although to a much smaller degree than Dr. Benson's complex at Searcy, and corporation and business contributions have helped keep the Manion Forum on the air.

In addition to their direct contributions, business firms also support organizations and publications of the American Right Wing by advertisements in Rightist periodicals and by sponsorship of radio and television broadcasts. While such magazine advertising and radio and television sponsorships are not, strictly speaking, contributions or donations to Rightist activity, they are a significant portion of the monetary life blood that flows to the American Right Wing.

Among the companies whose ads have appeared frequently in Right Wing publications are the Allen-Bradley Corporation; the Deering Milliken Research Corporation; the Schick Safety Razor Company, a division of Eversharp, Inc.; the Spindale and Cherokee Mills; the Flick-Reedy Corporation; Kennametal, Inc.; Knott's Berry Farm, and the Henry Regnery Company. The appearance of these ads in publications such as *American Opinion, National Review,* and the Liberty Amendment Committee's *Freedom Magazine* appear to reflect the political viewpoints of company officers and directors who support the American Right as individuals.

A most important example of corporate support for Rightist broadcasting is, perhaps, the sponsorship given to Dan Smoot's radio and television commentaries by the Dr. Ross Dog and Cat Food Company, headed by D. B. Lewis of Los Angeles. Other companies, some large, some quite small and very local, sponsor broadcasts by Life Line, the broadcasting operation of H. L. Hunt's Life Line Foundation. Hunt's oil company and his HLH Food Products also sponsor these broadcasts.

Individuals

A number of major organizations on the Right Wing are substantially dependent on individual contributions. These include the John Birch Society, Billy James Hargis' Christian Crusade, Americans for Constitutional Action, and the Christian Freedom Foundation.

There seems to be little question that Mr. J. Howard Pew of Philadelphia is one of the biggest individual contributors to Rightist causes, quite aside from the support provided such organizations by foundations established by him and his family. As has been noted, the individual contributions of Mr. Pew and Mrs. Mabel Pew Myrin account for the overwhelming proportion of the support received by the Christian Freedom Foundation, and exceeded $1,000,000 in recent years.

Pew support for the Christian Freedom Foundation is perhaps the most revealing example of how individual supporters can sustain an organization. But the key point to be borne in mind is that most organizations of the Right Wing which depend on individual supporters, receive contributions from large numbers of supporters who share the burden. Many of these donors contribute to a variety of Right Wing groups.

Research into the sources of funds for the American Right Wing reveals that, over and above the foundations and the corporate contributors, a group of approximately 250 men and women appear to constitute the major individual contributors. A fair proportion of these individual contributors are themselves the owners of business firms, corporation officials, or corporate directors. Some are prominent attorneys, retired men of wealth, or former political figures.

Among the more prominent individuals in this group of contributors are to be found such industrialists as Charles Edison of West Orange, New Jersey, William J. Grede of Milwaukee, Wisconsin, and F. Gano Chance of Centralia, Missouri. These men not only contribute large sums of money to the American Right Wing, but also give generously of their time and effort in leadership roles. Edison, for instance, is on the editorial advisory committee of the Birch Society magazine, while Grede and Chance are members of the Society's national council. In addition, Edison serves as treasurer of Americans for Constitutional Action and acts as advisor for a number of other Rightist organizations. Grede has helped raise funds for the Manion Forum, while Chance is an advisor of the Hargis Christian Crusade and a trustee of America's Future, Inc.

Other individuals, such as D. B. Lewis of Los Angeles, California, supplement their individual contributions to Rightist causes with commercial sponsorship of Rightist broadcasts and by advertising in Rightist publications. As noted, Lewis does this through his Dr. Ross Dog and Cat Food Company. A. G. Heinsohn, Jr., a Birch Society national council member and active in a number of other Rightist groups, also supplements his individual contributions with advertisements placed in Right Wing publications under the name of the companies in which he is a principal—Spindale and Cherokee Mills.

Moreover, men like Edison, Grede, Heinsohn, and Chance have, as has been mentioned, established foundations which also nourish the Right Wing with contributions.

There are other major supporters of the Right Wing who not only pump their individual funds into the cause, but who lend their names and appear time and again on sponsor lists of Right Wing organizations. In this category are such persons as General Robert E. Wood, Chicago industrialist; Roger Milliken, textile magnate of Spartanburg, South Carolina; and Harry Bradley, whose Allen-Bradley Corporation in Milwaukee was a leading supporter of Dr. Fred Schwarz's Christian Anti-Communism Crusade. And there are still other individual contributors, who apparently give money, but not too much personal time and effort. These include Robert Dresser, a Providence, Rhode Island, attorney; Frank deGanahl of New York; Bernard Peyton of Princeton, New Jersey; Patrick Frawley, Jr. of Hollywood, and a number of others.

Countess Rosalind Guardabassi of Prides Crossing, Massachusetts, is somewhat of a curiosity in the ranks of those who contribute generously to the Right Wing. Heiress to a woolens fortune, she has given to several Extreme Rightist organizations. But her largesse goes beyond even the Radical Right and extends to support for some organizations which are outside its limits and which peddle gutter-level anti-Semitism and racism. One of these, for instance, is Gerald Smith's Christian Nationalist Crusade. Another is the violently racist, anti-Semitic National States' Rights Party, based in Birmingham, Alabama.

Nonracist organizations to which Countess Guardabassi has contributed include For America, and she has been listed as a member of the National Advisory Board of We, The People!, a Chicago-based Radical Right organization.

Another woman of some affluence on the Right Wing scene, whose contributions go to a similar variety of causes, is Miss Olive Simes of Boston, Massachusetts. She has been listed as a contributor to the Christian Freedom Foundation, and other reliable sources indicate that she contributes, through a foundation called The Penthouse Fund, to the John Birch Society, of which she is an Endorser. But Miss Simes also contributed for a number of years to Gerald Smith's Christian Nationalist Crusade.

Index

About the Authors

ARNOLD FORSTER is General Counsel and National Civil Rights director of the Anti-Defamation League of B'nai B'rith. He conducts the League's program concerned with fundamental issues of civil rights and constitutional law.

BENJAMIN R. EPSTEIN, National Director of the Anti-Defamation League, has been its chief executive since 1947. His articles on anti-Semitism, human relations and postwar Germany have appeared in many publications, popular and learned.

Danger On The Right is the fourth book on which Mr. Epstein and Mr. Forster have collaborated. The others are *The Trouble Makers, Cross-Currents,* and *Some of My Best Friends. . . .*

The Anti-Defamation League is one of the nation's leading organizations combating bigotry and working to strengthen the nation's democratic institutions.